SOCIOLOGICAL PERSPECTIVES ON SCHOOL AND EDUCATION

is b   ke et

Sociology Now
A series sponsored by the British Sociological
Association

Sociological Perspectives
on
School and Education

Ivan Reid

Open Books

First published in 1978 by Open Books Publishing Limited,
West Compton House, Nr Shepton Mallet, Somerset, England

W 20328 £3.95. 3.83

Reprinted 1979 and 1980

Hardback ISBN 0 7291 0131 2
Paperback ISBN 0 7291 0126 6

British Library Cataloguing in Publication Data
Reid, Ivan
  Sociological perspectives on school and education.
  1. Educational sociology
  I. Title
  401.5'6   LC191
  ISBN 0–7291–0131–2
  ISBN 0–7291–0126–6 Pbk.

Phototypeset in 11/12 pt V.I.P. Garamond by
Western Printing Services Ltd, Bristol
Printed and bound by The Pitman Press, Bath

This book is dedicated to my Mum and Dad – for all they did and did not do to me as a child.

Also by Ivan Reid
Social Class Differences in Britain: a sourcebook
(Open Books 1977)
Sociology and Teacher Education (with Eileen Wormald)
(A.T.C.D.E. 1974)

Contents

List of tables

Acknowledgements

One quickly learns two things when writing a textbook. First, how little of what one writes can really be called one's own and consequently the debt owed to others. While, whenever possible, this is formally acknowledged by reference, it is here generally and genuinely professed. Second, one realises and appreciates how much help, support and encouragement are received in one's endeavour from others and how vital this is to the enterprise.

My thanks are due to the editorial board of this series for suggesting that I undertake this book. Without them, textbook writing would have remained for me a pipedream. From time to time I have thought they were wrong – for a variety of reasons – to invite me, but, if so, this is a mistake we have all learned to live with. Tony Marks and Henry Miller have been diligent and often useful in their efforts at reading and commenting on the manuscript.

My association with Open Books has remained happy and fruitful. Patrick Taylor's sociologically untutored publisher's mind has, I feel, helped to sharpen the clarity of my communication. Subediting, though essential, remains largely unrecognised but I wish to thank Linden Stafford for her diligence with the minutiae.

No acknowledgement would be complete without mention of my many students, mainly at the University of Bradford and Edge Hill College of Education, who over the years, through their willingness to listen – to be convinced or not – have contributed to my understanding of the discipline, and my insights into teaching and learning it. Some will recognise the fruits of our mutual explorations in the pages which follow. I wish also thank my colleagues at Bradford, many now departed for higher things, for their support. In particular I am grateful for having shared the teaching, literature and ideas of the sociology of education with Marie Macey.

My personal support team has remained remarkably intact and has surpassed its previous efforts. Brenda Carrington and Gladys Claridge have displayed enviable skills in putting my handwriting into typescript. Peter Taylor has provided another first-class subject index which will greatly benefit everyone who uses this book. Pat, Diane and Helen Reid have provided me with family support far beyond my expectations let alone my deserts.

The author and publisher would like to thank the following for permission to use material presented in this book: Granada Publishing Ltd, St Albans, for data from J. W. B. Douglas, *The Home and the School* (1964); Heinemann Educational Books Ltd, London, for a diagram from W. L. Wallace, *Sociological Theory* (1969); the Controller of Her Majesty's Stationery Office, London, for data from *Higher Education* (1963), *Public Schools Commission: First Report 1968*, and *Statistics of Education*, 1963, 1964, 1974, 1975; the Longman Group Ltd, Harlow, and the authors for data from R. Davie, M. Butler and H. Goldstein, *From Birth to Seven* (1972); N.F.E.R. Publishing Co. Ltd, Windsor, for data, and a diagram from J. C. Barker Lunn, *Streaming in the Primary School* (1970) and for diagrams from E. J. Goodacre, *Teachers and their Pupils' Home Backgrounds* (1968); the Office of Population Censuses and Surveys, Foreham, for data from *Education Tables (10 per cent sample)* (1966); the Social Surveys Division of the Office of Population Censuses and Surveys, London, for Crown Copyright data published by H.M.S.O., London, in *General Household Survey Introductory Report* (1973), *General Household Survey 1972* (1975), and A. J. Harris and R. Clausen, *Labour Mobility in Great Britain 1953–1963* (1967); Macmillan Press Ltd, London and Basingstoke, for data from A. H. Halsey, *Trends in British Society since 1900* (1972).

Preface

Since the number of British sociology of education textbooks is small, a sufficient justification, if needed, for producing another would be merely to add to available choice. Textbooks are often disappointing because readers lack a knowledge of the author's intentions and the contents of the book. The purpose of this preface is, then, to share with readers its author's aims and to outline the book's approach and content. Since no man or book can be all things to all men, it is only reasonable to expose at the outset what the reader can expect rather than to drag him through the book on his own assumptions or a tutor's preferences.

The discipline of the sociology of education is now both extensive and complex. It is extensive in terms of subject matter and research, and complex in the range of theoretical approaches it brings to bear upon its interests. Indeed it can be argued that there are now several sociologies of education and even some confusion among practitioners. It is the author's belief that the present condition of the discipline provides no reason for over-simplification or avoidance of the issues involved in teaching or writing about the subject. Fortunately the discipline has not yet reached the stage of some others where early teaching is over-simplified to the extent that a student has to unlearn early knowledge in order to progress with his study. And long may it remain so. This book is designed to help maintain that situation and to fill a gap in the literature. Its major aim is, at an introductory level, to come to grips with the reality of the discipline in a straightforward way. Hence there is no avoidance of current concerns in the discipline and there is an appreciation of both the quality and utility of the knowledge it contains, together with a recognition of what is not known. The novelty of the book lies in its attempt to present the discipline – as a particular approach to educational phenomena – as it now is.

The book begins with a review of the theoretical perspectives currently in use and sets these into their cultural background, offering a sort of sociology of the sociology of education. The application of these perspectives and a review of their findings and contributions are demonstrated in relation to a selected number of topics on school and education (Chapters 2–7). For example, schools are viewed as social systems from structuralist perspectives, as organisations from organisation-theory perspectives, and as social worlds from interpretative perspectives. The final chapter argues that the evidence in this book points to the existence of a single sociology of education, and an exploration is made of its nature and extent. Of course, ultimately, in order to produce a textbook an author must be selective, and this process is to some extent personal.

A guiding principle in writing this book has been the realisation that the audience for the sociology of education is composed of people involved in education. By definition all readers of this book have had educational experience, and a majority are or will be involved professionally. Thus the book sets out to display the discipline as a contribution to our understanding of educational phenomena rather than as merely a part of the body of knowledge called sociology. While the author is convinced that the utility of the sociology of education for education is dependent upon its being good sociology, he is also concerned with its relevance to education. Two aspects of the literature that consistently annoy involved readers are the over-use of material from other cultures, and statements or research which appear so naïve about educational reality as to suggest that the reader's own experience is superior in all respects to that of the sociologist. Hence, wherever possible in this book British material is used and an attempt made, where necessary, to avoid furthering educational naïvety, by pointing it out when it occurs.

Textbooks often vary between extremes. Some are full of fine-sounding overgeneralisations which leave the reader wondering how these relate to reality and what he has learned from his reading. Others take on the appearance of extensive bibliographies where readers have trouble seeing the wood for the trees. The present book attempts a course between these two. The topics covered have been limited in order to concentrate on what are seen as vital aspects, yet allowing, within the confines of a relatively small volume, for the fairly extensive use of the work of sociologists of education, including some quotation. This method was adopted to give readers a deeper familiarity with the literature and ideas of the discipline than is afforded by many other textbooks. It is hoped that this approach, together with referencing throughout the book, will stimulate and assist further reading.

One of the unfortunate outcomes of the timetables imposed by educational institutions is that disciplines become defined as a set of topics. Consequently textbooks tend to be used for specific and limited purposes rather than read from cover to cover. In the circumstances this is a natural and legitimate use, which the chapter layout of this book is designed to assist. At the same time such a segmented approach leads to unfortunately limited learning and compartmentalisation. One mark of the good student – perhaps only because of its rarity – is the ability to relate relevant material from one topic to his treatment of another. There are good reasons for seeing the content of this book as a cogent whole. First, as has been stated, it aims to provide an overall introduction to the discipline. Second, and more important, there are very definite interrelationships between the topics presented. For example, there are obvious limitations to an understanding of what goes on in the classroom which fails to take account of a whole set of other factors such as the biographies of the people involved, the nature of the institution of which they are part, and the structure and histories of the educational and social systems in which it operates.

While such exhortations may not inspire most people to read this book as an entity, the careful cross-referencing in the text and particularly the index will be noticed and should be used.

In spite of what might be seen as pretentious claims in this preface, these are in no way intended to suggest that this book is a presentation of the current state of the discipline addressed to my sociological peers or betters. It is essentially a book for students of education in its full sense, and is written in the belief that, while the sociology of education is of value in many directions (including itself), its major and vital value is for everyone interested in understanding education.

Ivan Reid
January 1978

1

The sociologies of education

Once upon a time, or so it seems, in British bookshops there were but two introductory textbooks in sociology – if any. It was the beginning of the 1960s, and in those days as students we chose between a MacIver and Page (1950) and a Davis (1949). Just before, and indeed for some time after, most of us who trained to be teachers did so at colleges in which the word sociology, like sex, was rarely if ever mentioned. In those days sociology appeared to live exclusively in universities and have a distinctly American accent. The sociology of education, in spite of Ottoway's book (1953) – which few of us, and even fewer of our tutors, stumbled across – was in a pre-infant stage. Thoughts of O and A level G.C.E. sociology may have flickered across the minds of an enterprising few, but were not made public. In those days people often and genuinely asked, 'What is sociology?' and received a confident answer, 'It's the scientific study of man in society.' It may be a myth that people said to sociology students, 'O.K., so you're a sociologist, say something in sociology.' But like most myths it contains some truth and reveals something of importance. I was often embarrassed in my first post in higher education by the sincere question, 'Well what do you as a sociologist think about . . .?' The question usually referred to some matter of college policy (like extending students' visiting hours!) and I was nonplussed: if only they had asked me about social class. Since I had been taught that sociology was only sometimes about people, demands that I apply it to professional or practical questions were too much!

However, the importance of the myth lies with the assumptions implicit in these sorts of question. People (other, that is, than sociologists) had both an ignorance of sociology and a belief or hope that whatever it was it had something to contribute. Sociologists, or at least those of us still wet behind the ears, were confident that we knew what sociology was – in those days one could manage to read nearly all the references supplied by a tutor – but lacked the knowledge or ability to see its direct application. Perhaps we were a bit like students of Greek history.

A decade and a half later, the situation has changed dramatically. In the late seventies, now that sociology is so much a part of academic, social and mass-media life, its earlier history sounds quaint. Such rapid growth and establishment of a discipline is perhaps without precedent. Students and teachers now find that their knowledge, like the books they read, rapidly becomes out of date. The growth of sociology has been as dramatic in variety as it has been in bulk. It is now acceptable to talk about sociologies in the plural. Each one of these claims to bring a new perspective to, or to add to, our understanding of social reality. The public is probably more certain of what sociology is than are many sociologists, and many believe, or hope, that sociology has nothing to offer. It is not too facetious to suggest that British sociology and sociology of education have, in the span of fifteen years or so, undergone a historical development similar in some respects to that of Christianity over nearly 2,000 years. From a few disciples with a basic truth has grown a sizeable army divided into a number of sects and denominations. These, while taking part in the same game and having distinctive ways of playing, compete with each other, and present a disunited front to the world. Some sociologists, as we shall see, are very sectarian, claiming to have the most, all or even the *only* light on the subject. Others see their sociology as being distinctive but only in terms of adding to the overall discipline. In this state of affairs it is perhaps only possible to talk of *a* sociology of education in the way in which one might say there is *a* Christianity or a single Christian church (though see Chapter 8).

Christianity and the sociology of education present a rather similar problem to the outsider wishing to understand them. He can either attempt to return to the original truth or immerse himself in the activities of each of the groups. In the latter case he has the opportunity to see what each has to offer and to compare, contrast and evaluate their contributions and usefulness. It is this approach that is adopted here, a sort of ecumenical (universal) sociology of education. In order to do this it is first necessary to identify the sociologies of education, or what are better termed the perspectives (or theoretical orientations) currently being used in the discipline. Having done that, the separate contributions of each to a number of topics in the sociology of education can be reviewed (Chapters 2–7). This review is not a balanced one. Some of the perspectives, perhaps because they are new, are not as well developed as others, and /or have concentrated on particular topics. Since this is a book for British readers it will have a bias, though not an exclusive one, towards British sociology of education. Further, since a major aim of the book is to illustrate the contribution of the discipline to an understanding of educational phenomena, there is an emphasis on empirical studies. Having defined the perspectives and reviewed their contributions, the final chapter explores the extent to which they are one, are interrelated, and form a cogent whole.

There are, however, a number of other perspectives or issues which must also concern us in our attempt to understand the sociologies of education. We need to explore something of the history of the discipline, short as it is, together with something of its cultural setting. The latter must consider the ideologies of the society and academic institutions in which the discipline is practised, and the demands and expectations these make upon it. This amounts to what could be called a sociology of the sociology of education. We begin, however, with theoretical considerations.

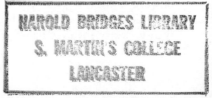

Theoretical perspectives

The importance of theoretical perspectives in the sociology of education, like any other area of study, can be simply stated. In spite of the common view that theory is abstract, difficult and detached from reality and practice, we all constantly use theories in experiencing reality. By theory in this context is meant, simply, universal categories, or basic assumptions about the nature of everyday things. For example, whenever we use language we rely (quite reasonably) on theory in this sense. Simple statements like 'This is hot' contain an assumed, common and accepted category 'hot' which has its own meaning and is in opposition to 'cold', and so on. A theory is, then, a supposition (assumption) which explains (or attempts to explain) something, especially a supposition based on principles that are independent of what is being explained; in fact it could be said that a theory must attempt an explanation in terms other than the characteristics of phenomena being explained. Hence it is not theoretical to say that children are naughty in school because it is of the nature of children to be naughty. It would be towards the theoretical if one attempted to explain the naughty behaviour in terms of a clash of interests between teachers and children and differences in their status, power and expectations – for example, that naughtiness was an attempt by children to avoid, or to negate, the demands of teachers that the children perform tasks that the children were unable or unwilling to do. It is also necessary to appreciate that, since theories always go beyond fact, it is never possible actually to prove a theory, at least exhaustively: it is impossible to make all the observations necessary for predicting with total confidence. However absurd it sounds, we do not know 'for a fact' that the next person to walk off the top of a nine-storey building will go downwards. This progression from fact to theory can be simply illustrated. I saw water flowing down a slope – that is a fact. I often see water flowing down a slope – that is a complex fact. Water always flows down slopes – that is a theory. At this stage, to accept the theory clearly involves belief. Further, all theories have their limitations: in both of the last two examples, the law of gravity is not universal. If blocks of flats are ever built on planets our theory will need modifying; it is certainly possible to see water flowing up a slope.

For our present purpose, however, it is another feature of theory that is most significant, and this is shown in table 1.1. Theory provides, through its assumptions, a framework or structure within which a person recognises problems to be solved and frames questions (hypotheses) to be answered, which in turn shape the observations he makes, the methods he will use to collect information or make observations, and finally a frame-work within which he will present his findings and make generalised statements. Table 1.1 also suggests two further points: that all the stages are interrelated – theory affects observation and in turn observations affect theory – and that the process has no obvious starting point. A common fallacy is that all science begins with theory, but a moment's thought about what has been said so far shows that an observation or an experience must precede, and be intimately related with, any theory.

Table 1.1
The components and process of scientific sociology

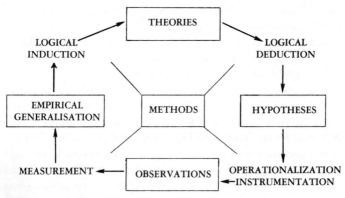

(Derived from Wallace 1969, p.ix)

It should be obvious, then, that in reviewing a body of knowledge like the sociology of education one must have some awareness of the basic theoretical stance or perspective from which particular research was conducted, or statements made. Only with such an appreciation is the reader able to compare, contrast and perhaps evaluate each such offering. It should even equip him to decide how well, in sum, the field of study is covered. To use a somewhat extreme analogy. Suppose we were to go for a walk on the Yorkshire Moors with four people. While we are enjoying the physical experience, we observe the behaviour and (since it's a story) peer into the minds of our companions. One, a geologist, stares into the distance, fascinated by an outcrop of unusual rock. Another, an archaeologist, looks at mid-distance to the site of a neolithic long barrow. The third, a botanist, is looking at his feet where he has just avoided crippling a rare flora. The last — this one an ornithologist — stands transfixed, eyes heavenward, homing in on a flock of migrating birds. The walkers are all human, all are sharing the same time and space, but viewing different aspects of the same reality because of their separate perspectives. Even if they were to pool their perspectives we would not have a total view, we should need others. Fortunately it is extremely unlikely, but, if they were so encapsulated in their separate perspectives, it is possible that they could overlook what many would assume to be the most important feature of the landscape — an isolated pub! The perspectives that sociologists bring to bear on the school and education are not as bizarre as those in our analogy. They can, as we shall find out, be seen to operate in a similar fashion and with similar consequences.

The following identifies the prevailing theoretical perspectives in the sociology of education, so that readers can trace their contributions to the issues outlined in subsequent chapters. The perspectives are dealt with here only briefly, as fuller explorations exist elsewhere; see, for example, Cohen (1968), Mennell (1974), Thompson and Tunstall (1971) and Wallace (1969). As Bernstein (1974) has suggested, the number of sociologies that can be identified depends on who is doing the counting. He, like others, and following Dawe (1970) and Horton (1966), recognises two main sociologies. Others do their sums differently; Wallace (1969), for example, lists eleven of what he terms 'viewpoints in contemporary sociological theory'. We shall follow convention and identify two sociologies while recognising that each of them contains a number and variety of perspectives. One good reason for being conventional − as is often the case − is that it would be difficult to be otherwise. In the present instance, an attempt to sustain the perspectives within each of the sociologies, shown in table 1.2, would be thwarted. Neither in purely theoretical works, nor in individual studies and papers are the distinctions within either of the two sociologies very clearly defined or agreed upon. In the face of such lack of agreed clarity only three strategies present themselves.

1 To accept and use the perspective claimed by each author. This is not feasible because many do not make such statements.
2 To adopt a working definition of one's own for each perspective, and then to classify studies according to it. Apart from being presumptuous and difficult, it would result in the redefining of some studies and add further confusion.
3 To avoid making too fine a distinction between the perspectives, by initially using the simple idea of the two sociologies, but maintaining a watchful eye for the subtle differences which exist within them.

It is the third strategy that we follow here. The two sociologies to be identified stem from a basic dilemma about the nature of social reality. This dilemma, which is no new idea, can be simply illustrated by two questions − 'To what extent is *society* made by man?' and 'To what extent is *man* made by society?' At this level the dilemma appears to be rather silly, since man and society are clearly products of each other − without man there would be no society, without society there would be no man. At an everyday level we can see the effect that society

Table 1.2
The sociologies of education

Structuralist	Main types	Interpretative
Systems Macro Normative Positivistic Traditional Holistic	Alternative labels	Action Micro Interactionalist Phenomenological Emergent Atomistic
Consensus Conflict Structural functionalism Marxist	Subtypes or perspectives	Symbolic interaction Phenomenology Ethnomethodology Marxist
Surveys Questionnaires Interviews Observation	Main types of methodology	Observation Participant observation Recording Interviews
Durkheim Parsons Merton Weber	Representative theorists	Mead Schutz Goffman Weber
Halsey, Flood and Anderson (1961) Banks (1968) Shipman (1968)* Ashley, Cohen and Slatter (1969)	Representative sociology of education texts	Young (1971) Cosin, Dale, Esland and Swift (1971) Hammersley and Woods (1976)

*Shipman (1975) spans both sociologies

has on man. Hence we recognise that there are similarities between people called teachers, and probably conclude that this has something to do with their social setting. They are as they are because of what they have to do, where and how they have to do it, and these rely on the expectations of people around them, the training they received, and so on. At the same time we recognise that each of them has a certain uniqueness. Mr X is not exactly like Mr Y – and for such mercies we are often thankful. No self-respecting sociologist will deny the existence of either side of this dilemma. What they do disagree about is the emphasis that each side should be given. Sometimes their statements amount almost to a denial of each other. Such statements should be viewed in terms of a debate, or, to return our earlier analogy between sociology and Christianity, as evangelism or semi-blind faith.

To further our understanding it is first necessary to indulge in a dangerous art, that of characterisation. It's only dangerous if you believe the characterisations, rather than seeing them as a means to understanding – so be warned! Structuralist sociology is accused of viewing man as a receiver of, and responder to, society. Social life, here, has been characterised as a play in which people act parts (roles) written for them by society. Interpretative sociology is accused of viewing man as a manipulator and creator of society. Social life here is likened to a game in which the players (people) have a great deal more tactical freedom than in a play. Readers will, at once, see through the analogies; both plays and games are governed by rules and both allow for (or even demand) interpretation. If you ponder on the differences between good and indifferent football or drama you will catch the subtlety involved, and at once become suspicious of characterisations of the two sociologies. Structuralist sociology does not totally ignore the meaning of social life to the people involved, nor deny the importance of the way people view their own social reality in affecting what actually exists in society. Nor does interpretative sociology have a view of man as constructing his own social reality completely uninhibited by structural factors such as wealth, sex, colour, power, and so on. They do, however, vary in their emphasis in such directions.

Structuralist sociology

This type of sociology has a long history as the mainstay of the discipline. It emanates from what sociologists for a long time viewed as their central problem − the explanation of social order. That is, why do societies, and social systems, exist and persist? − or, more pointedly, what makes them tick? There are two main types of structuralist sociology, one based on the idea of *consensus* (general agreement) and the other on *conflict*. The most common form of the first is structural functionalism, which has unique importance in the sociology of education; and the best-known example of the second is Marxist sociology. A useful introduction to these forms of structuralist sociology is to consider their theoretical defences.

Consensus theory

Social life would be impossible if there were no norms (recognised standards or patterns) in social situations, together with some commitment to these norms on the part of the people involved. This commitment, it is argued, comes from the fact that underlying the norms are shared values and beliefs about them (consensus). All apparent divisions in society − for example, differences in power − are countered by these values. Hence power is viewed as legitimate authority. In a similar fashion the social systems that make up society are in basic accord with each other. Society is viewed as being rather like a body: all parts are related to each other, change or movement in one affects the others, and parts cannot be autonomous from, or in conflict with, others. Functionalism has further implications. To appreciate these it is necessary to realise that the ideas were developed from problems faced by anthropologists attempting to understand societies which had no written history. A basic assumption that developed was that there is no such thing as a redundant social activity. If the participants in rain dances don't believe they dance to cause rain, then the dance must be fulfilling some other function for society and the dancers or else it would not happen. As Cohen (1968) has pointed out, the development of this is Parsons's (1949) claim that one of the major tasks of sociology is to analyse society as a system of functionally interrelated variables. Parsons (1951) treats personality needs and social needs as variables of the social system. Hence analysis of professional rules (for example those of doctors) displays that they have functions for (1) the profession — they regulate entry, maintain rights and obligations — (2) society — they provide and control a service — and (3) practitioners and clients — they regulate and structure their relationships allowing each to anticipate the other's behaviour and facilitate the exchange of the intimate without risk and involvement.

Conflict theory

Society exists because it serves man's interests; however, such interests are not the same for all groups in society. Groups vary in their access to scarce resources in society — wealth, power, prestige, knowledge etc. — and these differences are the basis of the conflict between interests and groups. Consensus exists only within a group with shared interests. General values in society are the values of the group which has control and hence the ability to impose (by coercion or inducement) their group values on the rest. Conflicts may not always be apparent — they become institutionalised or remain latent — but this situation cannot remain for long because group interests seek expression and autonomy. Marx saw the major axis in society as the relationship of groups to the means of production. The chief area of conflict was in social-class terms and between those who owned and those who did not own these means. Dahrendorf (1959) suggested that the axis was authority (power to impose one's will on others) and that the arena for viewing conflict should not be society as a whole but any area that was subject to the same authority (e.g. industrial enterprise, school); accordingly, there are many different conflicts within society and not one as suggested by Marx. Van Den Berghe (1963) has proposed that the theory be developed to include conflicts over all types of scarce goods in society.

Consensus and conflict theory

These are, then, two views which appear to be incompatible and directly opposed. They are not, however, mutually exclusive. Thus it is not a question of accepting one and rejecting the other (though in practice this is what sometimes happens). Indeed Dahrendorf has suggested that they vary in their utility depending on the particular situation one is observing (for an example of this, see table 2.1 and the discussion in Chapter 2). Cohen and Van Den Berghe agree that both theories contain elements of the reality of social life and of each other. The latter writer has identified how the two overlap or converge.

1 Both theories have a holistic view, seeing society as a system of interrelated parts, and may be criticised for overstressing this factor while underestimating the relative autonomy of some parts of society.

2 Conflict and consensus have dual roles. As Coser (1956) has pointed out, conflict can be a stabilising and integrative force for the groups involved. On the other hand, consensus about such norms as individual *laissez-faire* or competition is hardly likely to contribute to social solidarity.

3 Both share an evolutionary model of social change. Conflict theory sees a dialectical process towards progress, while consensus theory sees society moving towards greater structural complexity (See Chapter 5).

The conclusion, then, is that these two structuralist approaches are both partial and complementary. Their main objective is to produce theories that will show how structural features of social reality affect (or are related to) behaviour in social situations. They can be characterised as adopting the 'classical scientific' approach and being mainly concerned with the 'macro' aspects of society.

SOCIAL STRUCTURE	⟷	SOCIOLOGICAL THEORY	⟷	OBSERVED BEHAVIOUR

Interpretative sociology

This stems from the belief that structuralist sociology ignores or underrates important elements and processes between the two ends of the diagram above. Its concern is to put man back into sociology – not man as an individual (as in psychology or theology) but man as a process. Hence:

$$\text{SOCIOLOGICAL THEORY}$$

SOCIAL ←→   ↑   OBSERVED

STRUCTURE ←→   MAN AS A PROCESS ←→ BEHAVIOUR

There are three main types of interpretative sociology which are not as easily distinguishable from each other as the variants of structuralist sociology.

Symbolic interaction

This rests on the basic ideas of the classical social philosopher G. H. Mead, whose ideas have been neatly presented by Blumer (1965). Mead's central concept was that of the SELF, that man has the ability to be an object to himself – he can see himself, communicate with himself and even act towards himself. In a social situation he is, then, capable of deciding what his needs are and how they can be satisfied, he can review the possible ways of achieving them, anticipate the likely outcomes of possible actions, decide on the most appropriate action, undertake it and change course if his predictions prove to be incorrect. (Readers may find it useful to relate these ideas to such situations as boy meets girl (and vice versa) or headteacher interviews pupil.) The picture of social action that emerges is different from that gained from structural sociology. It is active, involving interpretation and definition on the part of the social actor, a far remove from pure response to external factors. Established social behaviour – the type we all rely on – is then an ongoing, dynamic process, maintained only through common definitions and reactions. Most importantly, and in contrast to structuralist sociology, it suggests the whole and full range of possible human associations – co-operation, conflict, domination, exploitation, compromise without duress, and so on.

The implications for the sociological enterprise and research are considerable. It suggests that the 'objective' or outside view of a social situation has very limited utility. It is only by gaining knowledge of the actor's perceptions and reactions to situations that an understanding of the action involved is to be achieved. Similarly one should not assume that when two or more people occupy the same relationship with another – say, pupils to a teacher – they share similar views or necessarily engage in the same behaviour towards him. Only by concentrating on the *subjective* meaning of the actor can one avoid a situation in which an investigator holds a different view or understanding of social reality from that held by the subjects of his study. This is not to claim that structural factors are to be dismissed, but that a clear change of emphasis is called for: rather than suggesting, for example, that the bureaucratic organisation of a tax office *determines* the behaviour of tax officers, the assertion is that it *affects* tax officers' definitions and interpretations.

Phenomenology and *Ethnomethodology* both have roots in philo-sophy, and clear distinctions between them are rare in the literature. We shall follow a notable exception, that of Mennell (1974).

Phenomenology
Phenomenology derives from the philosophy of Husserl who suggested that we should be concerned only with phenomena – that (literally) which can be directly understood by our senses, or how things appear to our consciousness. What remains behind the phenomena cannot be determined. Hence phenomenologists are concerned, after Schutz, with how reality is constructed through social process and how the individuals involved acquire ways of thinking. The major concern, then, is to explore the 'commonsense', 'everyday' world of how people understand each other and share similar perceptions of the world. Each person, it is claimed, has a unique stock of know-ledge and therefore to some degree views the world differently. Interaction takes place on the assumption that we can take for

granted other people's knowledge or views, and ignore some of the differences between them and us. Generally speaking, and particularly with people we know, such 'commonsense' assumptions work. With less familiar people and situations we must improvise, and this leads to some modifications in our 'typifications' (classifications or categories). Few distinctions are drawn between everyday life and the activities of social scientists, who construct typifications for scientific rather than 'practical' purposes. As Mennell suggests, 'to speak of multiple realities conveys an impression of the relativity and even subjectivity of truth, that all perspectives on reality are equally valid' (p. 49). Thus the abiding impression, or task, of phenomenology is to question and explore the commonsense assumptions pervading everyday life.

Ethnomethodology
Ethnomethodology considers the way people understand each other – communication and interaction – as being problematic. It claims that actions and statements have an infinite ambiguity, suggesting that generalisations brought from one situation to another are most difficult, if not impossible. Douglas (1971) distinguishes *situational* ethnomethodologists, who are concerned with the negotiation of social order; a basic research method here is to disrupt everyday situations in order to expose the underlying assumptions. Garfinkel (1967) asked students to act as 'lodgers' in their own homes (with predictably disruptive effects!). Douglas's other group are *linguistic* ethnomethodologists who concentrate on language exchanges. All conversations contain more than their words convey – think about your 'family talk' and how understandable it would be to an outsider. In conversations we all assume 'knowledge' on the part of others. Most sociologists believe that the participants could explain a conversation to outsiders, though some ethnomethodologists might not accept such as acceptable evidence of their meaning and intentions.

All interpretative sociologies can be seen as critical of structural sociology, especially phenomenology and ethnomethodology, which hold that the formulations and understandings ('common sense') of sociologists (as well as those whom they study) are problematic, and thus should be subject to investigation and reformulation.

Historical perspectives

Obviously one would expect the development of the sociology of education to be related to that of sociology itself. This, as we shall see, is certainly the contemporary case. In the past, however, few sociologists as such had any real concern with education; it should be remembered that, apart from the possibility that they had more important concerns, education as seen in economic, social and political terms is a comparative newcomer on any scale, even in Western society. Few classical sociologists (the main criteria of being 'classical' appear to be being dead and remembered) wrote much on education. In fact one of the few (and often forgotten) British classical sociologists, Spencer, had some very quotable things to say, for example:

Thoroughly to realise the truth that with the mind as with the body the ornamental precedes the useful, it is requisite to glance at its rationale. This lies in the fact that, from the far past down even to the present, social needs have subordinated individual needs, and the chief social need has been the control of individuals.

It is also true that sociologists like Mannheim were concerned with education, but, although his work has been available for some time (Mannheim and Stewart 1962), it has remained generally unrecognised. It was, however, only Durkheim who displayed any sustained interest in the subject – at one time holding the enchantingly titled professorial chair of 'the Science of Education and the Science of Sociology' at the Sorbonne (University of Paris). It is Durkheim alone who is consistently quoted by writers in the field and who has had a continuing influence on the discipline, as he has on much of the whole field of sociology. Since, without denying a European influence, most things sociological have their origins or developments in America, one is more or less obliged to review the early progress of the sociological study of education there. Writers in this field are fond of distinguishing between the early work, which they label *educational sociology*, and the subsequent and current work, which they call the *sociology of education*. While this terminology is useful, it is also somewhat misleading, since the distinctions are far from clear. Further, the use of the two terms suggests that the latter has replaced the former, though we can doubt the former's extinction. Initially, however, we follow convention.

Educational sociology

The term 'educational sociology' has a curious ring to it. It could suggest that this type of sociology is educational, implying either that the other types are not, or one might argue that it includes all sociology, since the subject itself is educational (i.e. helps with 'the systematic training and development of the moral and intellectual faculties'). However, the term is used to refer to that branch of the discipline which developed, early in this century, in America from what Corwin (1965) has described as a 'mixed marriage' of educationists and sociologists. Lee (1927) records that the number of colleges offering such courses grew from forty to ninety-four between 1910 and 1926, while Corwin states that twenty-five texts were published in the area between 1916 and 1936.

Educational sociology attempted to solve educational problems in a practical way using sociology. The main characteristics of the subject were an imbalance between educationists and sociologists in favour of the former, strong moral, political and practical overtones, and a lack of theory. Lester Ward is usually recognised as the most influential figure in the enterprise. His views – that the object of education was social progress, and particularly happiness; that only ignorance got in the way of righteousness – illustrate the moral and practical aspects which, it is claimed, took the discipline away from theory and research. Perhaps as importantly, because many of the courses were taught by educationists rather than sociologists, the main body of sociology had little to do with educational sociology. In Britain it is still true that much 'sociology of education' is taught in teacher-education institutions by people who, in terms of their qualifications, orientations and objectives, are basically education tutors rather than sociologists. Hence some of the criticisms of educational sociology could be applied to *some* contemporary sociology of education. The educational sociology outlined above had little real history or importance in Britain, since even sociology itself was not really established until after the Second World War. At about the same time it went into decline in America, largely replaced by the sociology of education.

Sociology of education

It is generally claimed that this can be recognised by the fact that it is the application of sociology to education. In other words, and in contrast to educational sociology, it is the socio-logical study of education, parallel to the sociology of the family, the sociology of religion, and so on. Probably the most notable difference was a shift towards the involvement of sociologists and the recognition of education as a useful and legitimate field for them to study. Some writers, for example Corwin (1965), have claimed that it is becoming a scientific study. Without debating the word scientific, we can agree that the sociology of education is concerned to solve problems that arise from a desire to understand education as a social institution – how it functions (i.e. what it does and how) and what are its relationships with other parts of society.

The sociology of education had then, as now, at least preten-sions, if not claims, in a number of directions. First, towards the theoretical: simply, to explain events in general terms, not solely on the basis of the events' own characteristics; hence one direction was to seek explanations of differences in children's classroom performance in areas outside the classroom itself. Second, towards the empirical: explanations were to be sought and verified through observations. Third, towards the objective: early flirtations with absolute objectivity – that is complete independence of an observer's attitudes – led to relative objectivity, a realisation of the effects of one's attitudes upon what is observed, and the recognition of the value and importance of others' attitudes and viewpoints. On these three criteria – theory, empiricism and objectivity – rested, and indeed still rests, the claim of the sociology of education to be 'scientific' and thus distinctive from educational sociology.

However attractive this simple division into two appears, it is misleading. The people involved, like the problems investigated, do not fall neatly into the categories of either sociological or educational. They lie between, across, over and around these categories. Even the purest-minded sociologist who went to study education as an institution would find the task impossible without becoming involved in educational problems, teachers' views, and so on. Indeed, unless he did so concern himself it is unlikely that his study would be very illuminating. The problem of explaining order and control in schools is at once a sociological challenge and a moral, educational, professional and practical problem for all involved – not forgetting the children, parents, administrators, politicians and the rest of society.

In Britain, though, some of these issues remain academic since here the development of the sociology of education is more closely connected to that of of sociology *per se*, and both have a history which only dates from the Second World War. It was not until 1961 that a second British university, Leicester, followed the London School of Economics in creating a professorial chair in sociology. Since then nearly all self-respecting universities have created them. Similarly the majority of other institutions of education, polytechnics, colleges of education, of higher education, of technical and further education, and even

some schools, have introduced sociology as part of their curricula and now have staff and/or departments teaching sociology.
Many courses leading to professional qualifications, including
such diverse professions as nursing, physiotherapy, accountancy, the church, social work, youth work, engineering and
architecture, now contain elements of sociology. Although
there are now signs that the expansion is over, the establishment
of sociology is real enough. In teacher education this establishment was unique, sociology being the first, and as yet the only,
social science to become a discrete and extensive curriculum
entity (a main course) as well as a contributory discipline to
education.

This book is clearly not the place to attempt to explain why
the period of the mid-1960s to the early 1970s should have been
an era of continual oversubscription to expanding sociology
courses in higher, further and professional education. Indeed
the history of this rapid development is not yet very well
defined, possibly because those who could write about it were
part of it themselves. As far as the teaching of sociology of
education was concerned, the most vital factors were the
changes in teacher education in Britain. The most significant of
these was its extension from two or three years in 1962 and an
increase in the number of students admitted to colleges of
education which rose from 16,785 in 1961 to 39,574 in 1968,
and peaked at 42,133 in 1972. Over the same period the
number of graduates in training increased by two-thirds (*Statistics of Education 1970 and 1975, Vol. 4*). At the same time there
was a move to make education, as a discipline, more academically respectable, by attempting to identify it with the separate
disciplines of which it is composed. Courses in education thus
became courses in the history, philosophy, psychology and
sociology of education. This is not to say that education courses
did not contain elements of these before. I can well remember
the vice-principal of the college I attended displaying in his
lectures an apparent fascination with the effects of living in the
slums of Scunthorpe on children's school performance. But in
those days it was all called education and, much like the

educational sociology outlined above, appeared to owe little to its contributory disciplines, but a good deal to its direct aim of producing people who would be adequate classroom performers.

One part of this curricula history which has interested the author (Reid and Wormald 1974; Reid 1975) is the very rapid development of sociology as a main (academic) course in teacher education. In 1960 only six colleges offered such a course, four years later it was twelve, by 1966 it was twenty-eight, and in 1968 no less than forty-six. It also displayed, indirectly, the dependence of sociology of education on sociology itself. In spite of there being very real pressures to make the sociology taught in teacher education relevant to teaching, Shipman claimed in 1968 that it was still possible to detect the influence of the university that the head of department had attended, simply by looking at the syllabus (Shipman 1969). The study of the school as an institution and the application of sociology to the classroom were not discernible as major elements in a survey of the syllabuses in 1968 (Ellis, McCready and Morgan 1969).

Nearly all commentators on the sociology of education have recognised the important part played in the immediate post-war period by the London School of Economics, whose brand of sociology held sway till the late 1960s. (See, for example, Banks 1976; Bernstein 1974; Shipman 1974). It was here that the work that forms the now classic book on social mobility in Britain (Glass 1954) was carried out. Rather more than a third of that book is about education. Two products of the L.S.E. — Floud, who contributed to Glass's book, and Halsey — must be recognised as very significant influences on the creation of the sociology of education in Britain. Not only did they write an extremely influential book (Floud, Halsey and Martin 1956) and many papers, but also a reader in the sociology of education (Halsey, Floud and Anderson 1961) which remains an important text today. At the time it was the only major and extensively used British book and remained so until Musgrave (1965) and Banks (1968). The importance of these associations was that they gave rise, for a period, to a monopoly of structural-functional theory in the sociology of education. The effect of this was that up to the mid-1960s, at least, the sociology of the education being taught and practised had, through the L.S.E. and to a lesser extent Leicester University, a fairly direct link with the sociology of Durkheim. Moreover, and in contrast to the present, there was little discussion about the theoretical basis of the sociology of education, almost entirely on account of the lack of alternative models. Indeed the only readily available alternative, Marxist or conflict structuralism, was ill organised and produced no textbook in this period.

But this situation was to change. The watershed, for most, was probably in 1970 when the British Sociological Association held a conference on the sociology of education. As a surprise to many of those who were teaching the sociology of education, a number of the papers presented revealed new, or at least different, theoretical perspectives (the papers have been published, Brown 1973). This is not to imply that the sociology of education was late into the field of the 'emergent paradigms', since in many ways, and for reasons outlined in the next section, it was to lead rather than to follow the main body of sociology. In fact, to see the 1970 conference as the watershed is only to pick out a significant national event – the writing had been on the wall for some time. The critics' reception of Shipman's book (1968), viewed by many as extremely useful – it had the virtue of presenting alongside a structural-functionalist analysis of the school a conflict-theory one – was a noticeable instance. Even allowing for the demands of the critic's role, the words of Young (1968) were forceful when he wrote:

> It will . . . give students a one sided and misleading idea of what sociologists are trying to do . . . Shipman's notion of sociology, alas all too common in the field, does lead one to ask the question whether such a book is worse than no book at all . . . It is one of the myths of conventional wisdom . . . that organisations can be thought of as having goals, independently of the goals of the various groups and individuals of which they consist.

From 1970 onwards the whole scene became less comfortable for those cosseted in structural functionalism and whose sociology of education contained few theoretical concerns. The most telling challenge, initially at least, came from the symbolic interactionalists and phenomenologists. The real bombshell was dropped by the Open University, who launched on a partly unsuspecting world the School and Society course, together with its reader (Cosin, Dale, Esland and Swift 1971). The effect of this publication was considerable, on account of its availability (as compared to other courses), its readability and most important, its appeal to students – most of whom were, initially, trained teachers. As we have seen, the message of this 'new' sociology was to put man back into sociology and to challenge the claim of my old professor of sociology that 'Sociology is only sometimes about people.'

In 1976 a revamped Open University course (E202) was released, which adopted a very clear Marxist theoretical approach. The course material covered both the micro and macro aspects of the sociology of education, from classroom interaction to its political significance and operation (Dale, Esland and Macdonald 1976; and Hammersley and Woods 1976). Such was the apparent or assumed political bias of the course that Gould (1977) held it to be indoctrination and not education, and a lengthy debate by correspondence was held in the national press. As far as the discipline of the sociology of education was concerned, it provided an alternative structuralist approach, one that attempted to span the 'old' and the 'new' sociologies in content and methodology and to re-establish the place of the European tradition. By 1977 these developments had led to the establishment of what can be called 'the sociologies of education', and to the need for the type of book you are now reading.

This section has traced, somewhat sketchily, a chronological history of the sociology of education in Britain. It is now necessary to identify two important aspects of the cultural setting in which these events took place.

Ideological and utilitarian perspectives

Academic disciplines do not develop in isolation, deciding on their own problems, producing new theories, presenting findings, and so on. They have a complex relationship with the social setting in which they operate. This is at once a simple and complicated point to make. If society, or its government, becomes interested in the effectiveness of education in relation to producing certain types of workers, then this interest, and probably the money made available, will encourage those disciplines involved to develop work and research in this area. Of course it works the other way round too: disciplines, because of their intrinsic interests, may reveal problems or research findings which capture the imagination or interest of society; or the interests of both society and disciplines may coincide. A good example from the sociology of education is the interest in the relationship between children's social class and their performance in education. As I have suggested elsewhere (Reid 1977a), a number of interrelated factors can be identified with this interest and the direction it took in the late 1950s and early 1960s. In its simplest form it can be seen as follows. On one side there was the continuing interest of the public, politicians and educationists in equality and equal opportunity in education, and in particular in the results of the 1944 Education Act. On the other, there were sociologists whose type of sociology (structural functionalism) gave them an interest in large-scale research and in seeking explanations for educational achievements outside the classroom, in the social structure. The coincidence of these two interests gave rise to a number of large national studies of social-class achievement in education.

For our present purpose it is necessary to pay some attention to two related aspects. First, to how the efforts of sociologists of education have been received into the ideology (body of ideas forming the basis for political, economic or social system) of society and educational institutions. Second, to the demands made upon the discipline by users of the sociology of education. These two aspects are intimately related and shed some light on the development and use of the current theoretical perspectives in the sociology of education. Our concern with these aspects will be limited to the main users of the sociology of education — teachers and teacher-education institutions. Somewhat similar points about sociology and society in general are available elsewhere (see, for example, Wright Mills 1959; Gouldner 1973).

Sociological theories, like most statements about man or society, can be seen to contain or reflect an ideology. A theory that sees the parts of society (institutions or systems) as related to each other, and conflicts between them as being underlaid with agreement or acceptance of certain values, can be characterised as being conservative. It suggests that existing society is basically right, or that it is in balance (equilibrium). Without stretching one's imagination too far, it can be seen that the above characterisation of structural functionalism suggests a possible reason for its acceptance and past monopoly in the sociology of education: it fitted in with the teaching profession's ideology. Teachers and teacher-education institutions have been found to be basically conservative (see, for example, McLeish 1970). The view of social reality presented by this type of sociology accorded reasonably well with teachers' perceptions of their teaching and their relationships with children and society. Moreover, and without being too cynical, its message was as appealing as that of the psychologists about intelligence: basically, that educational achievement was to some extent due to factors outside the classroom and teachers' control — in this case, the family and community as opposed to innate ability. Both these ideas to some extent protect the teacher from total responsibility for the end product of his teaching. In a difficult task like teaching such protection is welcome.

There was, however, another aspect of teachers' professional ideology which prevented them from accepting some of the structural-functional approach. This was their belief in the uniqueness of each teacher and each class. Hence there was a tendency to reject bold suggestions from sociologists of education that teachers were performing roles for society at large, such as occupational placing, and that it was possible to talk meaningfully in a generalised way about what *teachers* did in classrooms, rather than viewing them as helping children to realise their individual capabilities and goals.

In this sort of climate it was hardly surprising that the interpretative sociology of education, with its emphasis on the uniqueness of social situations, and a definite place for the individual, was welcomed and quickly assimilated by a profession where such an understanding of social reality was traditional and perhaps necessary. The way in which the new Open University course with its clear Marxist overtones is received by the teaching profession will provide an interesting test case. It is open to debate whether an approach that can be viewed as explicitly radical and political – in a direction opposite to that of the vast majority of the profession – can be acceptable, almost regardless of its usefulness within the discipline and practice. Only time will tell. If one is offered two or more sociologies, with no clear indication of superiority, the choice is likely to be based on how well each fits into one's ideology, beliefs and understandings of social reality. There is, however, a further factor to be considered – the use to which one wants to put sociology.

As has been argued, the sociology of education is mainly taught on teacher-education courses. Such courses have clear objectives: to prepare people for the professional role of teacher and educate them. There are fairly clear indications that the first of these is the overriding one, so that the content of such courses is both evaluated by teachers and taught in terms of its relevance and utility to professional goals. These criticisms were made public and shifted, between the mid-1960s and early 1970s, from questioning whether sociology and sociology of education had any value for teacher education to what type of sociology was most useful (Reid and Wormald 1974). McNamara used Jackson's (1968) 'summation of teacher talk' – that it was characterised by uncomplicated views of causality, an intuitive rather than a rational approach to events, opinionated stances regarding teaching practices, and a narrowness in applying abstract terms to work situations – to suggest that the sociology of education as currently taught was inappropriate to teachers and students, 'Not particularly because he does not want to but because the pressures of work and the practical demands of the situation in which he finds himself make it particularly difficult to stand back and look objectively at what he is doing' (McNamara 1972). He went on to claim that sociologists had, for too long, been interested only in developing and verifying general theories about social situations. The answer lay, he suggested, in grounded theory, which would 'develop a sociology of education . . . based upon observation and research in school situations . . . concerned with deriving explanations of the behaviour of individuals in schools from data collected in schools rather than applying theoretical perspectives from elsewhere'. Gorbutt (1972) argued that only by adopting the interpretative rather than the structuralist paradigm would the sociology of education produce a self-critical, researching teacher, a result he saw as necessary for revitalising schools and colleges. This emphasis towards what could be termed as utilitarian sociology (designed to be of use to schoolteachers) I noted was even true of main courses in sociology and social science in colleges of education. 'Of the 103 syllabuses in the Guide to Social Science Courses (McCready 1972) . . . only 38 are specifically referred to as sociology. The majority are directed towards more direct classroom skills or curricula, or to the extension of the role of the teacher' (Reid 1975).

This section has suggested that the professional ideology of teaching, together with the interests and demands of teachers in training and those of their tutors, provided a more fertile bed for interpretative than for structuralist sociology of education. Thus the ideological and utilitarian settings of the sociology of education must be seen as helping to shape the development of the discipline. Perhaps, however, the overriding influence is that of the nature of the phenomena dealt with by sociology, as well as the discipline itself.

Having reviewed the discipline's theoretical perspectives and something of the sociology of the sociology of education, our

concern is now with how these perspectives have been applied to
the content of the sociology of education. An obvious starting
point in any consideration of education is the school, and that is
where we begin.

Schools

Schools, as you may have noticed, are pretty odd places – there is
nothing else quite like them. They are, as sociologists would
have it, unique social institutions ('aspects of social life in which
distinctive values and interests, centring upon large and important social concerns are associated with distinctive patterns of
social interaction' Weeks 1972). Before exploring the ways
sociologists have viewed and researched schools, we can pick out
a number of commonly accepted but unique characteristics of
schools. The most important of these is that we all have to go to
school; the law insists upon it. Indeed, in Western society,
schools are the only social institution, of any real importance, of
which we must all be part. We can assume that virtually the
whole population experiences school – certainly a much larger
proportion than is involved in other institutions including the
family, marriage, religion, politics, and so on. Basically schools
are a significant part of people's lives, apart from anything else,
because of the large amount of time spent in them. At present
the minimum number of years at school is eleven (from
approximately five to sixteen years of age). This could amount
to something like 15,400 hours at school, or the equivalent of
10,266 football matches, 7,500 feature films or around 32,000
episodes of 'Coronation Street'! School is an important feature of
life, not only for the children in them but also for adults. It is to
be hoped that those who count schooldays as the happiest of
their lives are balanced by those who do not – otherwise it's a sad
reflection on the rest of society and adult life. Although not easy
to trace directly, our experiences at school, to varying degrees,
remain of some consequence throughout our lives. We can
suspect that our experiences at school affect our views, attitudes

and behaviour over a range of facets of adult life. It is certainly possible to see relationships between what people do, or do not do, at school, and income, style of life, occupation and social class in adulthood (see Chapter 7). The same experiences appear to be related to the educational performance of our children (see Chapter 6). It is in these terms that schools perform their very significant social role. Together with the family and other institutions, they produce a social adult in the full sense – that is a person who takes (or makes) his place in society. This implies that schools are about more than just learning in the cognitive sense – subjects on the timetable – and are about learning in the social sense. As will be seen below (e.g. p. 48) it is possible to argue that they are concerned more with social than cognitive learning.

There are other unique features of schools, many of which will be of concern throughout this book; some should be briefly identified at the outset. Schools bring together a small number of adults (teachers) with a much larger number of unrelated children (pupils) into an association. It would be difficult to see this association as purely voluntary. Children do not necessarily choose to go to school – either generally or regularly – neither do they choose the particular school or teachers. Likewise teachers have little real freedom of choice about the children they teach, or about where, what and how they teach (though in the latter cases their freedom is much greater than that of the children). This feature of schools, as we shall see raises interesting questions about social order in schools. What makes schools exist and endure, or what stops the children taking them over, or schools being almost deserted?

Schools can be seen, at one and the same time, to have quite specific and diffuse aims. In the first place they are instrumental, concerned with getting children to read, write, learn and pass exams. At the same time it is difficult to draw boundaries around schools and their activities since they attempt to influence pupils on a broad and deep front. They try, with varying degrees of success, to affect children's attitudes and beliefs, the way they dress and behave, not only in school but also outside.

It is interesting to speculate how much of a school's energy and time is spent on these non-instrumental aims, enforcing standards of dress and appearance, checking swearing, chewing and smoking, developing or demanding courtesy and attitudes of respect, and so on. It should also be noted that parents and society have high expectations of schools in terms of the non-academic characteristics of their products. Indeed the law holds schools wholly responsible for pupils from arrival to departure. All this is in stark contrast to institutions concerned with adults. Imagine a factory attempting to maintain a similar regime with its workers. Even colleges and universities don't try very hard. It needs bearing in mind too that schools set out to achieve their specific and diffuse aims with children who have widely different levels of ability and willingness to fulfil them. In some cases, and for a variety of reasons, schools are attempting the impossible. This should not only be seen with regard to the children they have to work with. Teachers, as we are all too aware, also vary in their ability and willingness to teach, or help children to learn, in these areas. Schools, their facilities and equipment, together with the educational systems in which they function, are often inadequate. Nor is competency and adequacy merely a question of having it or not – not all good scholars are paragons of virtue and no school or system works in all directions and with all its pupils. If we then put these considerations into a dynamic situation, with the demands made upon schools and the aims they set themselves changing over time, then we can begin to appreciate the complexity of the institutions we are viewing.

Another set of unique features of schools arise from the values and beliefs they exhibit. These can be seen to be different, rather than in opposition, to those of the general public or at least significant parts of it. Here we shall consider only two, the academic and the religious. Schools appear to believe that education is good in itself or for its own sake, whereas many people see it rather as a means to an end, say getting a particular type of job. Within education schools appear to give less regard to subjects which may have high intrinsic value (enjoyment) for pupils – like P.E., games and domestic science – and those most directly related to adult occupational roles – wood and metal work, typing and commerce. At the same time they give high regard to subjects like Latin, mathematics and foreign languages whose enjoyment and initial, or subsequent, utility pass many pupils by. This concern with education itself leads to a valuation of pupils within school on what is a narrow part of a person – academic ability. With this rewarding of academic ability goes what is often referred to as an élitist view of education. In schools the more gifted are treated differently and enjoy higher status than the less able. They are often taught different subjects differently by different teachers. Outside educational institutions, in the real world, a wider range of aspects of ability and personality are rewarded. In contrast to the family, for example, schools (particularly secondary ones) emphasize and demand a narrow and instrumental part of the person and pay less attention to the rich diversity of talents that make up a person.

Schools are more religious (or at least less secular) than other institutions in our society – that is, other than religious institutions. Section 25 of the Education Act 1944 says 'the school day in every county school and in every voluntary school shall begin with collective worship on the part of all pupils in attendance', and that 'religious instruction shall be given in every county school and in every voluntary school' (Dent 1958, p. 25). It is true that the Act gave parents the right to request that their children be excused from either or both and that at the present time not all schools abide by the letter of the law. Religious worship and instruction remain, however, the only legally demanded part of the curriculum of British schools. As a consequence, and in contrast to other aspects of life, schools, in general, are unique in including corporate acts of worship and religious instruction as regular elements of their everyday life.

So far we have identified schools as being universal, compulsory, effective in the short and the long term, complex, and displaying values and beliefs that are different from those of society at large. One further factor to be grasped is their scale. In

1975 there were 33,085 schools in England and Wales (*Statistics of Education 1975, Vol. 1*). These schools involved some 9,617,474 children, 492,303 full-time and full-time equivalent staff, and were administered by 104 local education authorities. They involved the expenditure of £4864 million which was 6.6 per cent of our gross national product. This amounts, then, to a vast and complex industry. Such simple facts suggest that the description, let alone the explanation, of schools as social institutions is a formidable task. Common sense suggests that in such a context any single approach is extremely unlikely to be meaningfully comprehensive. There is, however, an even more important consideration than that daunting one, to which we must now turn.

The sociology of schools

The sociological study of schools provides a good example of the paradox that characterises sociology. Because we are or have been part of schools, we have both an intimate knowledge and a set of values and beliefs about them, and so can frequently contradict statements both about schools in general and about specific schools and classrooms. These contradictions are similar to those involved in studying other social institutions – for example, the family. But one can go further and say that at one level we know what is going on in the schools and the classrooms of Britain while at the same time maintaining that we shall never know. These can be called levels of abstraction. They range from the very high – schools are places where knowledge and skills are passed from teachers to pupils – to the very low – our knowledge and experience of a particular classroom and teacher over a school year. The first gives very little insight into any particular school; the second may or may not give any insight into any other classroom. In the latter case it could well be that another person who shared the experience may have gathered different information. Neither of these forms of knowledge is very useful to an understanding of schools, and neither on its own is really sociology (see Chapter 8). Obviously we need something in between which will allow us to relate both to the general and the specific. These problems are, of course, true of many other phenomena. In the case of the human body, medical scientists know how bodies in general function, but such knowledge can be found lacking in relation to specific bodies, the abnormal or sick. Working in the other direction, that is from knowledge of a specific body, also has its dangers depending on which body it was. Clearly, to understand bodies, schools or any phenomena, both types of knowledge are needed, especially as it is difficult to see that they don't both contribute to each other. In the medical analogy a great deal of knowledge about the functioning of the normal body has come from the study of the sick and the dead.

At the outset it is, then, necessary to recognise that the sociological treatments being reviewed are limited in a number of ways. Our knowledge of schools is limited by being:

1) *Partial*	either	(a)	it is limited to only some aspects of the social reality of schools
	or	(b)	it is limited to only some (few) examples of schools
	or	(c)	both (a) and (b) above
2) *Dated*			Schools change constantly, if only because the people in them are replaced
3) *Problematic*			it will be difficult to move logically (a) from the specific to the general (b) from the general to the specific

From our considerations so far it will be realised that sociologists have adopted a number of approaches to the study of schools. It is quite acceptable to see these as arising both from the nature of the phenomena involved (schools) and from the body of the discipline (sociology). The next two chapters review these. The presentation is, however, to some extent artificial since its layout has taken into account two factors. First, the approaches have evolved over time, developing and/or becoming popular alongside the development of the sociology of education. This historical sequence has been heeded. Second, the presentation is at pains to point up the use of distinctive theoretical perspectives as outlined above. The artificiality arises because the historical sequence and the theoretical perspectives are not exclusive or really separate. It is also true that reviewing in this way can lead to a neglect of our central concern – a sociological understanding of schools. In reading what follows it should be borne in mind that it is not intended to suggest an evolution towards the truth, or of competing and conflicting perspectives, but rather an overall picture of contributions to the sociological study of the school.

2

Schools as social systems

The social-systems approach

Our first approach can be clearly seen as deriving from the structuralist or macro-sociological perspective. It involves viewing schools as social systems. 'The term social system may refer to small or large-scale social phenomena. Thus 'A' social system exists when two or more people are involved in social interactions; their behaviour is shaped by similar conceptions of the social norms and roles appropriate to that situation' (Weeks 1972). Traditionally sociology has sought theories which would apply to *the* social system (i.e. society) and the social systems of which the society is composed. Hence it is not surprising that the sociology of education has applied these approaches to schools. One central problem to which traditional sociological theory has addressed itself has already been identified as social order. Two main varieties of explanation have evolved, one based on consensus and the other on conflict. As was suggested in Chapter 1, the former has been more influential, particularly in the sociology of education. Perhaps the best-known exponent of structural functionalism is Talcott Parsons whose essay 'The School Class as a Social System' (1959) only rarely fails to be reproduced in readers on the sociology of education. As might be expected, the essay is about identifying the functions of schools for society and describing the processes involved. In spite of his title, Parsons talks both of class and schools, for example in his concluding paragraph he claims to have sketched 'a few major structural patterns of the public schools system . . . ' Parsons claims – and it is easy to agree with him – that schools are involved in four simultaneous functions:

1 Emancipation of the child from the family
2 Internalisation (learning) of social values and norms, at a higher level than is available in the family
3 Differentiation of the school class in terms of (*a*) actual achievement and (*b*) differential valuation of achievements
4 The selection and allocation of human resources into the adult role system.

It is the third function (differentiation) which he views as the most important. 'The essential point, then, seems to be that the elementary school . . . is an agency which differentiates the school class broadly along a single continuum of achievement, the content of which is relative excellence in living up to the expectations imposed by the teacher as an agent of the adult society.' It is on this process that we shall concentrate. Parsons recognises that 'Differentiation . . . along the achievement axis is inevitably a source of strain, because it confers higher rewards and privileges on one contingent (i.e. group) than on another within the same system.' This strain is alleviated by what he calls integrative mechanisms. Fundamental among these is the sharing of a common value, by the family and school, which recognises that it is fair to give differential rewards for differential achievement provided there has been fair access to opportunities. This he argues is the American value of equality of opportunity, that is, initial equality and differing subsequent achievement and rewards. This enables the parties involved, who presumably might otherwise object, to accept the differentiation. Parsons sees this as particularly important in relation to 'losers' in the competition. Certainly one has to agree with him that it is functional for the institution that losers should blame themselves rather than the teacher, school, educational system or society for their failure. It is also true that most failures in educational systems do not blame the system, at least openly, but it is more than a fair step from this to assume that it is because they share a common value of equality of opportunity. What is not clear, however, is what evidence there is that such values exist or that they are shared by the parties involved.

Presumably both can be answered by the fact that very few parents and children are in open revolt against schools for differentiating them from others. There are, however, a number of logical reasons, other than shared values, why this could be so, ignorance and perceived lack of power being obvious ones. It seems difficult to believe that parents can accept the idea of initial equality other than in a state of ignorance. Well- and widely reported evidence both in this country and America (albeit since Parsons's paper) has drawn attention to a variety of inequalities in educational provision (see Chapter 6 and, for example, *Half our Future* 1963; *Children and their Primary Schools* 1967; *Equality of Educational Opportunity* 1966). Further evidence suggests that parents have but a sketchy idea of what goes on in schools. Jackson (1964) reported that a third of parents with children in schools that streamed did not know what streaming was or which class their children were in. Those that did know overestimated the movement of children between streams and the chances of low-stream children having educational success. Government research reported similar findings (*Children and their Primary Schools* 1967), though here the percentage of ignorant parents was only 13 per cent. It has to be borne in mind that schools and educational systems are much more of a closed shop to parents in Britain than they are in America. For example, Benn and Simon (1972) point out that Circular 10/65 (*Organisation of Secondary Education* 1965), about the introduction of comprehensive schools, stated that parents' views were to be taken into account but that, since hardly any local authorities had machinery to consult parents, they were 'rarely involved in any systematic way'. Several studies, for example Pallister and Wilson (1970), have shown that knowledge of, and attitudes towards, education varies along social-class lines. In this study working-class mothers (who are the majority) had less knowledge of the educational system than middle-class ones. It is worth noting too that parents with the most knowledge of what

goes on in schools are in fact those most likely to object, via
parent-teacher associations and local politics, and by removing
their children from the local authority system and placing them
in the private sector. These sorts of considerations suggest that
an alternative view to that of Parsons is at least as acceptable.
This has been admirably stated by Friedenburg (1963): 'such
autonomy as it [i.e. the school system] possesses is derived from
their custody of the mysteries and records, rather than from any
considerable measure of popular deference to their authority'.

Parsons does not rest his case on the fact that a common value
is the sole integrative mechanism counteracting the strains
imposed by differentiation. He proposes three further factors.
In each case, as is illustrated below (and in the relevant parts of
the following chapters), the evidence for them and their operation is far from clear cut.

1 *Family differentiation cuts across achievement differentiation,
and the family supports the child in directions other than achievement*.
We can accept the latter statement with little comment. The
first is a bold claim, given the well-established evidence of the
relationship between family status and children's achievement
status (see Chapter 6). Indeed Parsons produces such evidence
himself while at the same time claiming 'The evidence also is
that the selective process is genuinely assortative.' What he
claims is that the group (minority) for whom the statuses do not
coincide are of considerable importance to the system. In other
words, the minority justifies the majority (this is further discussed below, pp. 110–11).

2 *Teachers like/respect pupils on grounds other than their achievement status*. While this has some truth – everybody loves a clown
– direct and indirect evidence suggests that teachers have a
preference for the able. Bush (1954) found a positive correlation
between teachers' liking for pupils and the pupils' academic
competence – they learn well, have good conduct and agree with
the teacher on social issues. This finding has been sustained by
recent studies (see for example, Taylor 1976). Herriot and St
John (1966) in America and government research in Britain

(*Half our Future* 1963; *Children and their Primary Schools* 1967) have shown that schools with low academic performance experience difficulty in recruiting staff and have high rates of staff turnover. There also appears to be a resistance to, or avoidance of, teaching the lower streams (a further discussion of these areas is to be found on pp. 50 and 129).

3 *Peer-group friendships cross-cut achievement status*. Again Parsons is resting his case on the fact that there are exceptions. In Britain, with its emphasis on streaming, ability has been consistently shown to be an important factor in friendship choice. For example, it is identified as such by Barker Lunn (1970) in primary schools and by Hargreaves (1967) and Ford (1969), among others, in secondary, including comprehensive schools.

Further, it needs to be recognised that Parsons appears to overemphasize that schools are about teachers and families and tends to forget the children. The essential element of schools is the direct face-to-face relationship of pupils and teachers. Finally it can be recognised that in writing about 'functions' and 'integrative mechanisms' Parsons has depersonalised the school and its social system. This criticism has been well sustained by Levitas (1974).

> . . . the function definition . . . [calls] the practice serving certain purposes a function. And in doing so the vital interests inherent in these purposes, the identities of their creators and executors and the social class intentions behind them are effectively hidden. When a sociologist talks about goals, anyone may ask 'Whose goals?' (p. 165)

Once one adopts the idea that schools (or any social system) are inhabited by distinct groups which have their own goals, then one has to accept that these goals may not coincide and there is therefore the potential for conflict. Certainly this was how Waller (1932) perceived schools.

> The teacher–pupil relationship is a form of institutional-ised dominance and subordination. Teacher and pupil con-

front each other in the school with an original conflict of desires, and however much that conflict may be reduced in amount, or however much it may be hidden, it still remains. The teacher represents the adult group, ever the enemy of the spontaneous life of groups of children. The teacher represents the formal curriculum, and his interest is in imposing that curriculum upon the children in the form of tasks; pupils are much more interested in life in their own world than in the dessicated bits of adult life which teachers have to offer. The teacher represents the established social order in the school, and his interest is in maintaining that order, whereas pupils have only a negative interest in that feudal superstructure. Teacher and pupil confront each other with attitudes from which the underlying hostility can never be altogether removed. Pupils are the material in which teachers are supposed to produce results. Pupils are human beings striving to realise themselves in their own spontaneous manner, striving to produce their own results in their own way. Each of these hostile parties stands in the way of the other; in so far as the aims of either are realised it is at the sacrifice of the aims of the other. (pp. 195–6)

Obviously we can recognise Waller as being a conflict-structuralist theorist, as he writes:

It does not seem extreme to say that those brilliant social philosophers who have developed the sociology of conflict might have found adequate material for their discussions without leaving their own classrooms. Nearly all the classic concepts apply to life in the school room, war, feud, litigation, conflict of ideals, victory, conciliation, compromise, conversion, accommodation, and assimilation. Not all these conflicts are visible to the naked eye, not visible, at least, as conflicts, but it is the part of the sociologist to learn to see the invisible world of social contexts. (p. 351)

It is of more than passing interest to note that the two best-known exponents of conflict theory applied to schools, Waller and Shipman (1968), are fairly unusual among sociologists of education in having had a good deal of classroom experience, including teaching. Waller has to be seen as a conflict-theory hardliner, while Shipman recognises consensus and conflict theories as two separate and valuable approaches. However much teachers and their like may wish to believe that education is about filling empty jars or feeding the hungry, reality is somewhat different. Anyone with classroom experience in secondary schools could hardly fail to be impressed by the centrality of discipline. While the problems of order are apparent and often recognised in such schools, it is also true that children in the reception classes of infant schools pose problems of control – as many a student teacher could witness. Indeed, even Sunday school teachers, working with very small groups (mostly between four and seven children), reported discipline problems as one of their major concerns in teaching (Reid 1977b).

The basis of a conflict-model approach to schools can be established by identifying the points of conflict. These lie with:

1 *The instrumental goal emphasis of the school* being imposed on children who vary in their ability and/or willingness to accept it (this was discussed on pp. 29–31 above; see also pp. 51–2 below). Together with this there is a *partial exclusion of affective goals* (see p. 49).
2 *The normative value emphasis*, with a concentration on what can be seen as middle-class norms (though see discussion on p. 50).
3 *Conflict between the young* (pupils) *and the old* (teachers), or between *the formal* (school and teacher) and *the informal* (pupil) *cultures* of schools (discussed at length below).
4 *Conflict inherent in the teaching process*. Greer (1968) has argued that, since teaching is about attempting to change pupils by introducing new ideas, it involves conflict and subordination (see also pp. 93–103 and 108).

From the above premisses it can be predicted that conflict will be greatest where

1 Children are of low ability and are in situations where instrumental demands are heavy.
2 Children come from widely different social-class and/or ethnic backgrounds from their teachers.
3 Where the age-group differences are accentuated (by their closeness).

What these conditions identify are the older, less able children in formal downtown city secondary schools, which is, of course, precisely where the greatest overt conflict is to be found. The conflict model has a great deal to offer by way of insights into school type B in table 2.1. Conflict is, of course, a fairly strong word, and it is necessary to describe it by reference to its manifestations. Given the differences in power between teachers and pupils, the most common overt reactions to conflict should be seen as forms of passive resistance. This involves playing up the teacher and playing down the class. Such activities use up a good deal of time in most classrooms. Hilsum and Cane (1971) found that the British teachers they surveyed spent 49 per cent of their time in the classrooms teaching (the average duration was about a minute). The average number of times that teachers indulged in direct discipline (reprimanding, glaring and smacking) during teaching time was forty, around once every seven minutes. Pupils can then be observed to develop the 'old lag syndrome' – well known in places like prisons and the armed forces – a form of mechanised semi-conformity. They laugh or hate teachers out of real existence and most effectively neutralise teachers' control by indulging in activities that are just outside his regime and so just avoid punishment, while causing the maximum disturbance. Teachers, on the other hand, withdraw mentally, and sometimes physically (I once worked next to a teacher who did little else in the classroom other than read novels – to himself). They use sarcasm and verbal haranguing, avoid direct conflict by permitting marginally unacceptable behaviours, allow themselves to be sidetracked from the lesson, and so on. You have probably done and seen it all yourself. Hence we can say that conflict and force must be features of

Table 2.1

Two 'ideal-type' schools and the relationship of two models
of structural theory

FEATURES	SCHOOL A	SCHOOL B
Type	Primary	Secondary
Intake	Middle class	Working class
Size	Small–medium	Medium–large
Educational climate	Progressive	Traditional
Staff orientation	Child	Subject, achievement
Teacher type	Ideographic*	Nomothetic*
Pupil control	Humanism †	Custodialism†
Child motivation	Expressive	Instrumental
Inter-staff relationships	Democratic	Authoritarian
Parent–staff relationships	Communicative/ reinforcing	Non-communicative/ antagonistic
Parental/community commitment	High	Low
Theory model basis+	Consensus (Model A)	Conflict (Model B)

MODEL A		MODEL B	
1	Shared norms and values are basic elements of school life	1	School life generates sectional interests
2	School life is based on reciprocity, co-operation, consensus	2	School life generates opposition, exclusion and hostility, and is based on structured conflict
3	School life involves commitment	3	School life involves inducement and coercion
4	School life is cohesive	4	School life is divisive
5	School order rests on legitimate authority	5	School order rests on power
6	School and non-school life (systems) are integrated	6	School life and non-school life (systems) are malintegrated and contradictory

*Derived from Getzels and Thelen (1960)

Ideographic means that the teacher emphasises the individual and personal more than the institutional role (helps person to know what *he* wants to know).

Nomothetic means that the teacher emphasises the institutional over the personal (handing down to those who do not yet know).

†Derived from Willower (1969)

Humanism means accepting and trusting pupils, optimism concerning self-discipline and responsibility.

Custodialism means maintenance of order, distrust of pupils, punitive and moralistic.

+Devised from Cohen 1968, p. 167.

schools since they are never really voluntary or democratic. In arriving at this conclusion we are in good company, including not only the sociologists mentioned but also philosophers of education. What is being suggested is that it is vital to view much of what goes on in schools as institutionalised conflict. The relative lack of overt conflict or violence appears to be due either to the very strong normative pressures in schools or to the fact that the balance of power in schools is very much in the teachers' favour. Conflict is ignored at peril by both sociologists and teachers. Shipman (1968) recounts the difficulties of student teachers in tough schools when headteachers refuse to see conflict as a school or group problem, viewing it only as that of individual teachers.

We have now arrived at the very unsurprising conclusion, that both conflict and consensus are parts of social reality! As is suggested in table 2.1 some schools (or social systems) appear to be characterised mainly by one or the other. It is possible to argue (cf. Dahrendorf 1959) that, in terms of systems like school A, consensus theory would be the most useful, and conversely that conflict theory would be more relevant to school B. A short reflection will reveal, however, that it is naïve to attempt to approach either solely in terms of one of the models. Some of the aspects of school A will undoubtedly be conflictual (actual or latent) but may well not be recognised unless a conflict model is applied. Hence it appears logical that the two should be used as a twin-headed approach, as Shipman (1968) suggested. Surprisingly enough sociologists have not been very active or successful in marrying the two models (though see Musgrave's (1968, 1970) ideas in a different context (Chapter 5) and Van Den Berghe's (1963) theoretical discussion).

The culture of schools

Since we have recognised schools as being relatively isolated social institutions with some explicit objectives, one approach to the sociological study of schools is via their culture. We are assuming that schools will have characteristic patterns of behaviour, values, beliefs and indeed physical environments which are to some degree different from those of other institutions in society. A further assumption is that, while we know there are variations from school to school, there is sufficient similarity between them for meaningful characterisations to be made.

Such an approach has considerable currency and history in the sociology of education. Waller (1932) identified 'a separate culture . . . within the school. This is a culture which is in part the creation of children . . . and in part devised by teachers in order to canalise the activities of children . . . The whole complex set of ceremonies centring around the school may be considered a part of the culture indigenous to the school' (p. 13). These two parts of the culture (or subcultures) we shall call the formal and the informal. In some ways they may be quite different, for example, the formal culture probably accords high status to academic ability while the informal may accord it to fighting/sporting ability or 'being one of *the* boys/girls'. As we shall see, the relationship between, and similarity of, the two cultures varies from school to school. Taken together they constitute the culture of the school, which can be defined as all that is *not* innate, that is, everything that is *not* both universal and unlearned. Clearly it includes nearly everything that happens in schools. One aspect which, surprisingly, is often neglected is the material environment. Perhaps this is because it is so obviously important. An extreme example would be the variation in potential classroom behaviours provided by tiered double-seater desks screwed to the floor as opposed to a few large tables and chairs. Schools appear to have a durability unknown in other types of buildings. In Bradford, for example, we have many large mills and factories which were built for methods of production in vogue in the nineteenth century. They stand empty, or are used for storage, partly because they are unsuitable for modern production processes. Schools built at the same time remain in use, even though the changes in educational methods are at least as great as industrial ones. While not prescribing how schools, teachers and children function, the buildings, their facilities and equipment certainly affect them. It is interesting, then, that such factors are usually not viewed in the literature as very important, being limited typically to a few descriptive sentences (though see Richardson 1973, Chapter 5).

The culture of the schools, like that of any social system, can be seen to have three broad aspects (Dahlke 1958):

1 *Instrumental* – from it people select the techniques of doing things, means to reach an objective.
2 *Regulative* – the actions of persons and the use of instruments are subject to the rules and regulations, the do's and don'ts of living. They specify what should be done or must be done.
3 *Directive* – from it individuals derive their ultimate as well as immediate values, their interpretation of life, the goals for which they strive.

As we would expect, the formal culture of schools is concerned with motivating and facilitating the achievement of children, and, as Parsons (1959) would have it, 'the content of which is relative excellence in living up to the expectations imposed by the teacher'. Although Parsons suggests that such achievement can, theoretically, be seen as cognitive and social, we have recognised that in reality these aspects are one, or at least inseparably interrelated. An interesting small-scale illustration of this interrelatedness is provided by Rist's (1970) observations of a classroom in a black American kindergarten (a rough British equivalent would be the reception class in an infant school). The school did not stream by ability. The teacher, who was herself black, very quickly grouped the children into three groups, which were seated at separate tables and given names to differentiate them. The children were allocated to these groups mainly on the basis of the teacher's observations and judgements of their behaviour (remember this was their first experience of school). Rist was able to show that the resulting groups were distinguishable by the following criteria – family income, family size and level of parental education. Observations revealed that the groups received differential treatment and experience. The lowest group received more control-orientated teacher behaviour, had less interaction with the teacher, and received more ridicule from the other children in the class, than did the other two groups. The initial groups were maintained, the only movement between them being the demotion of two children from the top group because of their inability to be as tidy as the teacher expected top group children to be. When the class reached the end of kindergarten their intelligence was tested. This revealed very slightly higher scores for the top group but overlaps between all the groups. The question now is the extent to which such initial decisions and treatments – based on social criteria – help to predetermine the school careers of children. Subsequent teachers will be affected by school records and will support initial grouping and labelling, while the children will respond with, or be socialised into, appropriate behaviours and achievements. Keddie (1971), in a study of a British secondary school, has displayed how teachers' 'knowledge' of the ability or stream of the classes they teach – based on previous teachers' assessments – affects which parts of the curriculum they teach, how they teach them and the way in which they respond to pupils' questions. The best illustration is that the question 'Why are we learning this?' is regarded as serious enough to require an answer if from a high-stream child, but as 'Why do we have to learn anything?' if from a low-stream child (see also Chapter 3).

The question of the mixture of the social and educational in schools can be taken further. We might, for example, reason that, since schools are consciously produced and maintained institutions (they don't happen by chance!), underlying their culture would be firm and clear educational principles. Or, to put it more forcefully, that it would be appropriate to attempt to explain what goes on in schools in terms of its contribution to learning and achievement. Of course, this is a somewhat mechanistic view of a human institution. Most schools are far from being factories since their 'products' are people not objects, and the processing involved has few similarities to that of production lines for a standard commodity like beer bottles. In other words, schools have to be affective – catering for the social needs of their members – as well as being instrumental – promoting the learning of certain types of knowledge. There is a third fact, briefly discussed above, which is the relationship of schools to society and other social institutions. Our present concerns have been admirably discussed by Young and Beardsley (1968), who argue that what goes on in classrooms is better understood in terms of systems theory rather than teaching or learning theory. The content of a lesson, which can be seen as an information exchange, is quite secondary to the importance of a lesson in structuring behaviour and socialising children to function in a social system. In other words, its purpose is more to socialise than to educate; social as opposed to cognitive learning is at a premiun. For example, a basic requirement of living in modern society is an ability to accept a common definition of social situations and to change readily from one situation to another. Young and Beardsley suggest that this is taught in schools via the timetable, as children have to move mentally and/or physically from subject to subject. When the bell rings, it breaks up what could be a useful learning situation in the hope of producing another one; alternatively, useless learning situations have to be maintained until the bell. As they comment, 'socialisation imperatives clearly outweigh the educational.' But it goes further: teachers' concern with making children indulge only in 'game-directed' behaviour acts in much the same way. Misbehaviour, however vital it may be to the individual, has to be checked. Examples of this would be reading a history book during a mathematics lesson (even where the latter was a waste of time), or the following piece of typical classroom conversation:

TEACHER. You are not paying attention.
PUPIL. Yes I am.
TEACHER. Well, what's the answer?
PUPIL. 362.

TEACHER. You don't know how lucky you were to get it
right, now stop looking out of the window and
pay attention.

In much the same way, experience of classrooms teaches children that many of their personal needs – affective, psychological
and even physiological – are irrelevant to that situation and
should be ignored. The overriding general rule is that behaviour
should be rule-directed, hence the preoccupation with rules in
school and class. If these are learnt properly, the child will be
able to function well in most social systems in the outside
world. Moreover, if schools do their job, social systems can
confidently be constructed in the knowledge that there are
suitable people to man them.

It has occurred to many writers that the formal culture of the
school is rather similar to middle-class culture. Havighurst and
Neugarten (1967) wrote:

> The orientation of the . . . school is predominantly that of
> the middle class. There is a strong emphasis upon the charac-
> ter traits of punctuality, honesty and responsibility. Respect
> for property . . . a premium upon sexual modesty and
> decorum. While both competitiveness and cooperation are
> valued to varying degrees, there is always stress upon master-
> ing and achievement. These middle class values are expected
> to be binding upon both children and adults. (p. 183)

The usual explanation is that teachers are by origin, and/or by
virtue of their occupation, middle class, and that they impose
their values on the school and the children. Another explanation, along Marxist lines, is that since the middle class is the
most powerful (as opposed to the largest) in society it attempts
to impose its values on the whole of society, and the most potent
means for this are schools and the legal and occupational systems. A rather different explanation has been put forward by
Dahlke (1958):

> A current interpretation of the public school is that it merely
> reflects and upholds middle-class values. The norms appar-

ently support this idea, but continuity of school and middle-class norms is incidental. Many of the norms and values emphases occur not because of middle-class influence but because the school is a group . . . [the norms and values] are necessary conditions if any group is to persist. (p. 253)

This idea – that the values and norms of the formal culture of the school arise from schools' institutional needs, that without them schools could not operate – has a certain appeal. Banks (1968) has commented on Becker's (1952) finding that teachers thought lower-class children unrewarding to teach because they had low motivation, were difficult to control and displayed habits such as aggression and indifference to hygiene which annoyed them. She wrote: 'However while some of these attitudes appear to reflect middle-class values, others are just as likely to be a reflection of the teachers' occupational needs. It is, for example, much easier to teach children who are highly motivated to learn, and who respond to the teachers' efforts' (p. 186). From one perspective the elements of school culture can be seen as middle class, from another as being requisites of teaching (as we know it). However, it is necessary to go further and question where the ideas of teaching came from, and why and how they are maintained, often in the face of a spectacular lack of success. The important factor to grasp is that, regardless of how it is caused, the formal culture of schools embodies strong elements of what can loosely be termed middle-class culture. The reality is that children from differing social-class (normative) backgrounds are differently equipped to respond to it. Given the intimacy of the social and the academic in schools, the ability to fit into these aspects of the formal culture is clearly a factor in achievement.

The objective of the formal culture of schools is to produce successful (achieving), well-behaved pupils. Common sense tells us that schools and teachers spend most of their time attempting to get pupils to behave in fairly closely prescribed ways (the ideal-pupil role) in order to achieve. At the same time, all schools to some degree or another fail in this aim – whether over all or for individuals. It is of sociological as well as professional interest to attempt to explain why this happens. Merton (1957) suggested that social systems exert definite pressures on certain people to be nonconforming rather than conforming; in other words, that social systems designed to produce saints also produce sinners, and that the explanation for this lies not with the nature of man, or original sin, but with the social system. Merton identified two theoretically separate elements in culture:

1 *Goals* (purposes and interests) – these apply to all members and are those things held up by the culture as worth striving for. In our present case we shall hold the overriding goal to be academic achievement.
2 *Means* – the ways in which the goals should be achieved that is, the socially acceptable way. We shall regard the major one as adopting the ideal-pupil role as defined by teachers (see pp. 57, 85–7 and 93–102).

Social systems, via their culture, provide both goals and means, but, even if the *goals* were accepted by all, groups of people would have different access to the *means* of achieving them. A good example, which Merton uses, is the goal of wealth or ownership in society at large which is very widely spread among the population. At the same time we must realise that the opportunity (access to the means) to achieve this goal, in a socially acceptable way, varies greatly – say from the wealthy businessman's clever son to the unskilled, unemployed person. Merton argues that people who are variously situated in a social structure can adapt to it in a number of ways. These are outlined in table 2.2 in the first three columns; the right-hand column describes these adaptations in the school setting. The extent to which the goals of the formal culture of schools are accepted by pupils is, because of our lack of knowledge, open to debate. It could be argued that, judging by pupil behaviour, they are more commonly accepted in infant schools than in secondary ones, possibly because the goals in infant schools are more realistic – can be achieved by the majority – than those in secondary schools. More important, however, is the fact that access to the means is differently distributed. The most important ingredient here is ability, both in the academic and the social sense. Almost as important is that aspects of the formal culture of schools actually provide structural barriers to access to the means for individuals. The most obvious example is streaming (discussed below, pp. 124–32) where staff, facilities and the curriculum are differently distributed, so that a low-stream pupil may be effectively denied the means to achieve O level G.C.E., even if that were his goal. At a more subtle level, teachers may categorise and group pupils, thus building barriers to some pupils' achievement and helping to determine their educational outcomes (see pp. 132–44).

In effect, then, we are saying two related things. First, that the formal culture, in operating, as it does, to produce well-behaved achieving pupils, at the same time produces delinquents and disruptive non-achieving pupils. This is, probably, partly explained by the culture's emphasis on rather narrow instrumental and normative standards; a broader-based culture *might* be more successful over all. (This is the essence of the arguments of the de- and free-schoolers, especially in respect of those children who don't achieve in traditional schools.) Second, that in order to achieve in school pupils must accept and be a part of the school's formal culture. Some evidence exists to show that some children have problems in relating to, and becoming part of, the formal culture. Jackson and Marsden (1962/1966) demonstrate that the able and successful working-class people they studied were still very aware of the clash between the culture of their family and community and that of their schools. In order to succeed they had either to forsake the former or else live a Jekyll-and-Hyde existence. Those who were unwilling or unable to do so either dropped out of, or failed at, school.

To return to Merton's schema (table 2.2): it is noticeable that there are problems in trying to characterise the adaptations to classroom or school behaviour. For example, innovation could well be disruptive to the school regime and also leads to a lack of

Table 2.2

Types of individual adaptations to the formal culture of schools

Adaptation	Goals*	Means	Description
Conformity	+	+	Successful pupil, well liked by teachers
Innovation	+	−	Orientated towards success but normative background, lack of ability/personality inhibits adoption of means
Ritualism	−	+	Well-behaved non-achiever
Retreatism	−	−	School is meaningless since pupil identifies with neither goals nor means
Rebellion	±	±	Uses school for purposes and in ways which are different to those of the formal culture

*Key	+ = acceptance
	− = rejection
	± = rejection and substitution

(Devised from Merton 1957, chapter 5)

achievement on the part of the pupil involved. It would also include, however, the pupil who was able (even very able), yet refused to do his homework or to work in the prescribed way (and not because he couldn't!). Here it is possible that if the means were strictly enforced the formal culture might stop or discourage this pupil from achieving. Schools depend on ritualism, especially since they contain a majority of children who will not achieve success (and who are aware of it) but who continue to play the game, abiding by the rules. If this were not so schools would quickly become unmanageable. Retreatism and rebellion are not necessarily distinguishable. As has been suggested, a common response of those who are not in tune with the formal culture of schools is passive resistance, which could stem from both these adaptations. The most dramatic and publicised response is a rebellion whereby the goals and norms substituted are in conflict with those of the formal culture. This can be seen as delinquent (Hargreaves 1967), and is a problem not only for the class teacher but also for the school. Behaviours in relation to these adaptations, then, clearly vary in degree; an extreme and not uncommon form of retreatism is truancy, where school is completely avoided. It is important that the adaptations are not seen as total responses by individuals to everything in the school's formal culture. Adaptations vary considerably over time and in regard to specific aspects, for example to particular teachers or parts of the curriculum. The class response that teachers receive or invoke will vary, while pupils who are conformist in academic settings can become rebellious in games or craft lessons (and vice versa). Bearing these strictures in mind, the reader is capable of applying his knowledge of the formal culture of school and its members to Merton's schema in order to illustrate it. This need not be limited to pupils, but may include the staff. Innovative teachers may be very success-ful (popular) with their classes, but are they with other teachers or the headteacher? See how well you can place pupils and teachers you know or have known into the types of adaptation. You will notice that so far our analysis has been at a fairly high level of abstraction. A section below (pp. 93–102) deals with analysis of classroom behaviour. First, though, we shall con-sider the other part of the culture of the school.

The informal culture of schools

As has been suggested, the idea of an informal or pupil culture of schools dates back to Waller (1932). Parsons's structural-functional analysis of the social system attempted to view facets of society in terms of the functions they performed (purposes they fulfilled), both for the social system and for the individuals in them. Writing about the 'youth culture' in society at large, Parsons (1942) claimed that its function for the social system was to hive off a potentially dangerous threat to the social structure into relatively harmless pursuits. In other words, while the young were busy making the 'pop' scene, they were unlikely to be actively criticising the political structure; their energies were being displaced. In much the same way the mere labelling of behaviour and ideas as 'adolescent' renders them harmless or insulates them from serious consideration by adults. For the individual Parsons saw the youth culture as helping to emancipate the child from his family by providing an inter-mediate culture between that of the family and that of adult independence. Following Parsons's thinking, one can see that, if there is an informal culture in schools which is different from the formal, then it could function in similar fashion. In secon-dary schools in particular, pupils who could pose problems for the school might not do so if interested and involved in the informal as opposed to the formal culture of the school. At the same time an alternative culture is provided which might particularly attract the under-achievers, the disinterested and the disenchanted, and which would allow them to become emancipated from the formal culture.

The now classical empirical work in this area was done by Coleman (1961) in ten schools in Northern Illinois and involved some 7,900 children (see also Coleman 1965). Coleman sug-gested that high-school pupils were orientated more towards their parents and peers than towards their teachers. His inter-view and questionnaire data indicated that the values of the informal culture displayed an anti-intellectualism which was in contrast to the formal culture. Status in the former was accorded to athletics and being popular. The 'leading crowd' (the most popular pupils) were slightly more anti-intellectual than the rest. Coleman shows that allegiance to the informal culture affected academic achievement to the extent that some able students hid or disguised their talents in order to remain 'with the crowd'. There was variation between schools: in some schools the informal culture was more supportive of academic performance than others. Coleman speculated that where this was so there would be greater competition and consequently the most able would succeed. He was unable to prove from his data that schools whose informal culture rewarded achievement more highly also had higher correlations between measured intelli-gence and school grades (marks). He did, however, show a relationship between the time spent on homework and plans to go to college and the level of academic support within the informal culture. His work, while being open to criticism on methodological grounds and leaving out a number of factors, poses some interesting questions. Are those who succeed in school either part of an informal culture which supports the formal, or alternatively are they individuals who can manage without belonging to the informal? In some schools does the informal culture work as a barrier to academic success?

Coleman's work has inspired a good deal of further work, both in America and Britain, much of which can be seen to be critical, and viewed under three headings.

Replication

Zenter and Parr (1968) and Hillman (1969) are two examples. Both disagreed with Coleman's study, finding that high status in the informal culture and academic achievement were related. Hillman argues that this is because of changes in the decade between the studies, mainly a decline in unskilled jobs and increased competition to get into college. He also showed that the pupil leaders valued academic achievement more highly than the rest of their peers. It has to be pointed out, however, that Hillman's study was of a single school with a very high percentage (75) of students with plans to enter college. Other studies have been supportive (see also below). McDill, Meyers and Rigsby (1967) analysed students' attitudes, finding that the most important factor was 'academic emulation'. In schools that rewarded intellectualism, competition and competence students tended to conform to these norms and achieve at higher levels.

The importance of the youth culture

Kandel and Lesser (1969), in a study based on three high schools, found that pupils' plans for higher education were more strongly related to their mothers' aspirations than those of their peers. While the study confirms that the informal culture of the American high school does not reward (value) academic achievement, it suggests that its effect on aspiration is less important than that of parents. In other words, adolescents distinguish between values related to their current peer relationships and those that are relevant to their future. Similarly Larson (1972) found that the importance to adolescents of peers' and parents' views and values was dependent upon the context in which they occurred. Peers were important in contexts with immediate implications and parents in those with long-term (future) ones. In comparing adolescents' and teachers' value systems Eve (1975) concluded that while these were statistically distinct there was little cause for concern. Adolescent values were largely derived from those of adults, were conventional in orientation and differed only in small measure from those of the adult world. Boocock (1973) has argued that the informal culture must be seen as part of the total school and social environment.

The conceptualisation of the informal culture

Synder (1966) argues that the youth culture is more diversified than Coleman had suggested, and that girls are both more involved and more affected than boys. He found that academic and athletic values were very close in popularity. It is, however, on Sugarman's work (1967) that we shall concentrate, not only because it is British but because it makes some significant contributions to the conceptualisation. Sugarman's study is based on data collected from 540 fourth-year boys in four London schools (two secondary modern, and one each of grammar and comprehensive, boys-only schools), mainly by questionnaire and some interviews. Sugarman argues that Coleman's work rest on two assumptions, and that his own study is concerned with the first.

1 There are distinct values and norms associated with youth which are in conflict with adults.
2 There are strong social pressures for youth to conform with youth culture.

He argues that schools are successful to the extent to which they can get children to play the *pupil role*, which is defined by teachers and has two characteristics.

1 Deferred gratification: the restriction of present pleasure in favour of the less agreeable but better in the long run (for example doing homework and not messing about in class, in order to achieve)
2 Subordination to all teachers (that is accepting and carrying out what teachers say because they are teachers)

Sugarman proposes that there is also a *teenage role* which is roughly opposite to the *pupil role*. In his research he operational-ises the two roles in what must be seen as a rather weak way. The measures he used are:

1 Commitment to the *teenage role* (self-reported and based on knowledge of the teenage scene, dating girls and smoking)
2 Commitment to the *pupil role* (both of these were based
3 Conduct as pupil   on teachers' reports)

His findings show, not surprisingly, that a high commitment to the teenage role is related to low commitment to the pupil role and poor conduct ratings. The question arises as to the direction of these relationships — does commitment to the teenage role produce poor conduct etc., or the other way round? Sugarman demonstrates that both are related to what he calls the 'intellectual quality' of the home (which is crudely measured by pupil reports about the number of books and type of news-papers in the home and museum and concert visits with the family). His data suggest that there are two distinct patterns — conformity across home, commitment and school behaviour; and deviancy. He claims, then, that the teenage role does not have equal appeal to all. He picks out two groups for whom it has strong appeal:

1 Pupils from poor, non-supportive homes, for whom the teenage role reinforces differences between their back-grounds and schools
2 Pupils who are beginning, through lack of success, to be alienated from school, who turn to the teenage role for support

His conclusion is that the youth culture is the culture of the non-mobile working class, the downwardly mobile middle class, and of individuals who seek mobility or goals along non-school lines.

In further papers Sugarman (1968, 1970) indentifies and classifies sixty-two peer groups involving just over half of his sample. These were:

	Achievement	Conduct	Number of groups
1	Good	Good	24
2	Good	Bad	17
3	Bad	Good	9
4	Bad	Bad	12

He reports that boys from low 'intellectual quality' home backgrounds in type 1 peer groups scored more highly on school adjustment than did boys from high 'intellectual quality' backgrounds who were not in peer groups and nearly as high as those who were members. Sugarman asks what this means. Does membership of a peer group result in a levelling of members' attitudes and behaviour, or must they have these in order to enter the peer group in the first place? In response to interview questions about the codes of behaviour of peer groups, and factors that led to a boy being admired, Sugarman found that none of the groups related either aspect to academic achievement.

Sugarman (1967) makes an interesting distinction between his own work and that of Coleman. The latter saw the informal culture of the school as having its institutional framework within the school itself. It was concerned with athletics and extra-curricular activities, and had the appearance of being a social system, a group activity. Sugarman viewed his as being a set of symbols, assumptions and standards that an individual pupil could use on his own. He seeks to explain the difference between the cultures in terms of the institutional differences between American high and British secondary schools. The former typically indulge in more public activities, especially sport, and a much wider range of activities than the latter. However, Polk and Pink (1970) in an American replication of Sugarman's study found evidence that the situation was similar in both countries. Obviously this raises questions about the initial conceptualisation, the questions asked and their relationship to results obtained. Murdock and Phelps (1972) have criticised Sugarman, suggesting that the evidence shows adolescents often to be involved in both the informal and the formal cultures of schools. Generally speaking, however, those who were not involved in the formal were likely to view themselves as part of the informal. They identify two distinct types of informal culture.

1 *Street culture*, involving mucking about in streets, playing football, going to cafes, and having a central value of solidarity of the group. They argue that it is basically working class.
2 *Pop-media culture*, where the central value is immediate gratification and expression of emotional and physical capabilities. It is individual and open to all, though characteristically middle class.

They argue that Sugarman confused the issue by calling both 'youth culture'. In their study, based on a working-class secondary modern and a middle-class grammar school, those with relatively low commitment to school were the most involved in the alternative cultures (the secondary modern almost exclusively with type 1 and the grammar with type 2).

However vaguely defined and inadequately researched the concept of the informal culture of the school is, it seems reasonable to conclude that groups of people within any social system will have their own ways of viewing and reacting to it. These will vary from more or less agreeing with others' views and the formal culture of the school as argued by Lambert with Millam (1968) in respect of pupils in boarding 'public' schools, to fairly direct conflict as illustrated by, for example, Hargreaves (1967). This is to take a rather simple view, as Sugarman and others have suggested that both the extremes and types in between coexist in most schools. In fact readers might like to join Davies (1973) in questioning the utility of the divide between the formal and informal in 'real' as opposed to analytical terms.

Teachers' informal culture

So far in this chapter an impression has been given that teachers are part of the formal culture of the school, that they help to devise it, and that they maintain it. Anyone with experience of a staffroom, however, will be more than aware that teachers' professional values and behaviours are subject to the influence of their peers. Together teachers can be seen to have an informal culture, a group understanding and solidarity with which they face the social situation of the school. Again, those with know-ledge of more than one staffroom will recognise variations on a basically similar theme. At one extreme some schools are like well-run navy boats, confident, well directed and with an identified purpose, while others appear disorganised, demoral-ised and antagonistic. Hargreaves (1972) has attempted the difficult task of generalising about the characteristic norms and values of school staffs. While not based on systematic research of any size, they 'ring true' to people who have been part of a staffroom. You will probably recognise them from your experi-ence of schoolteachers in general. The titles used are those of Hargreaves, though their description has been modified.

1 *Autonomy* – mainly concerned with the privacy of the classroom, providing the teacher with the freedom to do what he believes to be right in his own room
2 *Loyalty* – to each other, hence the avoidance of criticising other teachers, in front of pupils, the headteacher, and to some extent other teachers, and backing each other up
3 *Mediocrity* – much like the behaviour of many students, the avoidance of giving indications to one's peers that one works particularly hard or that one is over-keen
4 *Cynicism* – often humorous, but amounting to the derision of beliefs in the possible success of innovations or the achievement of objectives
5 *Anti-intellectualism* – a pragmatic, on-the-job (chalk-face) attitude, unencumbered by consideration of abstract theory
6 *Categorisation* – the characterisation or labelling of classes or pupils as, for example, bright, hardworking, or dumb yobbos etc. (see the section in Chapter 4).

In many ways the above can be seen as a corporate survival kit which helps to sustain individuals and the group in the face of the difficult demands of teaching and vagaries of the organisation in which they work. The teachers' informal culture then functions for them in a way precisely parallel to the pupils' informal culture in respect of the formal culture of the school.

Schools as organisations

A somewhat separate, though parallel, approach to the sociology of the school is provided by viewing it as an organisation. Some of the literature, for example Banks (1976), does not distinguish between schools as social systems and schools as organisations. Because of this, and because much of our discussion in this chapter already is relevant here too, we shall be mildly cavalier in our treatment of schools as organisations. Thus this review emphasises new contributions to, and reiterates the concerns of, the previous sections in this chapter. The application of sociological organisation theory to schools provides a particularly good example of the problems involved in applying general theory to specific situations and social systems, in this case partly because many of the ideas have emanated from the study of industrial and governmental organisations whose goals, procedures and market situations are far from identical to those of schools. Again, too, it points up the concerns of Chapter 1 as to which side of the basic dilemma of social reality it is best to approach from, in studying a social system.

Etzioni (1964), after Parsons (1960), defines organisations as 'social units [systems] deliberately constructed and reconstructed to seek specific goals'. He suggests that the division of labour, power and communication in an organisation is deliberately planned to help realise its goals, that its power centres review performance, make changes when necessary to increase efficiency and replace unsatisfactory people. Etzioni includes schools along with armies, hospitals and prisons in his examples of organisations, while claiming that other social units, such as the family, display similar though lower degrees of conscious planning. It is only possible to recognise schools as organisations in Etzioni's definition in a limited way. While schools do have organisational goals, these are far from easy to identify in a meaningful way. Shipman (1975), for example, defines them as instruction in subjects, moral training, social training and training for adult status. This, like other attempts, is at a very high level of abstraction, and defies specification because of the very wide variation of goals between types of schools, and schools within types. The organisational goals of schools are clearly different from those of an industrial or commercial concern producing a product or providing a service. A factory producing tins of baked beans provides a comparatively simple, contrasting example. A certain number of processes must proceed in sequence to convert raw materials into a finished product. The processes imply an organisational structure. The end product and its quality and quantity are easily recognisable, and hence the efficiency of the organisation can be assessed and compared with that of others. Furthermore, there are ready yardsticks for measuring the success or otherwise of changes in the organisation. Schools, on the other hand, do not start with raw materials like beans, tomatoes and tin, but highly complex and variable children who are capable (and willing) to react to, and with, those attempting to process them. The end product of schooling is also much more complicated. Very few people really see it solely in terms of somebody with five or more G.C.E. O-levels, but rather as a fairly complete person with many characteristics, most of which are unmeasurable. Indeed, take any two or three teachers and get them talking about the objectives of education and the means for achieving them and you have got a very long debate. Teaching and learning are seen as being essentially mysterious, though this must be seen as a purely cultural definition. The Jesuits had no such problems and produced a book that laid down precise details of how to instruct pupils; and most effective it was. Of course they had the advantage, or disadvantage, of complete consensus about the objectives of education. Where objectives are specific and agreed upon, then processes can become standardised; in this case it led to a simple, most authoritarian, teacher-dominated organisation. In present-day educational and social climates such approaches would be neither appropriate nor possible.

Another distinction between most schools and many other enterprises is that they are not independent to any large extent. They are part of a much larger structure – the local education authority, local and central government, and less formally pupils, parents and the community in which they exist. The importance of this is that schools have very little actual control over the amount of resources made available to them and only some control over the use made of such resources and policies pursued. In fact, they are faced with a whole host of potentially conflicting demands from parents, pupils, employers, the local authority, teachers, politicians and public opinion. At this point we may return to a previous question raised in this chapter: whose goals or objectives are schools trying to achieve? Failing, as we must, to identify a single source merely complicates the issue since we have very little knowledge of how schools combine the various objectives provided for them. Thus Etzioni's suggestion that schools, like other organisations, continually review their performance for greater efficiency becomes problematic. The situation is perhaps such as to suggest that schools do not appear particularly dynamic in themselves because in the face of conflicting demands they can legitimately fail to be dynamic in order to survive; or, alternatively, that schools do not function in this organisational way because most of the important decisions are made outside the school or in combination with outside agencies. The power of schools to change themselves is clearly limited, and certainly the ability to remove unsatisfactory people – be they pupils or staff – as Etzioni suggests, is most severely curtailed. Added to this is the fact that schools are not really in a competitive situation either among themselves or with other agencies.

Earlier in this chapter we considered the great range of types of schools (see also Chapter 4), and one aspect of this – size – is particularly important to our present concern. Although it is true that the average size of schools has grown since the last World War, it is easy to overemphasise the number of very large schools, which it is assumed create organisational and control problems. In 1976 there were only 257 (0.9 per cent) maintained schools in England and Wales with more than 1,501 pupils and 1,067 (3.8 per cent) of between 1,001 and 1,500. In contrast, of the total of 28,312 schools, 11,171 had fewer than 201 pupils and 22,030 (78 per cent) had under 401 (*Statistics of Education 1976*). Schools with over 1,000 pupils catered for only about 19 per cent of the school population. We can suspect that the majority of schools have little or no formal organisation. Schools of up to 200–300 pupils typically have an organisation consisting of only a headteacher and a timetable (which is often a loosely timed class rather than a school timetable) and perhaps a teacher or two who is paid to be responsible for some specific aspect of school (deputy head, music or library etc.). In this type of school, efforts to recognise an authority structure or decision-making process are likely to be thwarted. Given the uniqueness of the role of the British headteacher, the search often need not go far beyond him or her. It is then, only in large secondary, primary and middle schools that formal organisational structures exist and can be seen to function. A further observation would be that they exist most obviously and vitally in comparatively new or changing schools. A major impetus to new organisational thinking has been secondary-school reorganisation along comprehensive lines and the introduction of middle schools. Many older-established schools – some grammar schools, for example – started in a small way and developed personalised, autocratic regimes which have continued to cope without resort to the introduction of new organisation or institutions. Social systems do not necessarily change their organisation when faced with new problems. In education there appears to be a reverence for the established and historical; hence the new technological universities of the 1960s used existing organisational models, while many comprehensive schools have aped the public schools by introducing a house and/or tutor system.

A final consideration is that a whole range of organisational theories can be identified (for a useful overview, see Davies 1973). All the theoretical perspectives identified in Chapter 1 are again presented in organisation theory. Most commentators agree that, taken singly or together, the perspectives cannot be recognised as satisfactory in their application to schools. Indeed a reading of the literature soon assures one of the accuracy of Banks's (1976) echo of the feelings of Floud and Halsey (1958) that 'the study of schools as organisations remains one of the least satisfactory aspects of the sociology of education' (p. 190). The above factors, together with those outlined below, suggest the need for caution in the application of organisation theory to schools. Alternatively they suggest the need for more research and particularly for the development of specific theory based on careful empirical research in schools, or a 'grounded theory' approach as suggested by Gorbutt (1972) and demonstrated for hospitals by Glaser and Strauss (1968; see also 1967). There is one exception to this state of knowledge about schools as organisations – that which relates to the device of streaming. This area has been reasonably researched (see pp. 124–32 and Index).

The classical approach to organisations has been by way of Weber's concept of bureaucracy. This form of organisation he saw as a response to the growth in size and complexity of units of production and administration during the nineteenth century. Weber argued that bureaucracy introduced rationality into public life and that its main contribution was to increase efficiency in organisations. Weber's description of the 'ideal-type' bureaucracy (no evaluation here, merely the logical extension of the characteristics of actual examples) was of an organisation with some six characteristics (for a fuller account see Blau 1956). Here, these characteristics are reviewed in relation to schools, bearing in mind the strictures outlined above.

1 *A high degree of specialisation*. This factor clearly varies between types of school. In most infant and primary schools and some middle schools a teacher will teach a whole class the great majority, if not all, of its timetable. In secondary schools and

most middle schools teachers specialise in teaching a subject, a particular group of children (the sixth form, remedials), or have other specialisms, for example discipline, pastoral care, the library, the timetable, and so on.

2 *A hierarchy of authority*. All schools display something of this, even if only a simple dichotomy between the head and other teachers. The role of headteacher defines areas of responsibility and hence authority which cannot be totally shared. In larger schools it is normal for academic and administrative authority to flow from the headteacher to the heads of subject departments to assistant teachers (see table 2.3).

3 *Explicit rules which define people's responsibilities and how their tasks are to be co-ordinated*. In most schools, like other British institutions including the political constitution, little is actually committed to paper. Some schools have written school rules and a few have documents specifying the roles of members of staff, the meetings that will take place between the school, house and department staffs, and even timetables of when these meetings will take place and flow diagrams of the channels of communication and co-ordination of these meetings. Such documents are, however, either very rare or rarely made public. Table 2.3 is a hypothetical example of the organisational structure of a secondary school based on two examples to which the author was given access. Even where explicit formal structures exist, it should be remembered that the efficiency of an organisation depends at least as much on informal structures which grow up around it. (This is further discussed below.)

4 *The exclusion of personal considerations from official business*.

5 *Impartiality in the treatment of clients and subordinates*. These two aspects can be seen as problematic in regard to schools, since the art of teaching lies in the use of the teacher's personality and skills in motivating children to learn. Equality of treatment, or the exclusion of personal considerations on the part of teachers in respect to pupils, would, even if it were a possibility in the heady social climate of a classroom with thirty to forty pupils, amount to inequality because of the varying needs of children. It is here that the professional aspects of the teacher's role come

Table 2.3 The organisational structure of a devised secondary school

AREAS OF RESPONSIBILITY

Leadership, consultation, external relationships, executive decisions

Discipline, assemblies, timetable, examinations, sports and speech days, staff development, relationships with parents, social-welfare agencies, police, probation etc.

Pupil progress, pastoral care and welfare

Sport, social/extra-curricular activities

Academic/teaching co-ordination

Classroom teaching

HEAD TEACHER

Deputy head (female) ↔ Deputy head (male)

Senior mistress ↔ Senior master

Heads of years *OR* Heads of schools — Upper / Middle / Lower

Heads of houses

Heads of subject, departments or areas

Assistant or class teachers

Head's secretary
Clerks
Typists
Caretaker
Cleaners
Canteen staff
Auxiliary helpers
Groundsmen

N.B. Individual teachers may fulfil more than one role

Term 3 Meetings	Full staff meeting	Department meetings	Heads of Year meeting	Examination list/entries	Heads of Department meeting	Careers meetings
					Heads of House meeting	Full staff meeting	End of Term
Events	Parents' evening	School play	Option choice				Examination results	Reports	Re-streaming

into view. While gross unfairness and favouritism is shunned by most teachers and pupils, teachers have constantly to make decisions in respect of individuals and groups. Does this child need greater or smaller demands made upon it than the others, more encouragement or punishment? – and so on. These decisions can only rarely be made on the basis of tests and measurement; normally they must depend on the teachers' knowledge, skill and predispositions. In making such decisions (as discussed above and in Chapters 3 and 4) teachers – fortunately or unfortunately – appear to be human, react differently to different pupils on a variety of criteria and do not view their charges as interchangeable units. Similar processes may be suspected of inter-staff relationships.

6 *That a career exists*. While it is true that schools in the plural provide a career for teachers, this normally involves movement (promotion) between rather than within schools.

It will be gathered, then, that schools have an uneasy and incomplete approximation to the classical view of bureaucracy. Schools stand in a similar relationship to most other organisation theories (Davies 1973). There would appear to be two main factors involved in this uneasy relationship. The first stems from the emphasis placed by most organisation theory on the formal structure and functions of organisations. Since organisations are after all essentially human institutions, we should expect people in them to have relationships which do not follow the formal structure (as at table 2.3), to make attempts at 'playing the system', changing or ignoring it. This amounts to the recognition of an informal side to organisations, parallel to that which was recognised in the treatment of the culture of the school. In the present instance we can go further and state that the informal is crucial to the functioning of the formal. Many organisations, because of their design or their changing role and circumstances over time, would no longer function if the formal rules and organisational structure were obeyed. The simplest examples come from industry – complete havoc reigns if railways, airports, bus companies, the police and the like actually operate according to their written rules. Schoolteachers are continually faced with immediate problems relating to their pupils to which they must respond without recourse to the formal organisation. In schools where there is much less reliance on written rules, other aspects of the informal organisation are probably more important. It is quite simple for anybody with experience of teaching to point up the basis and functioning of informal groupings of the teaching staff (see, for example, Hargreaves 1972 Chapter 12). The author's experience has been that characteristics, from the professional (graduates and non-graduates, subject specialism, institution in which one was trained) through personal characteristics (age, sex and length of service) to individual's interests – both in school and out of school – produce groupings that affect the way the school organisation functions. Often such groupings cross and recross the formal groupings. In one boys' school in which I worked there was a clear divide between those who spent the lunch hour playing basketball and those who played bridge. Other than some difference between the groups in age and seniority, the two groups spanned most other divides among the staff. As a very junior (and relatively unskilled) member of the first group I was very conscious of how effective it was in supporting me as a teacher facing new problems. Although there were senior members of staff who had responsibility for inducting new staff, to use them meant an admission of a problem or failure, and in any case it seemed to me that answers from them were less valid than those of my peers. The latter were, after all, facing and apparently coping in a real way with precisely my situation. The anecdote serves to show that the informal not only served a function for the formal but probably also did it somewhat better (or, indeed, more comfortably for those involved). Of course the groupings were also dysfunctional in that they tended to emphasise formal status differences and reinforce unfortunate stereotypes of them, while curtailing communication and co-operation along the formal structures.

The second, intimately related factor concerns the job teachers have to do and how they have to do it. Teachers' jobs, their attitudes towards them and their aspirations can be viewed as professional. The term professional is problematic but here we can allude to the traditional professionals – the doctor, lawyer and clergyman. The most important factor for our consideration is that such professionals have a unique relationship with their clients. This relationship is based on trust, knowledge and authority and has a sacred aspect – it is not something that should be interfered with by other people. Clearly teachers, because they work in the sort of organisation described above and normally work simultaneously with large numbers of clients (pupils), are not in the same league. Etzioni (1969) has coined the term 'semi-professionals' for such occupations as teaching, social work and nursing. The most salient point he makes concerns the clash between professional and organisational principles, 'arising from the fact that the authority of knowledge and the authority of the administrative hierarchy are basically incompatible'. The principles of administrative authority – control and co-ordination by superiors – are diametrically opposed to the highly individual principle of the professional, who needs to be autonomous and responsible to his knowledge and conscience, free from social pressures, free to innovate, experiment and take risks in order to be effective. Whereas the 'real' professional makes his own decisions, the justification of an organisational decision is that it is in line with the organisation's rules and regulations, and that it has been approved – explicitly or implicitly – by a superior rank. It seems likely that this incompatibility is related to the vague approximation of schools to organisations and teaching to a profession, hence the confusion of those sociologists who have sought to apply either concept in 'pure' terms. What light it does shed illuminates the ongoing negotiation between teachers pursuing their professional goals and society pursuing its educational goals through various school-related agencies – not forgetting on the way, as sociologists and teachers too often do, the children in the middle, who also actively pursue their own goals. Such a model suggests that while the organisation believes it is achieving its goals (or is not having them interfered with) it will allow teachers their professionalism. Similarly, providing teachers do not feel that the organisation adversely affects their professional role performance (teaching), which is their major concern, they remain indifferent to it (Lortie 1969).

One further interesting point raised by Etzioni is that 'semi-professionals' are concerned with communicating their knowledge while the 'real' professionals are concerned with applying and creating knowledge. This reflects on our consideration of teacher education in Chapter 1, and on the underdeveloped nature of the technical as opposed to the academic parts of education. Teachers' education, practice, status and rewards appear to be more closely related to subject knowledge than to skills and methods of teaching children. This is in some contrast to other professions and may, as Etzioni suggests, make teachers more amenable to organisations.

The overriding impression gained from this chapter should be that there exist problems in applying sociological theory and models to the study of schools. This is not to deny that the enterprise has value in providing a new perspective and offering some valuable insights. It is as much a claim that there is a certain uniqueness about schools as it is that there is something wanting in the sociology of education. So far, however, we have concentrated mainly upon structuralist-theoretical perspectives and theories developed originally away from the 'chalk-face', and in non-educational situations. In the next chapter we change to the interpretative perspective, viewing schools as centres of interaction and, to some extent, through the eyes of the social actors they contain.

3

Schools as social worlds

Introduction

Our second approach to schools could be described as 'a real inside job'. It derives from the interpretative or micro sociological perspective and views schools not as social systems but as social worlds. An attempt is made to view schools directly through the eyes of the participants, the way in which they construct, interpret and negotiate the meaning of the social world they inhabit and the results of such activity. As was suggested in Chapter 1, such an approach refuses to take for granted many of the assumptions implicit and explicit in the structuralist view of schools, and relies on quite different research techniques.

In spite of the comparative newness of the approach, especially in its research application to schools, and hence its somewhat limited literature, certain considerations have been made in selecting and presenting the material below. First it has been chosen in order to provide some comparison and links with the material and areas dealt with elsewhere in the book. Therefore it concentrates on contributions to our knowledge of what goes on in schools rather than on the justification and utility of the approach and its research techniques, or its exponents' arguments for its superiority. Second, wherever possible, British studies have been used. While this is generally true for the book as a whole, here it is crucial. This perspective has a particular concern with, and sensitivity for, the meaning of social situations, and thus the applicability of knowledge of institutions in one society to another is more than questionable. One further factor needs to be borne in mind. The work in this field arises not only from shifts in sociological theory, towards the interpretative perspective, but also from other fields of interest (see Delamont and Hamilton 1974). Important contributions have been made by the allied disciplines of social psychology, social anthropology and sociolinguistics. Within the enterprise impetus has been provided by educational, particularly classroom, research. Apart from being relatively under-researched, classrooms have until recently been investigated mainly through 'interactional analysis', which involves recording teacher and pupil behaviour in prescribed categories. Critics have argued that these categories assumed a particular style of teaching – the traditional chalk and talk – and an overemphasis on the teacher's importance. This led to an ignoring of important aspects of social interaction in the classroom and of current trends towards different types of teaching. Further stimulus is identified as coming from the perceived failure of teacher education and lack of teacher interest in educational research, both being seen as due to the apparent distance of educational knowledge and research from real life.

Although the research reviewed below has used a variety of techniques, its major characteristic is the very full if not complete recording of events, interviews, and so on. Often this is achieved by the use of tape recordings which are subsequently transcribed and analysed. Writings in this field abound with numerous lengthy conversational or observational illustrations. The reason for these, it is argued, is that they allow a reader to reinterpret the material if he disagrees with the way in which the author has done it. Actually, however, this is rarely true or possible in that the researcher always has more 'evidence' available than can be presented in written form. The present book lacks the space to follow this convention of quotation just as it is severely limited in presenting many details of other work. For the full flavour of all research and particularly interpretative work, readers will need to consult the references given.

Pupils' worlds

In the last chapter an early criticism of the work was its comparative neglect of what should be regarded as the most important ingredient of schools – pupils (p. 39). That the importance of pupils in schools is not reflected in the amount of research directly conducted on them is surprising – and even more so in the present context of a perspective that emphasises the understanding of social reality through the meanings which members have of it. To neglect pupils is partly to ignore the vast majority – they outnumber teachers by around 20 to 1 in schools and by a larger number in classes. Probably such neglect is accounted for by the fact that researchers find teachers more amenable (easier and simpler) to investigate than pupils, rather than by any reflection of the latter's lack of status and importance in the minds of teachers, educationists and researchers. Certainly, from any perspective, indirect research on pupils, through teachers or parents, is problematic and unedifying (see also pp. 189–96).

However, some studies have been conducted on the way in which pupils see and relate to their teachers. For pupils, teachers are obviously a vital aspect of school: in a sense teachers and school are seen by pupils as being synonomous. After all, I can remember thinking as a pupil that schools would be fine places if they didn't have teachers in them! The teacher represents, or is, the school in the classroom; he or she is the front line. Consequently the way in which pupils see and react to teachers, and the basis on which they do, are of prime importance in understanding what goes on in classrooms and schools. In the last chapter it was suggested that some pupils were anti-school, rejected its values and those of teachers, and could be seen as behavioural problems or delinquents. The explanation for this was offered partly in terms of a cultural clash between pupils and teachers. An excellent introduction to the approach that is now our concern is provided by an early and important paper by Werthman (1963). He poses the question – which must have occurred to many readers with experience of schools – why it is that such pupils behave differently with different teachers? How is it that the culture clash appears to be applied (or operates) selectively? He set out to investigate this by observing and interviewing, over two years, the thirty members of a black gang in an American high (secondary) school. All the members were 'in trouble' to varying degrees in school, and more than two-thirds with the police. They were of mixed ability and school performance. His concern was to identify the criteria and process whereby the gang accepted or rejected the authority of their teachers. He found four criteria:

1 *Proper jurisdiction.* The gang did not give (accept), auto-matically, the teachers' right to punish bad behaviour (for example, lack of attention) but they would often accept good reasoning for avoiding bad and indulging in good behaviour.
2 *Irrelevance rules.* They would not stand for any reference to race, dress, hair or ability.
3 *Mode of address.* They preferred to be requested to do things and rejected demands or insistence.
4 *Fairness in the awarding of grades (marks).*

The last criterion, Werthman argues, was the most important. Whether a teacher was fair or not was determined by a set of criteria related to the first three and involved a process of judgement. The gang set about 'sampling' the grades awarded to other students by questioning them. The grades awarded were checked against a set of norms to decide whether fairness had prevailed. In the case of discrepancies the gang questioned the teacher concerned and considered his reply. If unfairness or discrimination against the gang was detected then that teacher's authority was denied. Behaviour that explicitly or implicitly recognised his authority was avoided: hence they refused to put up a hand in class; were late for, and attempted to leave early from, class; avoided the use of 'Sir'; and looked 'cool'.

Clearly the process whereby teachers are well received or not, and pupils' attendant behaviour, is more complex than perhaps might at first be expected and is illuminated by being viewed through the pupils' eyes. British research, using a variety of techniques, has provided similar insights. Nash (1974) gave a group of 34 Scottish twelve-year-olds a set of cards on which were the names of their teachers. In an interview the pupils were asked to make two piles of the cards: (1) teachers they 'got on with' and (2) teachers they 'didn't get on with'. One card from each pile was chosen by the interviewer who then asked in which ways the behaviour of the two teachers differed. In analysing the transcriptions of the interviews Nash found six common constructs (ways in which pupils discriminated between the two teachers): (1) keeps order/unable to keep order (this construct was the strongest and almost all the children used it); (2) teaches you/doesn't teach you; (3) explains/doesn't explain; (4) interesting/boring; (5) fair/unfair; (6) friendly/unfriendly (this construct was viewed as a bit of a bonus – teachers weren't really expected to be friendly!). These, Nash claims, are the 'members (pupils) rules', and the more in accord the teacher is with each of the first of the above alternatives the more 'acceptable' he will be to the pupils and consequently the more 'acceptable' will be their classroom behaviour. Similar findings are presented by Furlong (1976) from his observations of a small class of mainly black secondary school girls in a low-ability stream. Their acceptance of a teacher and their behaviour in the classroom was related to whether the teacher was:

1 *Strict or soft*. Observations suggested that there were also differences within the categories. When Mrs Alan tells off three pupils for being late for class, she meets abuse from the three, but the rest of the class don't join in the interaction. Mrs Newman's similar action met with a cheeky 'none of your business', and a discussion went on between half the class, ignoring the teacher. Obviously, says Furlong, the first teacher was seen as a more serious threat (less soft) than the latter.

2 *Effective or ineffective*, in terms of getting the girls to learn or not, or, as one of them put it, 'You can't talk in Mr Mark's lesson, you just have to work . . . so after a while

you work, and you enjoy it because you're learning a lot' (p. 35). The girls approached lessons knowing whether they were going to learn or not, and how they would behave, by reference to their past assessment of the teacher concerned.

Gannaway (1976) also reports that the overriding desirable characteristic of teachers as far as his group of comprehensive pupils was concerned was their ability to maintain order and authority in the classroom, though other factors were evident as can be seen from the following extract in which pupils were asked about their ideal teacher.

> JOHN. One who has a laugh with you.
> ANN. And one that understands you.
> JOHN. And one that won't let you get too stroppy . . . stops the lessons getting boring . . . whether he's human . . . He didn't sort of, you know, sort of being mucked about . . . sort of doing what we wanted him to.
> ANN. . . . took advantage of him (p. 51)

Gannaway identifies the other factors involved as 'can he have a laugh?', 'does he understand pupils?', 'has the subject (of the lesson) any utility?' (for examinations or job), 'is it mainly writing?' Other than in the last case, a positive answer was favourable and predicted 'good' classroom behaviour.

What is being suggested is that pupils are involved in 'sizing up' teachers and, having measured them, relating their own behaviour to how well the teacher matches their yardstick. A reading of Delamont (1976a) leaves the impression that the factors possibly involved in 'sizing up' are nearly limitless. Most of the following factors she identifies from her observation of a private academic girls' high school in Scotland, which she calls St Luke's. Pupils use such subtle factors as teachers' posture, gestures and their use of classroom space as well as speech, from which they often make judgements about a teacher's personality and mental condition (and, presumably, background). At St Luke's, pupils had their own views about acceptable fashion with respect to teachers' clothes. Again, age was a factor — younger staff were seen as more sympathetic, the older as more efficient and better at keeping order. Being married was associated with being placid in class and having a happy life out of school! Older unmarried women teachers were viewed within a narrow conventional role. Heads and deputies, when in the classroom, have an aura of authority that stems from their status in the school. Delamont even reveals that the girls of St Luke's 'sized up' teachers by the reputation of the university and department in which they gained their degrees and the academic achievement of their husbands! It is surprising, however, that no mention is made of the teacher's reputation in school. Pupils and teachers do not come 'cold' into the classroom; they have pasts (or careers) which are characterised in the school's folklore. Nicknames often contain cues of this. Among the more graphic (and respectable) I've come across are Bulldog, the Cow, the Pregnant Pussy (a man), Thumper, Mr Dillon and the Fairy Queen.

Such studies clearly suggest that pupils' reactions to teachers are in no way blanket responses to some generalised abstract concept of teacher. Rather they are the result of a process of considering a large number of factors related to specific teachers and pupils' past experience. Of course the fact that such differences exist may not affect the overall picture. Most of the research to date has been with odd (opportunity) groups of pupils, and no general picture has emerged. Comparing the accounts of Delamont with those of Furlong and Gannaway suggests that the first set of pupils see teachers along a line from positive to neutral (love to tolerance) and the latter from negative to neutral (hatred to tolerance). This calls, as all would accept, for more research which needs not only to be more extensive but also to have much deeper knowledge of the pupils and teachers involved, their careers and the contexts in which they meet.

There are several key areas of pupils' worlds that still await the perspective's research. Of prime consideration are inter-pupil relationships, but the research here has progressed scarcely further than that reviewed in Chapter 2 in the section on informal culture. There are considerable problems in research which attempts to capture interaction between pupils, the most powerful of which takes place in small groups and not in the classroom. Second, as has been hinted, the whole enterprise would be illuminated by information about the pupils' biographies out of school and their careers within school. Concentrating on the here and now of classrooms has dangers of limitation, since we must accept that 'making sense' of a situation depends to a large extent on what we bring to that situation and how it 'fits' or interacts with what is presented there and with the rest of our social world. Finally there are the often neglected parts of the school's social reality, both its physical aspects and its ethos or climate which, as yet 'mysteriously', touch upon the actors' social worlds.

Teachers' worlds

Although as has been implied this area has been more fertile in terms of research, it remains fragmentary. Again the literature appears to assume, not unreasonably, that the most important element of schools for teachers is the other actors with whom they are intimately concerned – pupils. The fairly direct research into how teachers see pupils appears contradictory.

The work of Nash (1973) and Taylor (1976) provides an interesting comparison, since both employed techniques based on Kelly's repertory-grid approach, whereby teachers identify and rank the constructs they use in evaluating pupils, and then rank the children they teach accordingly. It is rather similar to the technique outlined on p. 77 above. With eight teachers in one 'progressive' junior school, Nash identified three common constructs: hardworking/lazy; mature/immature; well-behaved/poorly-behaved. He concludes that the constructs relate to work habits, maturity and behaviour, which are, according to him, aspects of the child's personality. On the other hand, Taylor, using forty-eight teachers in eighteen schools teaching nine-year-old children, found that academic ability was more important than personality factors. What is important is that teachers are clearly using both academic and social or personality constructs in evaluating pupils. As such this research clearly supports the evidence reviewed in the last chapter. However, as in the previous section of this chapter, the present approach points to the complexity and process involved in people's evaluation of others, in this case teachers of pupils.

One of the most substantial British studies yet published in this area sought to discover how pupils become labelled as deviants (Hargreaves, Hester and Mellor 1975). It is a good example of what is called exploratory or illuminative research and reads rather like a detective story written by the detective in the first person. One could say that they enter the 'scene of the crime' as strangers and attempt to pick up and verify clues. Their main advantage over a detective is that 'the crime' is constantly committed and they observe it and question the participants fairly exhaustively. As you will see, they try to avoid coming to premature conclusions or imposing a structure on the scene, allowing it to develop and change over time. Although it is a long book the authors are anxious that readers appreciate how much they have omitted of their thinking; we shall be even more selective! While they accept that pupils have an important role in the process, the study is almost entirely directed at teachers. It was conducted in two secondary schools.

Deviancy is seen as involving three elements: (1) an act by party (person) one; (2) the interpretation of (1) by a second party as rule breaking, the labelling of the first party as deviant, and then according him suitable treatment; (3) the reaction of the first party to (2). Their study was limited to (2) above, hence their first concern was to identify rules in school. They found three main types. *Institutional* rules which were applied universally, such as punctuality, no litter etc. *Situational* rules which were applied in specific places, e.g. assembly, the classroom. *Personal* rules which were particular to individual teachers. They chose to concentrate upon situational rules and found that

[margin note: identifying deviance]

neither teachers nor pupils had any coherent concept of a set of rules. This, of course, does not mean that either party was unaware of the rules, but rather that they could not produce them in that manner. The researchers were able to identify the themes of the rules, which were related to talk, movement, time, teacher–pupil and pupil–pupil relationships. The importance and recognition of the rules appeared vitally related to the context in which they occurred. This was illustrated by the way in which the same words could either be an instruction or what they called an 'imputation of deviancy': for example, 'Pay attention' is an instruction when the pupils are working well but the teacher wants to give further instructions, but is an imputation of deviancy when the teacher is talking and the pupils are not listening. According to the researchers, the importance of the context was also revealed by the fact that the teachers could not always explain why they had said certain things in class and sought to explain them by tracing the context. The importance of the context to rules had not been expected by the researchers. In exploring rule contexts they found that lessons are typically composed of phases (or contexts) in which rules and their application change: entry – settling down – lesson proper – clearing up – exit. Teachers use 'switch signals' to define the change from one phase to another, whereupon all members move from one set to another. This suggests that members have a commonsense understanding of the classroom, a point further illustrated by the fact that teachers only rarely state which rule is being broken, expecting the rule breaker to know. Hence 'Reid!' in context would, as it often did, mean 'Pay attention!' The researchers' next concern was to find out how teachers interpret their pupils' behaviour as being deviant in the sense of breaking rules. They distinguish between *conviction rules* – where the teacher actually witnesses rule breaking or has direct evidence for it, for example, in relation to 'paying attention' when the pupil cannot answer a question – and *suspicion rules* which operate when there is ambiguity; for example, if there is talking or movement during a test it could amount to cheating but may not. The teacher is likely to adopt various strategies to find out, from direct questioning, physical searching or the later inspection of the two scripts. Teachers, as we may expect, have a vast knowledge of deviancy in classrooms and the ways in which it is disguised, as indeed pupils have of presenting plausible cover-ups! However, the research also reveals, as we might expect, that teachers also use their knowledge of the particular pupil involved in deciding whether behaviour is deviant. In investigating how teachers build up this knowledge of pupils, interviews were held to find out the constructs which teachers applied in their description of pupils (note the material on pp. 80–1). These were identified as appearance, conformity to discipline, conformity to the academic role, likability and peer-group relations. One of the major contributions of the study is the illustration that, while the teachers made initial identifications of pupils, not only were these qualified through more contact but a process of verification took place over time, resulting either in the initial reaction being substantiated or in a retyping. Over time, too, the teachers' greater knowledge of pupils led to more extensive (wider-range) typing of pupils which consequently became much more individualised. For example, motives were associated with deviancy of particular pupils. Some pupils appear, even at the early stage, to 'stand out' from the others. Three main factors are identified here. (1) *Sibling phenomena* – pupils with older siblings in the school are likely to be recognised early and their behaviour seen in the light of the latter's performance, both for good and bad. (2) *Staff discussion*: this can bring individuals to a teacher's attention before he meets them in class, or confirm or modify his own initial impressions. (3) *Particular problems*, for example, information received by the school about a medical condition. Note that, although it does not occur in this particular study, record cards and reports, where they exist and are used, could operate in this way. Finally, some 'spectacular' classroom happening or accident may make a pupil 'stand out'. Pupils who emerge from the teacher's process of typing as established deviants are seen as indulging in a diversity of types of deviancy, and as being persistent at it, incurable and not likable.

Having presented a very considerable amount of evidence on typing, the authors conclude:

"Although deviant pupils may be classified together under the diffuse label of 'troublemaker' there is nevertheless a uniqueness about every typing when pupils are considered as individuals. Deviant pupils emerge as distinct individuals, each with his own methods of deviating on particular occasions and for particular motives . . . There is a certainty and confidence to the teacher's knowledge of these pupils which, based on multitudinous events few of which are remembered . . . has been built over time into a coherent and resistant characterisation. (p. 215)

Their final concern was with how the teachers treated deviant acts. On detecting such an act the teacher has to decide (1) whether to intervene and (2) how to intervene. These decisions were explored by asking teachers to explain their behaviour in scenes of 'deviancy' observed by the researchers. The considerations relating to intervention were: would intervention be more disruptive than ignoring the act? how serious was the deviancy? who did it (what type of deviant)? what is the emotional state of the deviant? what is the likely outcome of the intervention (success or failure)? In choosing the type of action, teachers aim for the most effective (it'll work) and efficient (quickly and well) and this again is chosen in relation to the type of pupil committing the deviancy. Really stable deviants are subject to higher levels of threshold (will be acted upon less frequently) than other members because teachers do not expect anything from them – intervention is unlikely to be successful and will possibly cause more problems by giving rise to confrontation.

In a later paper (Hargreaves 1976) some thoughts are advanced on how pupils may react to being labelled deviant. The acceptance of the label is seen as being related to the frequency of the labelling; the extent to which the pupil sees the teacher who labels him as a person whose opinions count; the extent to which others (teachers, peers and parents) support (agree with) the labelling; how public the labelling is. Hargreaves suggests that pupils may have 'careers' as deviants through school. This involves a lengthy process rather similar in many aspects to that whereby teachers arrive at the stable-deviant label for a pupil.

It is, of course, important that teachers and pupils are not viewed only in relation to each other, or only in the classroom. They both relate outwards into the school as a whole, into the community and beyond to society. We turn now to studies that attempt to do just that. The first is a view of how teachers' values, incorporated in a new syllabus, are put into practice.

The importance of Keddie's work (1971) is its attempt to reveal the differences between what teachers as educationists think and how teachers as teachers operate. She found that the humanities staff in a comprehensive school disagreed with the rest of the staff about teaching methods but agreed with them about evaluating pupils. As educationists these teachers rejected the ideas of intelligence primarily determined by heredity, of streaming, and of a curriculum differentiated according to the ability of pupils, and thought of social class and ability as being separate. Such beliefs underlay the introduction to a new C.S.E. Mode 3 syllabus they introduced for all pupils — inquiry-based, and in which the pupils worked at their own pace using work cards. The objective of the course was to help pupils become more autonomous and rational beings, by developing modes of work and thought. Keddie points out that, while the course embodied a concept of the ideal pupil, this concept was identical to what already existed in the academically able child. The school was banded, pupils being broadly grouped by ability into bands A, B and C (see p. 125 below). Those in the A band were seen in ideal-pupil terms, those in C were not. Hence, as the A band worked more quickly than C and the course ran in a structured way from one topic to another, it could be seen to be more compatible with the A band than the C. Similarly the individualistic and competitive nature of pupil work (via work cards) favoured those who, through academic achievement, enjoyed and were good at this type of work. While the course appealed to A-band pupils in that they saw the manner of working as being valuable in terms of their future academic pursuits, pupils in C bands were more concerned with the immediacy of the course's content.

In operating the course the teachers appeared to Keddie to adopt (or fall back on?) the school's general ways of categorising and evaluating pupils, which as educationists they denied. This is illustrated by the following quotations from teachers:

> . . . it's 'O' level material . . . but some of the human elements may be C material (p. 144)

> I didn't know anymore than was on the workcard . . . this was all right with Cs but it wouldn't be with As (p. 143)

> The Cs who fail, can't meet [the head of department's] criteria [of autonomous work] . . . Many have working class parents . . . (pp. 141–2)

According to Keddie, teachers translated what they 'knew' about pupils in social, moral and psychological terms into what they knew about them as intellects. Similarly she argues, by implication, that teachers fail to appreciate that the pupils in different bands approach knowledge in different ways. The A-band pupils accept the teachers' definition of the subject and its framework, and ask 'relevant' questions, whereas C-band pupils used more immediate contexts for their approach.

> One unit of the socialization theme was work on isolated children, intended to show the necessity of socialization by presenting a negative case. In one account of an isolated child, Patrick, the description did not make clear that he was isolated in a henhouse because he was illegitimate and that the woman who put him there was his mother. In doing this workcard, A pupils generally did not raise problems about why the boy's mother treated him as she did, but got on with the workcard, although it emerged when they were questioned that they had not realized that the child was illegitimate. Some C pupils who wanted first to know why the woman had treated the child like this were told by their teacher: 'Well, we're not too interested in that but in the

actual influence on the development of the child.' Here not only is there a clear resemblance between the way that A pupils and the teacher had each shifted categories of meaning so that enquiry into the question 'Why would anyone treat a child like that?' becomes inappropriate, but also that the material is already in some sense 'real' and 'immediate' to C pupils, but that the teacher took no cognizance of this. It is often assumed by teachers that the comprehension of every-day meaning of material will be obvious to A pupils. Here it is suggested that this cannot be taken for granted. It may be clear to C pupils, whose first concern is likely to be with this kind of meaning.(pp. 151–2)

The differences are viewed by the teachers in terms of lack of ability – that is, the C band could not deal with concepts and subjects and required more concrete examples. It seems to Keddie that hierarchical categories of ability and particularly knowledge will persist even in unstreamed classes because teachers differentiate between pupils on what they see as high or low ability (see also Chapter 4).

There are some straightforward criticisms of Keddie's work. One can only wonder what the alternative model of the ideal pupil would be like, since she does not define it. Neither does she clearly identify the differences between teacher as educator and teacher as teacher, the extent to which the teachers sub-scribed to the ethos of the course as expressed by the head of department, or how well prepared the teachers were to under-take the new course. Further, we can question her assumption that one would expect to find a relationship between the values expressed in setting up a course and those displayed at the chalk-face, teaching it. Education abounds in such contradic-tions between theory or intent and practice; so why not with teachers? On the other hand, if her thesis was correct, then she is pointing to the persuasiveness of the cultural or situational climate of the school (the development of shared meanings) and how it affects staff members. In this way it would be very similar to Fuchs's (1968) intimate view of a single teacher in an American first school. This new teacher, on arrival, refuses to accept the school's categorisation of her pupils, seeing them more favourably in general terms. Four months of experience in the school and she becomes institutionalised, taking part in the very practices she once rejected. This aside, Keddie's contribution is valuable in offering a small insight into how teachers affect the distribution of knowledge by allowing some pupils access to it and in effect denying it to others. That this happened (and happens) between types of school has long been acknowledged (see Chapter 4); that it happens in situations where beliefs or syllabuses ostensibly reject differentiation of pupils or curriculum is revealing.

That teachers do differentiate between, or categorise, pupils according to social and personal factors can be accepted. Rist's (1970) American study (outlined on pp. 46–7 above) and the evidence reviewed in Chapters 2 and 4 (see, especially, the section on categorisation) show the predominance of factors associated with social class as well as other factors.

The next major study reviewed maintains this picture with a more detailed and intimate view of the individual teachers involved. Although the work of Sharp and Green (1975) is probably most important for its theoretical contribution, it is seen here as furthering the exploration of the relationship between teachers' thought and practice. It is a study of three teachers and their classrooms in a progressive, working-class infant school. Its importance stems from its attempts to illuminate the extent to which classroom practice is the result of, on the one hand, teachers' ideology and, on the other, the material and social constraints imposed by the classroom, school, its catchment area and society. The researchers identify the school's progressive ethos through an interview with the headmaster. They report that he combined a child-centred perspective on education with a social-pathological view of the community from which the pupils come. The major objective of the school, as he sees it, is to provide a socialising ('civilising' is his word), supportive context in which the children can develop. While he recognises an obligation to teach pupils to read and write, this is not the prime aim, which is to cater for the developmental needs of the whole child. Underlying this, the researchers report, is a pessimism about the effectiveness of the school in counteracting the effects of the home environment. The ambiguities are due, they argue, to a clash between the ideology of child-centred education and the conflicting pressures brought to bear on the headteacher.

From the study's reports of interviews and observation, the three classroom teachers can be characterised. As can be seen on pp. 90–1, the three are clearly individuals having their own views – from accord to mild disagreement with the ethos of the school – and variations in practice accordingly. The researchers argue, however, that they (or rather social phenomenologists) would expect such individuals to have differing forms of stratification (and differentiation) in their classrooms. In fact they found the stratification to be very similar in each of the classrooms and also little different to that of 'traditional' classrooms. This arises, argue Sharp and Green, because the common features of the material and social environment impinge on practice and cannot be 'merely intended away in consciousness'. The common features are seen as 'what to do in the classroom' (problems of management and control), the need to live up to (with) colleagues, superiors and parents, and the constraints of the classroom and of pupil numbers. The classrooms had stratification along a line from 'odd' (problematic) through 'normal' to 'successful'. This situation is a paradox, in that, while the three classrooms were 'child-centred', the children in them had reified identities which gave rise to differentiation. Those seen by teachers as being closest to their commonsense understanding of 'normal' or 'successful' received the most attention and were viewed most as individuals. Put the other way round, the authors see the style adopted by the child – the way he copes with the classroom situation – as being important in the way both he and his teacher construct his identity. At the same time the study does reveal some differences between the classrooms. Mrs L's classroom is relatively more dominated by teacher and rules and she used reified typing more often than the

Mrs C	Mrs L

1 Teachers' views on the children and their background

Can be summed up by the quotation 'thick and those who aren't thick are disturbed'. Sees this to some extent as related to deprivation. Of 36 children in her class she classed 30 as from 'odd' to 'mal-adjusted' and 3 as 'normal'.

Sees children as coming from unstable, uncultured backgrounds, particularly critical of mothers. Sees her jo as doing what the parents hav failed to do.

---

2 Teachers' attitudes towards the school and its ethos

Shares views with the headmaster and can be viewed as the 'ideal-type' child-centred teacher in the school.

Agrees in the broad sense but rejects ideas of complete in-formality and is therefore mor directive in the classroom.

---

3 Working in the classroom

High degree of pupil choice, specifically rejects idea of organising children into, say, groups and rotating them to all activities. Children do something because they have a need or interest. Records only kept for reading which was taught on a more routine basis.

Uses quite a large number of rules aimed to provide socialising experience which parents had failed to give. Les open choice than Mrs C; apparently keeps check that children do do work. Combine her knowledge of what childre need with a belief in choice. Has confidence and spends tin planning. Spends most time with brightest pupils.

Mrs B

Regards children as normal
from working-class backgrounds,
not as problems, nor does she see
their background as necessarily
producing problem kids.

Rejects the ideas and doubts the
efficiency of the methods propounded
by the head. Compromises between
traditional and progressive teaching,
does more direct teaching, believes
children to be more able than rest of
staff do.

Does not completely disagree with
free methods but thinks they are
wrong for these children. Since
constrained to use these methods,
adopts flexible planning and
organisation. Gets children together
and attempts to get them to make
up their minds what they will do.
Goes round to see that they are all
involved. Feels freedom should be
after pupils have done what teacher
thinks they ought.

other two. Hence, it is likely, argue the authors, that a higher proportion of pupils in this classroom will acquire low-status and deviant identities and there will be less mobility within a narrower range of identities.

Sharp and Green, in a rather Durkheimian way (see Chapter 4) though in a Marxist light, trace classroom practice to society and its 'need' to reproduce the economic and social system for the next generation. What they imply is that teachers, wittingly or not, are concerned with creating society in miniature in the classroom. 'The processes we have observed in the classroom . . . can be seen as the initial stages of the institutionalisation of social selection for the stratification system' (p.221). Like Keddie they see a difference between ideology and practice but their explanation, unlike hers, transcends the school: 'the educational ideology of child-centred progressivism fails to comprehend the realities of a given situation of a stratified society whose facilities, prestige and rewards are unequally distributed' (p. 226). While such reasoning has its attractions, particularly perhaps from a sociological standpoint, its demonstration is a long way off. Its value lies in indicating that there could be limits to the understanding of micro social realities gained only through the eyes of their actors. As they write, 'there may well be social situations where, for whatever reason, the individual may find it very difficult to give a meaning to his situation or his actions at all, or where he is completely constrained to do things irrespective of how he defines the situation' (p. 27)

To sum up this chapter so far. We have reviewed something of the social worlds of pupils and teachers as they are exposed in school and by certain research techniques. We have traced some of their implications in terms of classroom behaviour, and the 'ideologies' and society in which they occur. Much has been speculative and there have been considerable gaps. There are limitations to studies that concentrate on views through the eyes of one set of actors when there is more than one set, or which attempt to research in situations which are only reflective of, or different from 'the real scene'. In turning to studies that attempt a more complete view of classrooms, however, it should be borne in mind that such complexity causes further research problems.

The social world of the classroom

Our concern now shifts to observations of what happens when pupils and teachers meet in the classroom arena. How do they reconcile what can be seen as divergent interests, or, even if they are similar, how is a common understanding of the situation arrived at and then maintained? It is a common view of the studies we look at that the process involves, to varying degrees, an essential conflict (probably following Waller, see p. 40 above). This conflict is caused by teachers' attempts to enforce their definition of the classroom on pupils, – while pupils, whatever their definition, are trying to make the situation 'comfortable' for themselves. Obviously this entails negotiating or bargaining between the members. In approaching this area researchers have used all the familiar, everyday assumptions about classrooms – the centrality of the teacher, that they are there to teach, and that this involves controlling, motivating and evaluating pupils. What is novel in the approach is the isolation and detailed examination of the means teachers use to achieve these ends, and what happens to them in interaction with pupils. Here once again, however, there is an emphasis on research 'through' the teacher.

As you will have noticed (heard!), teachers talk a lot and, if you stop and think about it, they use some pretty odd language. In fact anywhere else but in the classroom they would be considered most rude. They often ask questions to which they already know the answer, and check up on, and interrogate, pupils almost constantly. Of course, this is teaching as we know it, so it is familiar and acceptable. The teacher is in fact stating his definition of appropriate pupil behaviour in the classroom, his definition of what constitutes knowledge, ability, and so on. One way in which teachers do this, and are allowed to, is by monopolising the conversation. Research (see Delamont 1976a) shows that secondary school teachers talk for around 70 per cent of their lesson time and speak three to four times as much as *all* the pupils in their class put together! Informal classrooms follow this general rule, though not all the children hear all the teacher says.

The centrality of teacher-talk, and the consequent subordination of pupils and pupil-talk, tells us quite a bit about classrooms, about the power, roles and expectations to be found there. Analysis of the language of teacher-talk goes further. Obviously in an 'ideal' setting it ought to aid learning — provided the teacher knows and pupils are there to learn. Studies of classroom language reveal, however, not only the complexity of its forms but, as might be expected, that it can stand in the way of learning. The style of language used by teachers often involves the use of academic terms (like parts of this book?) which the teacher finds 'natural' and necessary to his subject. On the other hand, pupils may find it most unfamiliar and confusing. Similarly teachers may find it difficult to understand, or be unwilling to accept, utterances from pupils who fail to use what the teacher sees as correct language style. Barnes (1969) has made the point that such language may not be necessary to explain certain ideas but that it is a convention to use it. At the same time, he argues, such language can be seen to support the role of the teacher. Respect for teachers' knowledge may stem from his language while teachers' recognition of pupils' learning may be related to the pupils' ability to use teacher-language as well as, or even rather than, pupil knowledge. Of course the two are not always separable, but it would appear easy to instance situations in which teachers fail to recognise valid ideas from their pupils. Asked how to remove a chlorophyll stain from a piece of material, a pupil suggested putting shoe polish on it and then washing it. He had the idea of using a solvent, but not the language with which to have his teacher realise he had the right idea.

It is important, then, to appreciate that teachers define not only knowledge but also pupils' ability. Teachers' knowledge, like education itself, can be fairly arbitrary, especially in the turmoil of a classroom. This is best exemplified in tests and examinations. The following example, from an eleven-plus selection examination, caused a long debate in the corres-pondence columns of *The Times*! Which of the following games is the odd one out – Football, Billiards, Cricket and Hoc-key? If you think about it you can make a case out for each and every one being the odd one! Only one was accepted as correct. Similar events occur in classrooms – you have probably witnessed some. Hammersley (1974) points out that pupils are judged as intelligent in the classroom on their behaviour, amounting mainly to how well they can answer teachers' ques-tions. This involves the pupils' acceptance of the role of the teacher and his definition and then behaving in appropriate ways.

Stubbs (1976) has also analysed teacher-talk, to show that the teacher constantly monitors pupils' language. A good deal of what teachers say is *metacommunication*, that is, communication about communication. Using material from his observations in a Scottish secondary school, he illustrates that metacommuni-cation involves (1) attracting or showing attention, 'Now, don't start, just listen', (2) controlling the amount of speech, 'Any-thing else you can say about it?' (3) checking or confirming understanding, (4) summarising; (5) defining; (6) editing, 'Now that's a good point'; (7) correcting, (8) specifying the topic, 'Now, we were talking about structures'. Stubbs argues that what teachers actually say – the style of language – is unimportant in comparison with what they (it) are doing. The teacher is about 'staying in touch' with his pupils and directing their discussion and language. This is very onesided since only very rarely do pupils use such words as 'That's an interesting question' or 'What do you mean by . . . ?' to their teachers. Again, Stubbs is pointing up the part played by language in supporting the teacher's role, his values and the mainten-ance of social order in the classroom: 'By the very way in which a teacher talks to his pupils, he inevitably communicates to them his definition of the situation and the form of teacher-pupil relationship which he considers appropriate' (pp. 167–8).

Other researchers have attempted to outline the structure of classroom communication rather than analysing its content. Sinclair and Coulthard (1974) say that the typical exchange structure of classroom communication is:

Teacher asks question $\rightarrow$ pupil responds $\rightarrow$ teacher evaluates
(initiation)   (response)   (feedback)

Notice that the sequence begins and ends with the teacher. In contrast, the much rarer initiations of pupils may receive a response but are unlikely to give feedback to the teacher. Again, these authors stress the role of language in the social structure of the classroom, well illustrating the complexity of these exchanges in the following example. A class have listened to a tape of someone speaking in a very 'posh' accent which is followed by laughter on the part of one pupil. The teacher asks 'What are you laughing at?' The pupil wrongly assumes that this is a disciplinary statement, when in fact it is a genuine question aimed at exploring the child's reaction and attitudes to the tape. A misunderstanding of a language form – as command instead of question – had taken place.

The complexity of the classroom as a social situation poses 'problems' not only for members but also for researchers. Walker and Adelman (1976) have argued that, particularly in informal classrooms, the mere recording of speech is not enough. Visual recording (film and videotape) is required in order to make sense of pauses, hesitations and fragments of speech together with non-verbal cues – facial expressions and gestures, for example. Actually, even this is not the whole answer. Anyone who attends a football match and then watches it on television appreciates the limitations of filming social reality. The essential message of their work is, however, that language can only really be understood if one has knowledge of the context in which it is used. Hence the incident from which the title of their paper comes:

TEACHER. Is that all you've done?
PUPILS.   Strawberries, strawberries.
           Laughter.

can only be fully appreciated if one knows that a favourite expression of this teacher about pupils' work was 'Like strawberries – good as far as it goes, but it doesn't last nearly long enough.' In other words, shared meanings have shared history.

As Delamont (1976a) points out, there are hardly any studies which reveal the processes so far discussed in terms of the pupils' perspectives. She presents an example (expanded in Delamont 1976b). The following classroom extract is from what she describes as a 'critical incident' in which the teacher is attempting to 'stage-manage' a discovery-method experiment in a science lesson on photosynthesis. It takes place, as the names of the characters suggest, at St Lukes (see also p. 78). (The experiment consists of covering leaves with silver foil with holes cut in it, exposing patches of leaf to the light. After a week or so the leaves are tested for starch, which is found in the exposed parts of the leaves and not in the covered parts.)

Mrs Linnaeus shouts for quiet and announces the last experiment.
SHARON.   Good!
   MRS L. (*Ignores Sharon, explains why they are doing it.*) If we cover the leaves with silver foil and leave them for a few days what will happen to them?
     ZOE. No sunlight can get through, so there won't be any starch.
   MRS L. (*Accepts that – states it formally as a hypothesis. Asks what would happen if they cut holes in the foil.*)
   KAREN. You'll get starch in the holes and not anywhere else.
   MRS L. (*Accepts that – states it formally as a hypothesis. Asks for volunteers to come and cut and cover leaves.*) You can cut your initials out if you like, then if it works you'll see your initials outlined in iodine.

Mary, Karen and Janice volunteer, and come to the front to get on with it. The others revert to their own activities . . . Michelle puts up her hand. Mrs Linnaeus acknowledges her . . .

MICHELLE.   Mrs Linnaeus, I don't see how that will prove it – it could be all sorts of other things we don't know anything about.

MRS L.   (*Comes down the lab to Michelle's bench. Asks her to expand her question, explain what she doesn't see.*)

MICHELLE.   Well you said if there was starch in the bare patches it would mean there was . . . it was because of the light, but it could be the chemicals in the foil, or something we know nothing about.

SHARON.   (*butts in*). Of course it'll prove it, we wouldn't be wasting our time doing the experiment if it didn't.

MRS L.   I don't think that's a very good reason, Sharon . . . (*She laughs and then goes into great detail about experimental design, the atomic structure of carbohydrates, and other things in an attempt to satisfy Michelle. Few other girls listen, Henrietta does.*)

MRS L.   You look worried Lorraine.

LORRAINE.   (*says she isn't.*) (pp. 124–5)

The teacher is 'caught' between Sharon who sees through the illusion of discovery to the fact that the lesson is heavily teacher-structured, and Michelle who accepts the illusion but challenges the experimental design, wanting to know whether it meets the criteria of scientific proof. They have two quite different perspectives on, and therefore strategies in, science lessons. Sharon is instrumental and trusting, while Michelle is matching school science against real science. Delamont points out that Michelle's parents were research scientists! Michelle's challenge is serious to the teacher, since it highlights the difference between real and school learning, and the teacher is faced with a choice between explaining that she is 'stage-managing' or using her greater knowledge to justify the procedure. In doing the latter, and defending her teaching method, the teacher runs slap into Sharon's exposure, which she avoids by laughing (perhaps rather than saying she is wrong). Of course the teacher might have got angry, dismissed the question, or even set Michelle on testing her hypothesis. Delamont concludes that what is needed is more research on the relationship between actors' thoughts and their actions.

Discipline and the maintenance of order were seen as crucial elements of schools and classrooms in Chapter 2. These have also occurred as part of some of the studies discussed in this chapter, and we now view some specific research. Hammersley (1976) has identified three basic strategies adopted by teachers in the classroom in order to generate and maintain their authority. His observation was made in a boys' secondary school during fairly formal traditional-type lessons. First teachers present themselves to their pupils as figures of assumed (not to be questioned) authority. Second, they demonstrate their superiority by asking questions to which they have the answers, but which the pupils are unable to answer, and also by challenging pupils to confrontations. Third, they skilfully modify their normal requirements in the classroom when they anticipate problems in their enforcement.

Woods (1975) has analysed what he sees as a common informal type of discipline strategy used in schools. This he delightfully titles 'showing-up', a term from pupils' language in a secondary modern school. Showing-up involves the public embarrassment (or attempt at it) of an individual or group of pupils. We have all probably witnessed such when a teacher has discovered us in a noisy situation and said something like 'Who are you?' 'We are 4B, Sir.' 'Hmm more like 4Z I'd have thought!' Woods describes the functions of showings-up as: socialisation, negative sanctioning, a means of establishing and maintaining power, a means of motivation, and revenge or counter-attack. Woods' research consists of interviews with pupils, and the following extract gives a vivid firsthand reflection of a showing-up and possibly an indication of its effectiveness!

CHRISTINE. I was sitting next to Kevin, and he'd got this
cartridge in his pen and he was going like that
(*she indicates an obscene gesture*), and I just pushed
him away, and the teacher was writing on the
board and he must have eyes in the back of his
head . . . and he says . . . he turns around with a
fuming face and he says 'will you two stop fidd-
ling with each other!' I never went so bright red
in all my life, and he pushed me over one side
and him on the other . . . and everbody turned
round, didn't they . . . in front of all my friends!
You know . . . he made me such a . . . mockery
. . . can't stand him! Everybody was scared stiff
in that class, everyone just sits there, all quiet.
(pp. 134–5)

A very direct piece of research into teacher-talk and its
relationship with discipline is that of Torode (1976). He con-
trasts the classroom styles of two teachers of a lower-middle-
stream class of boys in a Scottish secondary school. One teacher,
who is successful in maintaining discipline, constantly defines
the social facts of his classroom with statements in which the 'I'
and the 'you' are immersed. As in, 'When we do compositions
we don't have any talking at all I hope that is clear . . . ' (p.
178). The other teacher, who appears to have constant trouble
in his classroom, does not follow the same rules, for example:
'Right would you all stop talking please?' 'Cannon sit down' (p.
187). Torode suggests of the latter that 'The incessant and
sometimes violent conflict which characterised his lessons was
directly attributable to the teacher's failure to give an enduring
definition of the situation while that situation was being
enacted' (p. 191). His account amounts to the suggestion that
the effective teacher may state his definition of the situation by
portraying numerous 'persons', sometimes including himself,
situated within a social context posed as a social fact external to
them as individuals. While accepting that language, its form,
style and use, may be important in classroom discipline, this

claim can be seen to go rather too far. On the one hand, we know nothing of the biographies or careers of these teachers except that the second was in his first year of teaching; the other, we can suspect, was well experienced. To what extent is the superior language form a function of experience, authority and status, and what part of the boys' obedience arises from their recognition of the same factors? On the other hand, if discipline were simply a question of using appropriate teacher-talk — something that can be quickly taught and learnt — presumably few teachers would still have disciplinary problems.

Outside the classroom, in the school, the application and enforcement of rules becomes the concern of all teachers as a group. Schools, as we know, vary as institutions in this respect, some having very rigid regimes over their pupils and others with regimes that are difficult to identify. Reynolds's work (1976) is most interesting in that it also displays the utility for research of a double-headed, sociological perspective approach. In surveying nine secondary modern schools in a former mining community, he is interested in explaining why some of the schools were more successful — produced fewer delinquents, had better pupil attendance and performance — than others. His initial approach is to analyse a number of existing traditional sources in relation to the schools. All the schools used corporal punishment and can be characterised as 'unprogressive, traditional and working class'. The more successful schools tended to be smaller, have lower staff turnovers, smaller classes and older and less adequate buildings. The major difference, according to Reynolds, is the way in which teachers apply the school rules. This aspect of the research involved observation and interviews. Successful schools had a sort of truce between staff and pupils.

This truce is in the nature of an unofficial arrangement for the mutual convenience of both sides of the school, made between working-class pupils of low aspirations who seek a stress-free time . . . and teachers who realise that many of the rules and regulations which should, in theory, govern the interaction between them and their pupils would, if applied, only make their task as teachers more difficult. (p. 225)

While he does not claim to have discovered what it is about schools which promotes deviance or conformity to social norms, Reynolds's claim is that his study shows that individual schools do have 'a substantial effect on the sort of young people they turn out'.

In Walker and Adelman's work, jokes and laughter are identified as a means by which teachers who have strong and positive relationships with their pupils control their classes. In the strawberries incident (p. 97 above) they argue: 'the class is signalling to the teacher that they know what he wants and the quoting of the rule becomes a joke' (p. 139). In contrast, Woods (1975) shows that sarcasm is used by teachers as a form of class control in the process of 'showing-up'. 'The lowest form of wit', as we used to tell our English teacher, who was a master at the art. 'But the most useful,' he used to reply. Woods (1976) puts forward the idea that laughter is an important element in school for pupils. Apart from being a natural part of children's way of life, for some it makes sense of school; pupils used humour as one of the criteria on which they judged teachers. Woods argues that there are two forms of what he calls institutionalised laughter: 'mucking about' – rather aimless behaviour often called 'silly' by teachers – and 'subversive laughter' – aimed at undermining the authority of school or teacher. The amount to which these are indulged in is related to the degree of commitment to school. Achieving pupils, being more committed, were less involved in both types than pupils in non-examination classes. 'Mucking about' was associated with the boredom of class and school felt by the latter group of pupils. 'Subversive laughter' was more political in nature and was directed against the authority and routine of school and teachers while serving to maintain the interests of the pupils' peer groups. Laughter, then, can be viewed as a means of coping with the situation.

In concluding this view of schools as social worlds, it is not necessary to rehearse the comments made about it at the beginning of this chapter and at the end of each section. Research in this area, as opposed to the ideas from which it emanates, is both new and rare in Britain. Its potential, viewed by some as very considerable, awaits demonstration, and its contribution is distinctive and yet supplements or complements the schools-as-social-systems approach. This is discussed in Chapter 8, but readers should consider it here.

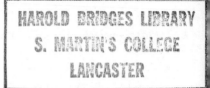

4

Differentiation in school and class

Differentiation in school and society

This chapter is concerned with the full range of differentiations found in our schools and their classes. Differentiation is used here in its literal sense – a noun from the verb 'to differentiate', meaning 'to constitute a difference; render unlike; recognise differences between; distinguish, discriminate' and even 'develop characteristic differences'. Note that these dictionary definitions clearly suggest an *active* process. In our present context the word refers to a whole range of factors – the separation and segregation of children into different schools, within schools into different classes, including streaming, the categorisation of children in the same class into separate groups and, at the micro level, verbal and non-verbal differentiation by a teacher in his interaction with individual pupils. Before looking at these processes in detail, we return to the question discussed in Chapter 2, namely the extent to which educational practices and processes are unique and based on pedagogical principles as opposed to being more directly related to practices and processes in society at large. Initially, to explore this relationship and to gain an overall picture, our approach is at the macro level and uses the structuralist views of Durkheim. Note, however, that the Durkheim quotations are being used as illustrations rather than justifications for the argument put forward. For Durkheim there appear to have been few problems about our question. He wrote 'Education is only the image of and reflection of society. It imitates and reproduces the latter in abbreviated form, it does not create it' (Durkheim 1952, p. 379). This viewpoint suggests that explanations for school-based phenomena might well be assisted by a knowledge of the features of the society or culture in which the schools in question exist; simply that educational institutional processes are linked with societal processes. A further theoretical assumption will be that equal weight must be given to both '*Manifest functions* . . . those objective consequences contributing to the adjustment or adaptation of the system which are intended and recognised by participants in the system' and '*Latent functions* . . . those which are neither intended or recognised' (Merton 1957, p. 51). It is thus necessary to view streaming not only in terms of its basic rationale – that it produces groups of children with reasonably similar ability, which make viable groups for teaching – but also in terms of its more hidden (unfortunate?) outcomes – it leads to social as well as ability segregation and children appear to live up, or down, to the labels they are given.

Differentiation and segregation are, of course, characteristics of society at large. Few would refuse to accept that there are differences in the general population in terms of wealth, power and prestige or, to use a simpler term, social class. A whole welter of data on social class (based on occupation) shows that differences exist between classes in income, employment, health, housing, family structure, child rearing, education, politics, religion, leisure and opinion (for a review, see Reid 1977a). Moreover classes tend to be segregated in terms of where they live and where they work, and display differences in attitudes, beliefs and behaviour. The residential segregation is pretty obvious in any journey across one of our cities. It can be argued that this form of segregation works towards the perpetuation or maintenance of differences and inequalities. Thus poor people's actual knowledge of the wealthy's homes, way of life, schools, local services, and so on, let alone the unequal distribution of society's resources used to maintain them, remains relatively limited, certainly at the experiential level. The converse is also true, the wealthy having only a sketchy idea of life in the slum areas of our cities.

In much the same way, the segregation of children into schools hides from pupils, parents and even teachers any real knowledge of the differences between types of schools. Secondary-modern school children have a hazy and often inaccurate knowledge of the facilities in grammar schools and even less in 'public' schools. Differences in the provisions, facilities and expenditure are thus hidden. Comprehensive schools show just as wide variations, similarly hidden, even within the same area. Such differences also exist in higher and further education, between universities, polytechnics, colleges of education, technical and further-education colleges.

Scholastic (or academic) and social-class differences often come together. The social-class composition of the types of school and higher-education institutions varies very considerably (see Chapter 6). The higher the status of the institution the higher the proportion of the middle class. Even within a particular category of school, differences can be found. Government research showed, for example, that among secondary modern schools in slum and problem areas 79 per cent were 'materially grossly inadequate' (*Half our Future* 1963). In much the same way, forms of in-school segregation, like streaming, hide an unequal distribution of staff, facilities, the curriculum and expenditure from pupil and parent eyes, especially because of the relationship between social class and school stream – the lower the stream the higher the percentage of the lower-class children (see p. 127 below), the parents of whom are less knowledgeable about schooling (see, for example, Pallister and Wilson 1970, and p. 37 above). As we shall see, once the divisions have been made, their subsequent performance can be used to justify them, and even where streaming does not exist formally similar processes can happen (pp. 124–32).

A further functional aspect of differentiation can be developed from the ideas of Durkheim (1956) and Hopper (1971). Durkheim argued that education had the job of fitting out the child not only for society but also for that particular level of society in which he was going to operate as an adult – that is his occupational role. Hopper wrote about the 'warming-up' and 'cooling-out' processes in education. Since it is neither feasible nor desirable initially to select those children who are destined for high-status jobs, schools need to 'warm up' and keep warm the aspirations and endeavour of all children; but education has also to 'cool out' unrealistic aspirations. Presumably the latter process partly accounts for the fact that very few overweight, myopic, low-achieving schoolboys (and girls) aspire to be airline pilots! The two processes are 'designed' to produce in children aspirations that are realistic in terms of their own ability and of the ability of society to provide such occupational roles for them. That the processes are imprecise has been more than adequately illustrated by the overproduction of several thousand schoolteachers in 1976. The ideas do, however, give us some insight into the possible utility of differentiation in schools. Streaming, for example, gives the A stream higher status than B, C, D, E; if you like, a feeling of superiority, the 'comfort' of groups below them. Generally this status in school is a reflection of the status of their family origin in society at large, and is even more likely to reflect the status of the occupational life to which they will progress after leaving school. The experiences of the lower streams are similar but reversed. The suggestion is, then, simply that the divisions between schools, and within them, reinforce and indeed increase (see p. 173 below) initial differences between children. Collins (1971) suggested that this produces two groups:

1 The carriers of élite knowledge and social skills. The minority who are successful in education.
2 Those who have a respect for, or acceptance of, the first group. The majority who are not successful in education.

Schools can be seen to pave the way for, and legitimise, the long-term separation and differential reward system operating in society at large (see Chapter 7). In their structural arrangements, then, schools fulfil Durkheim's (1956) claim that 'Education is, then, only the means by which society prepares, within, the children, the essential conditions of its very existence' (p. 71).

A further insight can be gained from Durkheim's lectures to his student teachers. Here he drew an analogy between education and hypnotism, arguing that if the teacher could hypnotise his pupils into a state of blank consciousness and exceptional passivity then pupils would have maximal receptivity for assimilating the teacher's ideas. However, Durkheim saw that this ideal condition (from the teacher's point of view) was never wholly achievable and therefore that the teacher must always play a dominant role: 'one can say that education must be essentially a matter of authority' (1956, p. 87). The centre of a teacher's power would seem to be his ability to differentiate between pupils in terms of his interaction, the marking of written work, and so on – and his part in differentiation within the school – helping to determine the pupil's future, which class he will be in, whether he sits examinations etc. Forms of differentiation also reflect the relationship between passivity and educability, or ease of teaching. Hargreaves (1967), King (1969) and Lacey (1970), in their participant studies of secondary schools, all showed that as one moved up the streams D to A the children became more in accord with the values and interests of the teachers, the school and education. Those in the bottom streams, lacking passivity, are often contained rather than taught and in general are avoided by experienced teachers. The school system treats them as relatively unimportant and keeps them in ineffective situations where they won't disturb the status quo or the real purposes of the school. In many ways, it can be suggested, schools exploit them as society will when they enter the adult world. They are the ones who run messages and help the caretaker; their treatment and lack of status is a direct and anticipatory socialisation for life after school. 'Just as the priest is the interpreter of his god, the teacher is the interpreter of the great moral (social) ideas of his time and of his country' (Durkheim 1956, p. 89). One basic means by which this is achieved is the separation and segregation of children within and between schools, thus avoiding the problems caused by 'warming up' or 'cooling out' the wrong individuals or groups of children; or teaching inappropriate parts of the curriculum, values and interests to those who are destined never to need them.

The argument so far — that differentiation in education reflects and is related to differentiation in the social structure of society — can be tested by reviewing the controversy around three possible educational innovations: (1) the abolition of 'public' schools; (2) the introduction of real and full comprehensive schools; (3) the abolition of streaming. Whatever educational principles are involved in these controversies, they are not the main feature of the arguments of lay or professional supporters and opposers. The debates are all centred round social as opposed to educational principles and concerns. This is not particularly surprising, since these innovations are no mere tinkering around with the educational system but are challenges to the social fabric of society. The net result of such changes would be to cause groups who have beliefs in their justified or desirable separation to mix. At one level, this would be seen to cause clashes of values, beliefs and behaviour; a common assumption is that human beings gravitate towards the worst. More importantly, however, such changes would greatly increase competition and hence the possibility of social and occupational mobility. For example, the public schools' monopoly of élite jobs (see table 4.2a below) might be broken. Probably a larger proportion of the children of those parents comfortably established at the top end of the social structure would find themselves faced with a decline in status. Nor would it be onesided, since the increased potential for upward mobility might well be resented by those who have been successfully socialised to accept and value their place in the social order (see, for example, Jackson and Marsden 1962/1966). These arguments bring into focus the question of the relationship between education and society. What is suggested here is more than the common assumption that they are related (which nearly all sociology of education texts point out). Here they are seen as the products of each other, with the implication that the stronger (society) will believe that the weaker (education) should not be allowed autonomy in any more than an apparent sense because of the seriousness of the issues involved. In other words education is far too serious a matter to be left either to educationists or to teachers. Under the guise of such ideologies as academic freedom and the power and authority of headteachers lies a very real force of social control. This is interestingly illustrated by the events surrounding Risinghill Comprehensive School in London during the mid-sixties (for an account see Berg 1968), and more recently at William Tyndale School. It is further evidenced by the small part played by schoolteachers in educational policy-making at government, local-authority and even school level.

A number of objections can be made about the picture presented so far. In particular it can be argued that it is far too comprehensive and generalised. Pupils succeed and fail in school and afterwards both because of, and in spite of, the educational system and its relationship with the social structure. Many teachers fail, through enlightenment or inability, to process their charges adequately in the manner outlined. These limitations can be accepted, particularly since they do not refute the argument. It is the subtlety of social institutions that makes them effective. The blatant and absolute use of power always runs the danger of evoking powerful reactions. In the present case, as in many others, exceptions to rules are commonly used to justify whole systems. Implicit in this thinking is the justifiable assumption that all human institutions are imperfect, and that if individual cases of justice can be demonstrated any underlying fundamental injustice fades into unimportance. If our educational system allows John Bull, who is from a disadvantaged home and school, to be successful, then if Joe Soap is not successful it is obvious that the fault lies with him and not the system. Clearly, while this line of thinking is common, it is faulty. It is at this stage that quantitative analysis becomes vital. We need to know not so much of Joe Soap and John Bull but of their relative proportions in the population at large. Alongside this we need to know similar factors about the other groups, composed of the Jeremy Bypass-Smythes, who also inhabit the educational and social systems of our society. This has been, and should remain, a major role for macro-sociology, and some of its evidence is presented below (Chapter 6).

It is also worth noting that, while the argument has been based on the relationship between one form of differentiation in society – namely social class – and education, other forms could be considered. While these forms have not been traditional concerns of the sociology of education, and consequently their literature is not extensive, they can be seen to operate in a similar fashion. Interestingly enough, social class can again be recognised as an associated variable with respect to these forms of differentiation. The most obvious form of differentiation in society is that of sex, which is becoming a major area of study in sociology.

Broadly speaking, sex differentiation in social life generally, and in education specifically, can be seen in terms of the assumed primary adult roles the sexes occupy – wives and mothers on the one hand and occupation on the other. Most commentators (for a most readable, female account see Sharpe 1976) point out that the social-role differences of the sexes are established very early in the family and that schooling, along with other social processes, reinforces them. Girls in primary school tend to perform better than boys (see pp. 135–9 below) and maintain a measure of superiority in verbal ability at secondary school level. What appears to happen, however, is that at some point in adolescence girls begin to underachieve in relation to their real capacity, or alternatively do not make as much of their talents as do boys. Explanations for this are mainly sought in respect of sex roles, teachers' part in support-ing them and pupils' response to them. For our purpose it is perhaps best illustrated by reference to differences in the cur-riculum, subject choices and school performance of the sexes.

Secondary-school curriculum can be seen as sexist in that the sexes are offered different fare. Benn and Simon (1972) found that in the 589 mixed schools they studied 50 per cent had subjects that only boys could take (e.g. woodwork, metalwork, and technical drawing) and 49 per cent subjects for girls only (e.g. needlework, domestic science and typing). Of course, where the curriculum is not closed in this way the exercise of 'choice' may amount to the same thing. As a study by the Department of Education and Science (*Education Survey 21*) concluded:

> It may be that society can justify the striking differences that exist between the subjects studied by boys and girls in secondary schools, but it is more likely that a society that needs to develop to the full the talents and skills of all its people will find the discrepancies disturbing. (p. 24)

The last part of this quotation makes a suitable epigraph for the whole chapter. Douglas and Cherry (1977), reporting the progress of a national cohort of children, point out that, while girls were less likely to fail O level G.C.E. completely, they gained passes in fewer subjects than boys. In particular, fewer passed in mathematics and science. Girls of high ability at sixteen were less likely to have ambitions for full-time education, and only 10 per cent passed A level G C.E. compared to 14 per cent of boys. National figures revealing that over the past twenty years differences between the sexes have been closing are at tables 7.7b and 7.8a below. Writers in the field agree with Sharpe that the factors of sex and social class are compounded so that working-class girls are at a greater disadvantage in education than their middle-class sisters.

The clearest examples of culturally distinctive children in our educational system are, obviously, those of ethnic minorities. Surprisingly little information is available, since statistics are not kept on this basis and little research has been undertaken. Little (1975), surveying ethnic-minority achievement in London schools, reports 'Just as the educational system has in a sense failed to meet the needs of the child from a working-class background, so now, to an even greater extent, it is failing to meet the needs of the child from a different cultural background, and this is demonstrated by differences in mean levels of attainment.' While explanations for ethnic minorities' poor showing in educational achievement are usually in terms of cultural and linguistic differences, the common combination of colour and low social class is also prominent (Milner 1975). Little displays from his data that 'immigrants' perform less well than 'underprivileged' white pupils. Both he and Milner make a strong point concerning the role of the school system: 'it is the inability (or unwillingness) of the existing system to modify its practice to meet the needs of new types of pupil that should be stressed . . . what goes on in school is a factor determining differences in performance' (p. 68).

The main emphasis of the argument is simply that social differentiations in society are of importance in educational situations. And, indeed, that the educational system cannot be fully understood without such an appreciation, since explanations along pedagogic lines, or in individual terms, are unsatisfactory. Having suggested a causal direction – from society to education – we now turn to the major forms of differentiation in schooling before continuing a discussion of their implications.

Schools

The existence of different types of schools and educational institutions in a society implies that children will be segregated from others and receive different education. While this *may* be uncontroversial in respect of some groups – for example, the blind, the deaf, the mentally handicapped, and so on – it is far from so in respect of the general population. It is particularly controversial when viewed within a cultural value set that emphasises equality or equality of opportunity, and within a society in which education is directly related to occupation, life chance and lifestyle opportunities (see Chapter 7). In Britain the segregation of groups of children into separate types of school has to be viewed in a historical context. Prior to the nineteenth century, education was really only for the rich, who had tutors, and a very few others who attended charity schools. The development through voluntary educational institutions, mainly provided by the churches, to compulsory education for all (Forster Act 1870), has been marked by segregation and differentiation. A number of criteria have been used for differentiation.

1 *Religion*. An interesting fact is that it was only in 1871 that religious tests were abolished at Oxford and Cambridge; previously Nonconformists and Catholics were denied such education on the grounds of their inability to swear to the 39 Articles of the Church of England. Most of the early nineteenth-century Sunday schools and church day schools, the only education available for most, made denominational subscription a factor. Denominational schools and colleges exist today, though their importance, in general terms, can be seen to have declined.

2 *Sex*. Originally real education was for boys only. Vestiges of this still exist, notably in curriculum differences between the sexes and the lower entry of girls into further and higher education (see Chapters 6 and 7). Single-sex schools have become quite rare other than in the 'public'-school sector, where the most prestigious are boys' schools (though even these now have a nominal few girls). It can probably be argued that sex has become, like religion, a less important factor at the formal level.

3 *Age*. Early schools catered for all ages and often taught them in classes of mixed age. Age segregation became much more prevalent with the development of larger schools, the identification of infant, primary, secondary and tertiary stages of education, and the institution of streaming. A minor counter-trend has been those infant schools that have vertical age- or family-grouping teaching units.

4 *Ability*. Similarly, early schools generally taught children of all abilities, as do infant, primary and most middle schools today. The institution of secondary schools and particularly the 1944 Education Act tripartite system segregated children of different abilities into particular types of school. Recently comprehensive schools have in many areas removed segregation by ability in local education authority schools.

5 *Social class and/or wealth*. This has remained a constant and central factor, and is our main concern.

The 1870 Education Act created two types of education – elementary for working-class and secondary for middle-class children (Silver 1973). The former can be characterised as providing suitable education for the manual worker while the latter provided education for non-manual occupations and for entry into higher and further education. A major factor here was the way powerful sectors of society used schools to maintain or enhance the status and life chances of their children. Thus alongside the elementary and secondary schools were the 'public' schools, so called because most were originally charity schools for the poor – as were many of the older grammar schools. These were suitably revamped by the emerging upper middle class of the Industrial Revolution for their children. Such schools became increasingly exclusive by charging fees, being boarding establishments, teaching idiosyncratic curricula (classics and dead languages), and establishing special relationships with universities, the civil service, church and commerce (see table 4.2). They remain an important and divisive element in education today.

The most significant historical change came with the 1944 Education Act, which abolished fees for secondary schooling. This was seen as removing the last economic barrier to education and making a significant contribution to equality of opportunity for all, regardless of class or wealth. The Act had as its aim the provision of education for each child according to its age, aptitude and ability. Efforts were directed mainly towards the secondary-school stage, establishing the tripartite system – grammar schools for the academically able, technical schools for those who, while not particularly able, could be taught a trade or skill, and secondary modern schools for those who were not examinable. The Act did little about 'public' and independent schools, which remained outside the local authority system. Since there were very few technical schools the system is best viewed as bipartite – grammar and secondary modern. Government research in the late 1950s revealed that the social-class composition of the types of school were quite different (*15—18* 1960). While 71 per cent of the male children of professional workers went to selective (49 per cent) or independent schools (22 per cent), only 18 per cent of semiskilled and 12 per cent of unskilled workers' male children attended selective and none independent schools. There had been little change. In much the same way as the system that it had replaced, the new one, with minor regional variations, functioned so that grammar and independent schools catered for the middle and secondary modern schools for the working class.

During the 1960s unsystematic local moves were made to introduce comprehensive secondary education – simply a school for all children. Many supporters saw this as a major step towards a less socially divisive system of education. However, not only is the comprehensivisation still incomplete but the multitude of different types introduced make it a nonsense to talk of *a* system of secondary education. In some areas the development of community schools, drawing on all children in the immediate area around the school, makes the segregation of the social classes starker than before. The coexistence of grammar and independent schools (recently swollen by the non-Catholic ex-direct-grant schools) means that children of ability and the middle class may be 'creamed off' the comprehensives. On the national scene the impression gained is that more middle-class children now attend 'non-selective' schools than previously, about 24 per cent in the mid 1950s as compared to 49 per cent in the early 1970s. This is largely a result of comprehensivisation, but does not necessarily entail any more mixing of the social classes in particular schools. Table 4.1 suggests that the remaining grammar schools are still basically middle class (classes 1–3), and the secondary modern working class (classes 4–6). Comprehensive schools were attended by similar percentages of each social class, other than class 1. Particularly noticeable is that a sizeable proportion of middle-class children (30 per cent from class 1) attended schools other than those provided by local education authorities.

Whether intentional or not, the net effect of our present, like our past, educational system is to keep apart children from different sections of the social structure and to treat them to

Table 4.1

Type of secondary school attended by children aged 11–14 years by social class* of father or head of household (percentages)

	1	2	3	4	5	6	All†
Secondary modern	29	34	32	49	53	49	44
Comprehensive	20	29	34	32	29	30	30
Grammar	19	19	24	12	9	6	15
Direct grant/							
independent	30	15	4	1	–	–	5
Other/special	1	3	6	6	8	15	6
All	6	16	17	41	15	5	100

* For details of social-class classification see Appendix p. 257
† Including unclassified
Note Type of school attended was identified by parent.

(Derived from Reid 1977, table 6.10, devised from *General Household Survey 1972* 1975, table 4.1)

educational fare of differing types. This can be no better illustrated than by reference to 'public' schools. The Public Schools Commision (1968) showed that pupils in such schools were almost exclusively from the middle classes, only 1 per cent being working class (classes I and II, which comprise 18 per cent of the male population, provided 85 per cent of the pupils), with independent schools being very similar. It would be difficult, then, to disagree with the Public Schools Commission finding that 'public' schools are 'socially divisive', in that they recruit and segregate a very particular group of children from the majority. The significance of 'public' schools lies not only with their almost exclusively middle-class intakes but also with the destinations of their outputs. Public-school products are remarkably successful in gaining entry into universities and in securing élite jobs in our society. This is clearly demonstrated in table 4.2. When looking at the proportion of public-school-educated holders of these positions, it should be remembered that only 2.6 per cent of the school population aged fourteen were so educated.

Given that there is a relationship between parental social class and children's educational achievement (see Chapter 6), the question arises as to whether public schools provide a superior

Table 4.2a
Percentage* of public-school-educated holders of various élite jobs in Britain

The establishment

The civil service, under-secretary and above (1970)	62
High-court and appeal judges (1971)	80
Church of England bishops (1971)	67

Education

Vice-chancellors, principals and professors in English and Welsh universities (1967)	33
Heads of colleges and professors at Oxford and Cambridge (1967)	49

Commerce and industry

Directors of 40 major industrial firms (1971)	68
Directors of clearing banks (1971)	80
Directors of major insurance companies (1971)	83

Politics

Conservative Members of Parliament (1970)	64
Conservative Members of Parliament (1974)	73
Conservative Cabinet (1970)	78
Labour Members of Parliament (1970)	8
Labour Members of Parliament (1974)	9
Labour Cabinet (1970)	29

* Percentages rounded. The percentages are the total in each group whose education is known. All public schools are included, but not other independent or direct-grant grammar schools.
Devised from: (1) Boyd 1973, tables 4–11; (2) Public Schools Commission: First Report 1968, vol. 11, appendix 8, section 4, table 4.28; (3) Whitley 1973; (4) The Times House of Commons 1970 and 1974, p. 257, and Punnett 1971, table xx.)

and advantageous education or merely reinforce the educational and social advantages of middle-class children. Would these children be equally successful in ordinary schools? One approach would be to look at some aspects of the educational differences between public and local-authority schools. Like many other educational questions, however, there are no simple answers. A number of studies have shown that the educational achievements of pupils known to have failed the eleven-plus selection examination and who attended public schools have been superior to those of similar children in local-authority schools. Masters and Hockey (1963) reported that 70 per cent of such boys attending Headmasters' Conference schools gained five or more G.C.E. O-levels. Kalton (1966) compared the 72 per cent of public-school eleven-plus failures who gained four or more O-levels (of whom 15 per cent gained university places) with the three per cent of secondary-modern-school pupils who achieved four or more O-levels. In the Lancing College study it was found that of the 23 per cent of the intake who had I.Q.s of below 112 some 93 per cent gained five or more O-levels. Holding social class constant and comparing the O-level achievements of public and grammar-school pupils, Douglas, Ross and Simpson (1968) found grammar schools to have the better record other than among the highest-ability boys where there was a marginal advantage for the public schools. These sorts of findings suggest that there is no clear-cut evidence of an overall educational superiority of public schools. However, it can be argued that such evidence is difficult to interpret given the very real differences within the types of schools compared and the variety of catchment areas they serve.

Much the same conclusions can be drawn from the educational provisions of public schools. The proportions of staff in such schools who have degrees, whose degrees are of first-class honours standard, and whose degrees were obtained at Oxford and Cambridge, are higher than in local-authority schools. It would be more than bold to claim this suggests that the instruction given is superior, especially since a lower proportion have undertaken teacher-education courses. It is true that there are more teachers to pupils in public schools where the ratio in 1967 was 1:12 compared to 1:23 in local-authority schools, though the grammar schools' ratio was 1:17 (*Public Schools Commission*). Given the extra duties and proportionately larger sixth forms of public schools, the difference is perhaps not large. Teaching groups do appear to be smaller in public schools, and certainly the length of the supervised day and week are longer. Over all the facilities of such schools, other than libraries and playing fields, have not been shown to be consistently superior to those of other schools.

It is in those aspects of education which most defy measurement that the advantages of public schools can be seen to lie. First, and in contrast to other schools, they have considerable control over pupil entry, recruiting pupils whose parents have a firm commitment to this particular type of education and over half of whom were themselves so educated. We can suspect, then, that the congruence between home and school is quite direct and shows much less variation than is the case with other schools, as indicated by the parents' willingness to support the schools financially – in addition to paying fees – and the higher rate of entry into the sixth form and higher education (see table 4.2b). Burt (1961) summed it up when he wrote 'Professional parents want the training in character, manners, speech and social ideals which, with few exceptions only the better type of public schools at present seems able to impart.' The Public Schools Commission is almost sceptical (perhaps because of its evidence) when it reports 'Public schools claim to provide a better education whether it is on better facilities, better teachers or the advantages of boarding. Parents presumably accept this and anecdotal evidence to the Commission suggests that employers do (e.g. Public school boys have more self-assurance).' Here, once again, is a clear message that education is most and

Table 4.2b

Percentage of 14- and 17-year-olds educated at public schools and percentage of entrants to university educated at public schools, England and Wales (1967)*

(a)	14-year-olds at school (1967)	2.6
	17-year-olds at school (1967)	9.3
(b)	School-leavers going to university (1967)	16
	School-leavers going to Oxford and Cambridge (1967)	35

* The percentages are the total in each group whose education is known. All public schools are included, but not other independent or direct-grant grammar schools. Derived from Public Schools Commission: First Report 1968, vol. 11, appendix 8, section 4, table 4.28

vitally important in the social sense; it is the confirmation of a status culture, the legitimisation of privilege (see also Chapter 7).

It is, of course, the boarding element of public schools which is their most distinctive feature. This, together with the home backgrounds of the pupils, is probably the key to their success in socialising a recognisable standard product with a real market value. Attempts have been made, via Goffman's (1962) concept of 'total institutions', to liken the processes in public schools to those in prisons and mental hospitals. Pupils are similarly supervised for twenty-four hours a day, learn respect for their superiors (masters and prefects), allegiance to the rules of the organisation over their personal desires, and loyalty to their peers and the ideals of the institution which mirror those of their parents and the status group to which they belong. The continuous and protracted experience of a school run by teachers for parents, both of whom share the same values, and supported by the informal culture of the pupils (see Chapter 2), is in some contrast to the regime of most local-authority schools. Quite apart from the existence of any 'old school tie' type of recruitment into the élite jobs by well placed 'old boys', the social rather than necessarily the educational advantages of a public-school education suggest that Floud (1950) was accurate in claiming 'In England, professional qualifications for the foremost positions generally include an important social ingredient which is not supplied by the maintained grammar school and the provincial university' (p. 132).

While public schools are the most blatant example of differentiation and segregation in education by school, numerous other examples exist. Some of these can be seen as chance happenings and others as partly or wholly contrived. As is pointed out elsewhere in this book, there would appear to be a relationship between the socio-economic-cum-geographical situation of a child and the schooling it receives (see also Chapter 6). Within this overall relationship there are, of course, further variations. Schools are not good, bad or indifferent *only* because of the age and extent of their buildings and facilities, their situation, the children they contain and their ability to attract and keep staff. However, a general association may be observed in that the oldest, poorest schools, with staff recruitment and turnover problems (at least until the recent overproduction of teachers), with low academic achievement of pupils are to be found in inner-city areas serving predominantly working-class clienteles.

While it is possible to argue that the effects of separate and different education of children from differing social-class backgrounds is functional – it is part of the process of the reproduction of the existing social structure and order – it can also be seen as undesirable. Such separation can be viewed as contributing, for example, to industrial and political problems in that those in control of resources and those who work, or provide, them have little understanding of each other as they experienced quite separate educations. There have also been more immediate concerns, for example, that the continued separation of the social classes in education produced continual inequality in educational provision and also that the absence of middle-class and able children adversely affected the achievements of other children and the ability of schools to realise the untapped talent which was assumed to exist. Although the most common belief about the move towards comprehensive secondary education is that it was to end the selective examination at eleven-plus, the authors of the scheme were also interested in ending social separation and segregation. 'It is the government's declared objective to end selection at eleven-plus and to eliminate separatism in secondary education' (*Organisation of Secondary Education* 1965). Marsden (1971) declares that, in the same year, Labour Party policy presented comprehensive reorganisation as a response to 'overwhelming technological and popular demands' together with 'research evidence of waste and social divisiveness in the bipartite system', and the Public Schools Commission was set up: 'The main function of the Commission . . . will be to advise in the best way of integrating the public schools with the State system of education'. The reality, twelve years on, in reviewing the progress on both these fronts clearly underlines the arguments presented in the first section of this chapter. With respect to public schools it suggests the obvious political power of those involved in maintaining them intact – the independent-school sector has actually grown! Alternatively it displays the political naïvety, lack of power, or even insincerity on the part of the politicians and others who framed the policies of change; or, some compromise or negotiation between conflicting views (for a fuller discussion of factors involved in educational change, see Chapter 5).

With regard to comprehensive schools the situation is far more complicated. The variation in their implementation is vast. While definitions of what constitutes a comprehensive school vary similarly, it is true that its pure form – a school for all – has only exceptionally been achieved. The salient questions here are: is a school comprehensive when it is single sex? – it is denominational? – it is in competition with independent/public/grammar schools? – it caters only for children up to the legal minimum school-leaving age? – its catchment area provides an intake limited in respect to a particular social class or ethnic group? – it continues to stream (see next section of this chapter) or to segregate children within it, in much the same fashion as under the bipartite system? At this point it becomes necessary to consider what could be done to end social segregation and differentiation in schooling. Logically it would be that each school would reflect, in the correct proportions, the social composition of the surrounding area according to the criteria of say, ability, social class, ethnic and religious background and sex. A problem here would be defining what area the school was to reflect. A school in a city could recruit *all* the relevant children in its catchment area and yet be most unrepresentative of the social structure of the city as a whole. Does this imply 'bussing' children on an immense scale from one area to another? Would such an undertaking rather interfere with children's education than contribute to it? Certainly it would not take into account regional differences in the social structure (that could mean 'flying' rather than 'bussing'!). Almost implicit here is the fact that some differentiation and segregation by school is probably inevitable. At the same time the implications and results of this fact are not necessarily inevitable. Schools in poor areas do not have to be poor schools. To be otherwise, however, would require positive planning and expenditure in ways that have not been practised, to any real extent, so far. Some positive (in the real sense) discrimination would have to be attempted in certain areas, and this could be seen to imply the establishment of national standards and policy. Having reviewed some of the factors contributing to differentiation in education by schools, and some of the implications of these, our attention now turns to differentiation within the school.

Streaming

This form of differentiation has been, and remains, a very common feature of British schools. Its rationale is firmly set in the psychological tradition of education, with its belief that a child's ability is measurable, and remains fairly constant over time. The origins of streaming, as we know it, can be traced to the evidence that Cyril Burt gave to the Consultative Committee on the Primary School (Hadow) in 1931: 'By the age of ten, the children of a single age group must be spread over at least three different standards. And by the age of twelve . . . children need to be grouped . . . not merely in separate classes . . . but in separate types of schools' (quoted in Van Der Eyken 1973, p. 320). The British use of streaming is unique, particularly with regard to its extent – it is illegal in Norway, was abolished in the Soviet Union (1963) and is not used in the United States or France (Jackson 1964).

Before discussing streaming any further, it is necessary to define our terms:

1 *Streaming*. The placing of children of the same age into different classes on the basis of ability, normally involving one or more of the following: performance on a school-based attainment test; performance on an external intelligence and/or

attainment test; teacher's personal and/or professional assessment; the child's age.

2 *Non-streaming*. Mixed ability grouping.

(*a*) *Indirect or random*; the placing of children into classes, say, by name, alphabetically.

(*b*) *Direct*: the forming of *parallel groups* by first ascertaining the ability/attainment of the age group and then ensuring that each class has representative numbers across the range.

3 *Banding*. Some large schools, mainly secondary, do not stream but divide pupils into, say three, ability groups – above average, average and below average. This can result in a number of classes composed of pupils from each band (a loose form of streaming) or can be the basis for direct non-streaming (each class containing the three bands).

4 *Covert streaming*. The allocation of children in an overtly non-streamed class to relatively closed groups (see Rist 1970, outlined above on pp. 46–7).

5 *Setting*. The allocation of children to classes for particular subjects on the basis of their ability in that subject. Although this system is more likely to occur in a non-streamed school, it could operate to some extent in a streamed one.

6 *Grading*. The allocation to a class depends on the pupil's attainment and progress and not on his age or measured ability. It is widely used in American and Soviet schools but not in Britain.

Streaming rests on two simple beliefs: that since children vary in their ability (however defined) they learn best in classes of children with similar ability, and such classes are more easily, or better, taught. In contrast, mixed ability classes are believed to hamper the learning of dull and bright children and make teaching more difficult. It is important to appreciate that these views, expressed by large majorities of teachers in studies by Daniels (1961) and Jackson (1964) and a good proportion of those in Barker Lunn (1970), have to be seen in context. Streaming had been a characteristic of primary-school organisation since the 1930's, and most of the teachers were the products of such schools, and had trained and worked in them. We might expect people so involved in an organisation to have some acceptance of it, but the situation is changing. Jackson reports that 96 per cent of the schools in his study were streamed, while Barker Lunn found only 65 per cent. Although primary schools are changing towards non-streaming, this is less the case in secondary schools (Ferri 1971). It seems likely, then, that streaming remains an important feature of the majority of British schools. This is particularly true, since, as has been suggested and as will be seen, covert streaming can feature in 'unstreamed' schools and classes.

Our present concern with streaming will be limited to three main aspects – the composition of streams, the effects of streaming, and the importance of streaming as an organisational basis of schools. These aspects will be reviewed mainly in the light of empirical research stemming from the structuralist perspective. The last chapter, and to some extent the next section of this chapter, review evidence from the interpretative perspective, much of which is relevant to streaming.

The composition of streams

Given the rationale of streaming, an initial expectation is that the basic difference in the composition of streams would be ability. Over all this expectation is born out. Douglas (1964), using common-attainment tests (standardised, so that the average score of all children was 50), showed that children in the upper streams of two-stream primary schools had higher scores than those in the lower ones (55 marks compared with 45); there was, however, a considerable overlap between them. Barker Lunn found that 15 per cent of the children in her sample were, according to either their English or arithmetic scores, in the wrong stream. This could mean either that assessment of ability was not as accurate as it could or should be, or that factors other than ability were taken into account. In the first place psychologists only claim 90 per cent accuracy for the best tests, so that even when these are used 10 per cent of pupils may be misplaced. Further the 'averaging out' of ability, by the use of either 'intelligence' tests or a series of subject tests (which are averaged together) to produce a list of children in ability order, clearly disguises or enhances some pupils' particular strengths or weaknesses. Second, considerable research exists to suggest that streaming appears to favour children with certain ascribed (as opposed to achieved) characteristics. The most famous of these is parental social class. Douglas found that on the basis of their performance, in his ability tests, 11 per cent more middle-class children were in upper streams and 26 per cent fewer in lower streams than would be expected. He also found that children who had had poor maternal care, or who came from large families, were more likely to be in the lower streams. Jackson and Barker Lunn support the social-class finding and further suggest that children born in the autumn are favoured. The underlying reason for this is that they are older and spent longer in the infant school – three years as opposed to two years and a term for summer-born children. Barker Lunn shows that girls fare better than boys. The former are more often found in the upper streams and boys in the lower than would be expected.

The ascribed factors outlined are, of course, related to ability. The value of the research reported here lies in the fact that when ability is held constant the ascribed factors still operate. To some extent streaming involves social as well as academic differentiation. There is, as we have seen, evidence to suggest that teachers, consciously or unconsciously, discriminate among pupils according to social criteria (see also the next section of this chapter). In relation to the most obvious, neutral and educational factor – the length of infant schooling – it is surprising that many schools fail to make an age allowance in placing children into streams (Barker Lunn 1970).

These considerations are not limited to streamed schools. Covert streaming can be a feature of unstreamed schools and classes. The grouping of children by ability, in some form or other, appears to be more closely related to teacher type than school organisation (see the following sections). It seems likely, too, that 'covert' streaming takes place in streamed classes. Indeed, schools appear to be very much like societies and most other social groups, in that forms of stratification are almost universal, if not inevitable (see below). Even an ideal-typical unstreamed school is almost bound to stratify to some extent by age.

The effects of streaming

There is a good deal of evidence to show that streaming is a self-fulfilling prophecy — that the original decision to put children into streams is proved 'right' by their subsequent performance. Douglas, for example, showed that children in the upper streams improved their attainment-test scores between the ages of eight and eleven, the less able children improving the most. Between the same ages children's scores in the lower streams deteriorated, the most able among them deteriorating most. The net effect was that the two streams had a bigger difference between them at the end than at the beginning. Marginal children in both streams had moved towards the stream's norm. An important contributory factor here is the lack of movement of children between streams. Barker Lunn points out that over a three-year period 75 per cent of children who were in the wrong stream (according to their ability) remained in the wrong stream. Those who were promoted tended to make good progress while demoted children tended to get worse. Of course it is probable that other factors are at work alongside streaming. In the last example, it could be that promoted and demoted children differed in personality and motivation as well as in ability and stream. Douglas demonstrates how social class and stream operate together. While middle- and working-class children in upper streams both improved their scores, it was the middle class who improved the most. In the lower streams middle-class children's scores improved (not as much as in higher streams), while the working-class children's deteriorated.

A notable effect of streaming is that it helps to structure

pupils' friendships and the development of informal cultures. This effect has been extensively explored, particularly in secondary schools (Partridge 1966; Hargreaves 1967; Ford 1969; King 1969; Lacey 1970). All these studies show that friends tend to be chosen from within the same stream. The reason is obvious. Streaming results in limited interaction with pupils in different streams. They also reveal that, as one descends stream, so commitment to school declines and distinctive 'anti-school' informal cultures become more apparent and common. Lacey (1974) points up the role of streaming in this, by looking at it in process. In the unstreamed first year of the grammar school he studied, all boys displayed a high commitment to the norms of the school. In the second year came streaming, the differentiation of pupils and, progressively, their polarisation into pro-school and anti-school subcultures.

The streaming of children has implications for the staff, who in effect become streamed themselves, by association. In primary schools the older, more experienced teachers normally teach older children and the higher streams. In secondary schools those with most experience, qualifications and the highest graded posts spend more of their time teaching the higher than the lower streams. The young, inexperienced, low-status staff tend to be most associated with the lower streams. While this state of affairs reflects the salary and reward structure of the teaching profession and, to an extent, its value system, it can be seen as influencing the effects of streaming. It would be a bold claim that the evidence shows that the best teachers teach the best children. But, given that it is partly true, it could go some way to explain the growing separation in terms of performance of different streams through the school system. It is, then, interesting to speculate what the net effect would be if the situation were to be reversed – if the less able received the best teaching.

The effect of streaming on children's learning has been abundantly researched, mainly in comparison with non-streaming. Such research has tended to be inconclusive. Studies can be quoted which support the superiority of streaming and others of non-streaming. Much of this research can be criticised on methodological grounds, for often involving small samples and being limited in time, span and scope. The largest British study (Barker Lunn 1970) reported that 'Comparable pupils made similar progress in the two types of school' (streamed and non-streamed). However, as has been suggested, achievement is only one aspect of education, as indeed is streaming, and we now turn to another consideration of the latter's importance.

The organisational importance of streaming

The most interesting finding from the Barker Lunn research was that the actual teachers involved were more important than the organisational basis of the school. This will, of course, not surprise readers intimately involved in schools. She identified two types of teacher, based on their attitudes and teaching methods. Table 4.3 illustrates the two types and shows that

Table 4.3

Two different types of teachers and their distribution in streamed and non-streamed schools

Type 1 teachers	Type 2 teachers
Believed in *non-streaming*	Believed in *streaming*
No streaming by seating	Some streaming by seating
More favourable attitude to slow child	Less interested in slow child
'Permissive'	Non-permissive
Tolerant of noise and talking	Low tolerance of noise and talking
Less favourable attitude to physical punishment	Favoured physical punishment
Less use of 'traditional' lessons	Frequent use of 'traditional' lessons
Frequent 'progressive' lessons	Less use of 'progressive' lessons
Formal sums about once a week	Formal sums every 2–3 days
Non-streamed schools	*Streamed schools*
52 per cent were type 1	17 per cent were type 1
48 per cent were type 2	83 per cent were type 2

(Derived from Barker Lunn 1970, table 4.3 and text, p.52)

each type was to be found in both streamed and non-streamed schools. In spite of the fact the sample used was balanced (thirty-six of each type of school), it is noticeable that over all 66 per cent of the teachers believed in streaming, and that these were only just in the minority (48 per cent), even in non-streamed schools. Implicit here, and explicit in the research, is the fact that some classes in unstreamed schools are non-streamed in name only. This limits the value of comparing the progress of children by school type. In the study no differences were found in the average academic performance of pupils of comparable ability and social class taught in either type of school. Neither did teacher type seem to affect academic outcomes, though this could have been blurred by children changing from one type to another, year by year. Similarly, in more general aspects, neither school organisation nor teacher type had any noticeable effect on children of above-average ability. However, the social, emotional and attitudinal development of average and below-average pupils was affected by both, and particularly by teacher type. Such children, taught by teachers of type 1 in non-streamed schools, had better relationships with their teachers and held higher academic self-images than other children. The poorest attitudes to schools were found among children taught by teachers of type 2 in non-streamed schools. Pupils in non-streamed schools had better images of their class and also thought that others had a better image of it, than their counterparts in streamed schools. While in both types of school ability and social class were factors in pupil friendship, there were more mixed-ability friendships in non-streamed schools. Below-average-ability children taught by teachers of type 2 were more likely to be friendless or neglected by their peers (perhaps reflecting the attitudes of their teachers). In non-streamed schools a greater ability range of children participated in non-academic school activities than in streamed schools where those of high ability tended to monopolise. Parents, too, appeared to be affected by school organisation. Streaming was interpreted as an indication of their children's future. Parental aspirations for children in non-streamed schools were linked less to the child's ability than to parental hopes. Most of the differences between streaming and non-streaming are then to be found in spheres other than academic achievement.

The organisational and educational importance of streaming, like other organisational aspects, is mediated by the teachers who operate the system. It can be argued that the crucial factor is the level of involvement of the teachers. Streaming might be a more effective form of organisation if it were operated in its full sense by committed teachers. A good example of how it is not is the lack of movement between streams of wrongly placed or changing pupils, and this in spite of teachers' beliefs to the contrary. The deployment of teachers and school resources, together with teachers' behaviour and attitudes, appear to some extent fortuitous or accidental to the ideas behind streaming. A reasonable conclusion is that teachers behave and operate in particular ways in spite of, as well as because of, the organisation of schools. The next section is concerned with a form of differentiation which appears to be characteristic of teaching and learning whatever the context.

Categorisation

This refers to the less formal processes involved in the differentiation of children in class and school. While the processes are related to the structure and organisation of schools and education in our society, they are more importantly related to personal and professional aspects of teachers' role performance, and, in turn, to a very general facet of social life. In our everyday life we all constantly categorise (label or classify) people, events and situations, which is to say we make generalisations about them from limited information. Where people are concerned, categorisation involves having expectations and making predictions about their behaviour, attitudes, interests and reactions. Reflection upon our everyday life quickly brings to mind the whole concept. We would find life intolerable without categorisation – if each new encounter had to be built up from scratch.

Teachers are continually faced with large groups of children; a secondary school teacher may teach, say, 200 individuals in groups of thirty in the course of a week. Not surprisingly, then, teachers categorise their pupils – some as bright, hardworking, well-behaved scholars, and others as thick, idle and ill behaved, with shades in-between. There are two consequences of this. First, since the teacher (like us) is likely to resist having to recategorise pupils, behaviour that is contrary to his predictions is likely to be accommodated as out of character (or category); for example, bad behaviour by the school captain is differently perceived and dealt with from that of the most consistent miscreant of 4 G, whose good behaviour is similarly likely to be overlooked. Second, the teacher directly, or through his behaviour, is likely to communicate his categorisation to the pupil(s) involved. This, in turn, is likely to affect the pupils' own self-image, since the balance of power in schools creates pressures to accept teachers' definitions.

We have touched on this process in various places in this book, so far. In the last section of this chapter, and in Chapters 2 and 3, it is suggested that formal aspects of the school, streaming in particular, provide a certain institutionalised categorisation of pupils. Further, that in the process of education selection, ranking and segregation appear to be rife and that these rely not only on academic but also on social criteria. Our present concern is to review some of the criteria used by teachers to categorise and subsequently to differentiate their pupils.

It is possible to identify two major types of differences which form the basis of teacher categorisation – group differences and individual differences (Brophy and Good 1974). In following this 'convention' it will be realised that these differences are intimately interrelated.

Group differences

Social class

The most significant and specific British study is that of

Goodacre (1968), which evolved from an earlier observation (Goodacre 1967) that, while infant school teachers' estimates of children's reading ranked in order of merit – middle class, upper (skilled manual) working class and lower (semi- and unskilled manual) working class – this was not reflected in the children's performance on standardised reading comprehension tests. The tests failed to display the superiority of the middle class, showed that upper-working-class children performed better than was suggested by their teachers' evaluations, and confirmed that lower-working-class children were the poorest readers. Briefly the investigation revealed that teachers regarded pupils' home backgrounds as an important factor in learning to read and that they frequently categorised pupils as coming from 'good' or 'poor' homes. A description of the characteristics of the two types of home was gained from a sample of teachers in London infant schools. As table 4.4a shows, the descriptions were detailed and complex. The important point to grasp here is that these descriptions were not based on experience since three out of every four teachers had never visited the home of a pupil (9 per cent said they had and 18 per cent that they might in exceptional circumstances). The study also identified the sources of clues teachers used in order to categorise pupils according to their homes. Table 4.4b gives a list of such clues in regard to material circumstances. Goodacre suggests that there is strong evidence that differentiation is based upon well-structured stereotypes, dependent upon such clues. She writes: 'These findings suggest that teachers tend to think of the 'good' home as the one which facilitates their task . . . teachers of young children may be equating the 'good' home with middle-class values, and therefore discriminating against working-class children and their parents . . .' (pp. 29–30). Similarly Nash (1973) reports that some teachers thought, quite wrongly, that less able and attractive children were from poor homes. Readers may draw strong parallels here with the study by Rist (1970) outlined in Chapter 2. It should also be appreciated that this happens at an early and crucial period in a child's education – learning to read in the infant school. These early categorisations can be seen to affect not only initial but also subsequent school experiences, through the passing on of school records, their incremental effect on the child's progress, and the continued categorisation by subsequent teachers. Social-class or background categorisation appears to be a very general phenomenon in schools. Delamont (1976a) reports that, even in the fee-paying upper-middle-class girls' school she studied, the staff differentiated between pupils from intellectual homes and those from merely wealthy ones.

Ethnic background or race

Perhaps surprisingly, hardly any research has yet been done in this area in Britain, and not very much in America – although there, evidence points to the fact that teachers are likely to have negative attitudes towards minority groups and to differentiate them in classrooms (Brophy and Good 1974). Datta, Schaefer and Davis (1968) analysed the descriptions of seventh-graders (thirteen-year-old pupils) by forty teachers. Blacks were described in less favourable terms than non-blacks, though distinctions were made on the criterion of ability. High-ability blacks were seen as hardworking, well behaved and studious; low-ability ones as poorly adjusted, more rebellious and asocial. Holding ability, and hence to an extent social class, constant, and comparing colour, it emerged that, while able blacks and whites were seen just as favourably, low-ability blacks were viewed in a poorer light than their white counterparts. Katz (1973) looked at integrated schools and found that white students initiated interaction more often than blacks and that teachers either accepted or reinforced this rather than attempting to compensate for it. Similarly, observations of white, female teachers' interaction with black and white seventh and eighth grade pupils, arbitrarily labelled 'gifted' or 'non-gifted', revealed that blacks received less attention, were ignored and criticised more and praised less. 'Gifted' blacks fared worst (Rubovits and Maehr 1973).

Sex

Douglas (1964) reports that British primary school teachers tend to see boys as less hardworking, less able to concentrate and

Table 4.4a

Teachers' characterisations of 'good' and 'poor' homes

	'Good' home			'Poor' home	
Rank order all teachers	Category of items	Examples of the items in the different groupings	Rank order all teachers	Category of items	Examples of the items in the different groupings
1	MOTIVATIONAL	Parents interested in child's activities, spend time with child, answer questions, parents educated	1	EMOTIONAL	Insecurity, lack of affection, constant bickering, parents divorced, separated, broken homes
2	EMOTIONAL	Stable home life, child loved, family unity, mutual consideration	2	MOTIVATIONAL	Parents not interested in child's activities, questions not answered, parents low intelligence
3	CULTURAL	'Good' conversation, visits to interesting places, the 'right' amusements, sensible toys	3	MORAL TRAINING	Laxity, little discipline, children run the streets, lack of faith, indulged
4	MATERIAL	'Good' food, clothing, adequate sleep, physical provision	4	ECONOMIC	Overcrowding, financial insecurity, hire-purchase, mother working, absent from home
5	MORAL TRAINING	Firm but kindly discipline, moral values, religious faith	5	CULTURAL	No conversation, poor manners, too much street play, poverty of interests, lack of books

REGULARITY, ORGANIZATION, AND TRAINING	Regular meals, sleep, habits, cleanliness, television watching supervised	6	MATERIAL	Poor food, clothing, insufficient sleep, neglect, lack of physical care
ECONOMIC	Attractive housing, space to play, mother at home or makes provision, financial security, regular parental employment	7	INTEREST IN CHILD'S PROGRESS	No parental interest in schoolwork, education
INTEREST IN CHILD'S PROGRESS	Parental help with school work, interested in education, co-operate with school	8	REGULARITY, ORGANIZATION, AND TRAINING	Irregular meals, sleep, habits, dirtiness, television watching not supervised
UNCLASSIFIABLE	Quiet, tidy, settled schooling, care of toys	9	UNCLASSIFIABLE	Noisy, untidy, broken schooling, etc.

(Derived from Goodacre 1968, tables D/1 and D/11)

Table 4.4b
Teachers' clues* to a child's material circumstances

1 The child's possessions at school and quality of clothes
2 The types of holidays and visits described by children
3 The amount of pocket money
4 Whether the school photograph was purchased and school uniform
5 Buying National Savings Stamps at school
6 Children's response to appeals and their gifts for others
7 Whether a child had free dinners or was in receipt of other welfare
8 Information (unspecified) gained by talking to parents or children
9 Information from child's drawings, stories or 'News' periods
10 Child's cleanliness, quality of underclothes and condition, language, speech, behaviour and manners
11 Their respect for equipment and property
12 Their general knowledge and familiarity with books
13 Their father's job or occupation
14 The family's hire-purchase commitments
15 Parental interest in child's activities
16 Whether family received welfare benefits
17 Parental appearance
18 Whether parents were saving for a home of their own
19 Whether the mother was working

* Given in order of frequency of mention by teachers
(Derived from Goodacre 1968, pp. 37 and 38)

less willing to submit to discipline than girls (see table 4.5). Although higher-social-class children were seen as generally better behaved than others, these boys still received more criticism than girls. It should be borne in mind that such observations were made by predominantly female teachers. Although test scores revealed that girls were only slightly superior in school work, teachers' assessments appeared to reflect their sexist attitude in that they underrated boys' and overrated girls' performance. As Douglas comments:

> These views are heavily influenced by the behaviour of boys in class. The unruly boy or the boy who is idle tends to be graded by his teacher as unsuitable for a grammar school education even when, by his scores in the survey tests, he should get a place. In the 11+ examinations . . . although they do less well than would be expected from their test scores

Table 4.5

The percentage of primary school boys and girls seen by teachers to have certain unfavourable characteristics by social class

	Poor worker or lazy	Lacks concentration	Lacks discipline
Middle class			
Boys	11.3	17.2	3.3
Girls	6.1	8.7	1.2
Manual working class			
Boys	23.8	27.8	3.9
Girls	14.7	17.6	1.6

(Derived from Douglas 1964, p. 75)

[they] do considerably better than their teachers anticipated. The women teachers . . . appear to find boys difficult and unresponsive . . . These differences [between boys and girls] . . . suggest a lack of sympathy and understanding of boys. p. 74)

One can expect that, with the objective influence of the eleven-plus examination removed, this form of categorisation is now more important. It would seem to be an important factor in the frequently reported phenomenon that boys have less favourable attitudes towards school than girls (see, for example, Barker Lunn 1970; Jackson 1968). Unfortunately, for our purpose, this analysis was not continued in the follow-up study at secondary age (Douglas, Ross and Simpson 1968). Given that the sexes perform somewhat differently at secondary than primary level (see p. 112) and that male teachers are much more prevalent, it is interesting to speculate both about secondary teachers' categorisation of pupils along sex lines and as to why, as yet, it awaits empirical investigation on any scale. It may well be that along with curricular and other factors teachers' categorisation of pupils in terms of 'appropriate' sex roles affects achievement and attitudes towards sixth-form, further and higher education.

Individual differences

Achievement

Given the existence of streaming in British schools and the importance of children's attainment in education, it is no surprise that achievement or ability plays an important part in teachers' categorisations. Indeed it can be recognised as the most important, though it is often confused with other factors. As has been suggested, where pupils are streamed teachers tend to apply 'appropriate' stereotypes to the classes, involving behaviour and performance expectations. They adapt the curriculum in 'suitable' ways (Keddie 1971) and probably help to bring about a self-fulfilling prophecy (see the previous section of this chapter, and pp. 85–8 and 47 above). Barker Lunn (1970) has shown that in non-streamed schools many teachers still categorise and differentiate their charges along similar lines. Wittingly or otherwise teachers communicate their categorisations to the children. Barker Lunn and Nash (1973) have shown a relationship between teachers' perception of children and the children's self-perception. There is some not uncontroversial evidence that given reason to change their categorisation teachers modify their behaviour, with a consequent change in pupils' performance (Rosenthal and Jacobson 1968). Pupils in this study who were randomly identified as 'spurters' became such in the following year. What this type of research at least indicates is that teachers, quite correctly, adapt their approaches to the assumed ability of those they teach. Not to do so would be absurd. However, a problem arises when their assumptions are incorrect, inaccurate or result from categorisation based on inappropriate clues, many of which are being identified in this chapter. It is hardly surprising, given their job, that teachers have a preference for more able children and thus devote more time to teaching these than the less able. It can also be argued that it is not surprising that teachers are more favourably disposed towards children from middle-class homes and that they often see ability and home background as synonymous.

Personality

Fesbach's work (1969), which has been successfully replicated, suggests that teachers have a preference for pupils with particular types of personality. They tend to prefer conforming and acquiescent pupils and reject the active and assertive. This can be seen to be related to the sex differences mentioned above, in that the first qualities are more typical of the young female role in Western society and the latter of the male.

Categorisation by teachers can also be shown as being based on more bizarre factors.

Physical appearance

The Open University (Bynner, Cashden and Commings 1972) conducted an experiment in which teachers were asked to group eight photographs of children into two groups of four – bright and dull. Some were always categorised correctly in relation to I.Q. and measured ability, others incorrectly and others inconsistently. The study reveals, perhaps surprisingly, that many teachers are prepared to make judgements on such evidence (probably in classrooms too). The consistently wrongly categorised boys were a very smart and bright-looking chap with an I.Q. of 82 – 46 out of 54 categorised him as *bright* – and a less smart, rather dull-looking chap with an I.Q. of 110 – 40 out of 54 categorised him as *dull*.

First names

Harai and McDavid (1973) found that teachers made more favourable judgements of essays which were apparently written by children with common names (which had in fact been randomly assigned) and less favourable to ones bearing unusual names. The author suspects that this may partly explain some of his experiences as a pupil!

Speech

Crowl and MacGinitie (1974) found that teachers listening to pupils' taped answers were more favourably disposed to those rendered in a 'white' accent as opposed to a 'black' one. Similarly teachers reported higher academic expectations of pupils who spoke in a standard way than those whose English was non-standard (Williams, Whitehead and Miller 1972)

Writing

Yes, teachers do knock off marks for sloppy presentation, poor handwriting, and so on. Soloff (1973) asked teachers to mark two identical essays for content only. One was neat, the other was not; the first consistently gained higher marks.

Having reviewed some forms of teachers' categorisation of pupils, certain implications and considerations need to be identified. Clearly the most important implication is that categorisation leads to the differentiation of pupils by teachers and that this, in turn, affects pupils' learning and achievement, their self-image, attitudes to school and education and probably, eventually, life chances and views of the world in adult life. It can be argued that, for those who are categorised in undesirable directions, the whole process is rather disastrous, and even that it involves unprofessional behaviour on the part of teachers. On the other hand, but perhaps still unfairly, those favourably categorised benefit from the process. At the same time teachers are human, and it is difficult for them either to avoid categorising pupils or to treat pupils as identical units. Indeed, as has been suggested, in some cases the latter would be equally undesirable. Two important factors must be borne in mind. First, teacher–pupil relationships are clearly a two-way process. Pupils affect teachers' behaviour in much the same way as teachers affect their pupils'. Second, it would be a false assumption that categorisation necessarily involved the conscious recognition of differences and application of varying treatments. Obviously both these factors must be viewed within the context of the classroom, the reality in which the drama is played out. Teachers' preferences for middle-class, bright, able and co-operative children can then be seen in behavioural and situational terms. Simply, it is easier, and possibly more rewarding, to teach well-behaved, able and motivated pupils. Hence, whether teachers consciously discriminate in favour of, say, middle-class or female children, or whether the preference arises from coincidence between ideal-pupil role performance and ascribed factors is open to debate. Sociologists, in general, are more concerned to illuminate processes than to impute motivations to social actions. Therefore this section is not necessarily critical of teachers as individuals (not *all* of whom fit the description), but it does suggest the importance of a knowledge and awareness of categorisation for those wishing to understand schooling. There is another way in which categorisation is a two-way process. As was shown in Chapter 3, pupils categorise their teachers – often very cruelly. This affects both pupils' behaviour towards the teacher and that of the teacher involved. It can, then, be very difficult to love 4G who have you down as an élitest, academic, 'square' bore, whose major interest in life is their discomfort, or to avoid loving 4A who see you as a young, dashing, 'with it', brilliant historian, their gateway to O-level!

There are three main considerations. Since the evidence is far from conclusive, these are best viewed as open-ended questions.

1 What is the role of knowledge in the production and reinforcement of categorisation?

The existence of records and information about, and the institutional categorisation of, pupils does appear to structure teachers' categories. Fuchs (1968) and Keddie (1971) have described how persuasive schools are at inducting members of staff into this aspect of their role. It has also been shown (Goodacre 1968) that, independently of such 'official' sources, teachers have access to 'knowledge' or form opinions about their pupils. Since this has been shown to happen in the reception classes of infant schools, it seems unlikely that categorisation would not be a characteristic of teaching even if teachers were ignorant of the pupils.

2 Does categorisation (*a*) reinforce existing differences between children or (*b*) instrumentally create differences?

The evidence suggests that its role is rather towards reinforcing existing differences than towards creating them. However, it is also true that over the school career categorisation widens the differences. In terms of ability, achievement, behaviour and motivation, infant school children are more alike than those in the final year of a secondary school. In this sense, it could be argued, supposed initial differences have been intensified so that they become real ones.

3 Are the categorisations especially professional (i.e. products of teachers and teaching) or are they reflections of public and generally held views?

While explanations can be sought in terms of teachers' role performance and schooling practices, the coincidence between teachers' categorisations and those in society at large can not be ignored.

Overview

In this chapter some of the main forms of differentiation in school education have been outlined. The structure and content of the presentation have demonstrated that differentiation in the social structure is mirrored by that in schools and classrooms; however, the implied direction of influence although illustrated in this chapter can be questioned. Obviously the reverse could not be held – that differentiation in the classroom directly produces the same in society. It is more reasonable to accept, as was argued in the Introduction, that school and society are intimately related and therefore that the forms of differentiation are very similar, if not the same, in both. However undesirable – educationally, morally or ideologically – the effects of differentiation in and between schools may be, it is probably unrealistic to expect schools and teachers to change radically, if at all, the social facts of life. This may go part way to explaining the limited success of educational changes, which often appear to be only partly or poorly implemented, in changing society. It suggests, as Chapter 5 illustrates, that in general social change precedes educational change.

So far our considerations, while centred on the school, have also clearly moved beyond those walls and into society. The picture that has emerged is that education can – indeed must – be viewed as a social enterprise. The next chapters broaden out to consider the relationships between education (mainly schooling) and the family, the economy and industry, the social structure, government, politics and religion. Given this subject matter – macro-social factors – what follows relies almost exclusively on structuralist perspectives. Interpretative sociology has been mainly concerned with a critique of existing sociology of education rather than with substantive contributions in these areas. Mostly this criticism has followed that outlined in Chapter 1 and is not again fully rehearsed. The following chapter picks up an aspect of our discussion of schools – namely, that they are dynamic – and takes a view of their history from the sociological perspectives outlined in the first chapter. In so doing, the historical foundations are exposed of many of the concerns, practices and controversies surrounding schools and education today.

5

Educational change

Introduction

This chapter has two major themes. It emphasises that present social reality cannot be properly understood solely in terms of the present. It also pursues the common theme of the whole book – the variety of perspectives in the sociology of education. The two themes are linked in that we shall consider various sociological interpretations of historical social change and their effects on education.

The importance of the first theme can be illustrated by thinking about what would be made by that now classical visiting Martian of a typical lecture-room scene. He might well be forgiven for assuming that, since one person was orally giving others information, the printing press had not been invented, that the students could not read, or that everything the lecturer said was his own created knowledge, unobtainable elsewhere. His understanding would be assisted by knowing that the lecture method has a history going back to the medieval universities, when much knowledge was carried around in a few heads and the only way for many people to gain it was to sit at another's feet and listen. An explanation of why the method had survived would demand both historical and further social considerations. Certainly it is impossible for all the lectures taking place in the country on any given day of term to be spontaneous events created by individuals who happen to come together. Probably the continued predominance of lecturing has to do with its social appeal or comfort. It can be seen to 'justify' both parties – lecturers and students feel they have been working when they have delivered or attended a lecture. The lecture system can also be seen to help support the role of lecturer and student, the superiority of one over the other (this has been discussed in relation to teacher and pupil in Chapters 2 and 3). Leaving our Martian to his own devices, it is obvious and important that an appreciation of history be built into any, including the sociological, approach to education.

This historical dimension could be provided in a number of ways, most obviously by a historical chapter. However, this chapter will incorporate a second dimension, illustrating the differences between, and contributions of, theoretical perspectives. History is then not merely sets of facts, the knowledge of which provides a single understanding. All history, like sociology, involves interpretation. Apart from a variety of historical treatments, a number of sociological models (or perspectives) have been applied to educational history. In order to evaluate the contribution of each model, perhaps a standard historical account of educational history should first be presented. However, since all history involves interpretation – at the very least in the selection of events or facts to be presented – this is not possible in the space available here. The historical events recorded here are not in question, though their selection, interpretation, the importance given them and the inter-relationships traced between them can be challenged. Interested readers will find a most readable treatment of the area by two historians is Lawson and Silver (1973).

Further, the material presented in this chapter discusses a number of general areas of concern about the whole nature of sociology and the sociology of education, which are taken up in the overview at the end of this chapter.

A structural-functional model

Shipman (1971) provides a good illustration of this approach. His book traces the educational consequences of modernisation in society. Modernisation has two major characteristics – industrialisation and urbanisation. In the movement towards these there is an increase in the use of science, a decline in the importance of religion and a growth of impersonality in interpersonal relationships. Most features of social life are taken over by specialist organisations and structures. The emergence of schools is part of this structural differentiation. They are concerned with education, which Shipman defines as that part of socialisation (the total transmission of a culture) that is considered so important that its teaching must be organised to ensure learning takes place. As might be expected, an important part of Shipman's thesis rests on the statement that 'Social life is only possible if there is some degree of order in the relations between people' (p. 124). Through modernisation the teaching and maintenance of this aspect of social order passes from the undifferentiated family and community into the hands of specialist organisations. It is important to realise that, while formal agencies destroy the monopoly of kinship groups in this respect, they do not replace the family, community, religion or work. The societal problem of modernisation is that the specialist organisations present sets of uncoordinated value systems. In order to maintain social order, these possibly conflicting value systems and the interests they represent need co-ordinating – a task increasingly undertaken by central government.

A major requirement for modern society, Shipman argues, is the need for commitment to a set of values which fit the norms of bureaucratic organisations, these norms being that the environment is impersonal and that assessment is based on performance and not affected by status away from work. Hence it is often not what is taught that matters but rather the organisation of the teaching and learning (see also Chapter 2, pp. 48–9). Education also functions as an important element in controlling the mobilisation of Society to modernisation. It has been used to attack established power, to subordinate the masses, and its control has been vital to those wanting to determine the direction of the process. Schooling, as has been stated, is only one set of specialist agencies involved in education which is also undertaken by other agencies such as the churches, armed forces, political parties, mass communications, the work place, and so on. The inevitability of conflict, suggests Shipman, leads to the increasing supervision of schools by government. Education then fulfils a number of functions, but its role in the maintenance of social order is the most significant.

Order rests partly on individuals having learnt to behave according to a culture, and partly on the existence of controls to ensure that they do. However, social order is never solely maintained by reinforcing the effects of home, school, church, work, and so on, but also by the force of dominant groups in society. In education and schooling this could involve indoctrination, which has, through the development of certain techniques, become potentially more effective but at the same time more difficult to use because of the conflicting influences in society. Schooling is often not reinforced by other agencies. Consequently a more typical response has been the separation of the élite's education from that of the masses. The tendency for adult status to remain related to that of family or origin (see Chapters 6 and 7) is a function of education's involvement with other features of the social structure, mainly stratification. To concentrate on schooling is to ignore other influences on education (pre-school facilities, private tuition, intellectual quality and stimulus of the home etc.) which are accumulative and persistent.

According to Shipman, school occupies a central place in the maintenance of social order in modern societies and typifies how organisations work as social control agents.

> The school operates . . . not only in enforcing values such as honesty, obedience, loyalty and industry, but in actively defining deviance and merit, selecting and labelling delinquents and successes, and using these distinctions to reinforce order and indirectly to stabilise the society of large units . . . A school therefore incorporates the norms of modern society and children are exposed to these in a situation where they must rely on their individual efforts. The

school bell and factory hooter symbolise similar types of
organisation . . . Another way . . . schools . . . reinforce social
control is through the moral climate that the teachers try to
establish and maintain . . . Punctuality, quiet, orderly work
in large groups, response to orders, bells and timetables,
respect for authority, even tolerance of monotony, boredom,
punishment, lack of reward and regular attendance at place of
work are habits to be learned in school. (pp. 52–5)

The model at work

Shipman considers education in England from pre-1780
through to the post-1944 era, as well as education in Japan.
Our consideration is limited to Britain during the period
1780–1850, the period that saw a phase of uprooting and
disturbance, of transition from an agrarian to an industrial
society. These changes – from agriculture to industry, from
village to urban life and the attendant increase in population –
Shipman identifies as the causes of problems of social control.
The existing institutions, which had provided for control in the
mid-eighteenth century, were disrupted and became less effective. The stable social conditions, based on work, the family and
community and reinforced by religion, were the experience of a
declining proportion of the population. Increasingly these were
supplemented by a range of government and voluntary bodies,
including schools.

In the early part of the period working-class children were
extensively employed. Apart from a few charity schools for the
poor, schooling was increasingly supplied by Sunday schools
provided by churches. As institutions these can be seen to have
had several advantages. Since Sunday was the day of rest,
attendance did not interfere with the children's contribution to
industry and at the same time kept them off the streets and away
from trouble. Indeed the social control of children was a major
concern of Robert Raikes, the national populariser of Sunday
schools. These schools were religiously motivated and thus
involved the then very powerful institution of the church in

education. Finally they were cheap, using volunteers alongside paid teachers.

After the turn of the century, day schools were established, again mainly by the churches. These used the monitorial system of instruction in which one teacher 'taught' a large number (often hundreds) of children by using older, able pupils (monitors) to teach groups of younger pupils. Shipman argues that this system was admirably suited to the day because it appealed to the supporters of education, it was cheap and efficient, and was able to cope with a school population that was growing at a prodigious rate – a growth due to legislation which progressively controlled the hours of children's work and the age at which they could be employed. Ragged and other philanthropic schools were established with the aim of solving the problem of the urban slum children. Until the end of the period government intervention was limited to the inspection of schools and the provision of some funds for the voluntary bodies who ran the schools. The quite separate schooling of the middle classes also underwent reform. Private schools thrived, many being established by Nonconformist churches, while the 'public' schools began to cater no longer for the poor but for the rich who were turning away from private tutoring.

Shipman's main argument is that education was concerned with social control. He identifies a debate between those who thought education would discipline the workers and those who thought it would make them a disruptive element in society. However, all those involved in providing education agreed that the existing social hierarchy should be maintained, that the prime function of education was to control, and that the importance of religion in education was not in dispute – only the particular brand to be used. According to Shipman, schooling developed as work became limited for children. The monitorial system that replaced work exhibited the same regime and characteristics, and provided a sound preparation for life in work (see the quotations on pp. 149–50). This regime, aptly called 'the steam engine of the moral world', was reflected in the curriculum and teaching methods of the schools. They were

harsh places in which children were expected to receive knowledge without question from teachers who had the supreme
backing of the church. The learning was systematic and often by
rote; failure to learn was punished because it was taken to
indicate idleness or vice. Shipman reinforces his claim that
education was about social control by showing that there was no
demand for education for economic advance at this time, since
in that respect England led the world. Further, from manual to
professional worker, actual work knowledge and skills were
learnt 'on the job' rather than in school or university. The
clearest indication of the disciplinary function was to be found
in the way employers used their own schools. Even the enlight-
ened, like Robert Owen, saw schools not for teaching technical
skills but for teaching all a new morality. Shipman claims that
the schooling of this period was successful in that the popular
social disturbances that characterised the early part of the period
were contained by its end. The challenge to social order had
been diverted; attempts to destroy the social system had become
attempts to change it.

The model's contribution and an evaluation
The value of Shipman's contribution is that it places education
very squarely in the whole set of social institutions that society
comprises. It views education very much in a service role,
fulfilling certain functions, like social control and the socialisation of the workforce, which are seen as the needs of society. As
such needs change, so do the functions of education. That an
intimate relationship between education and society exists is
not in dispute, and is a constant theme of this book.

The criticisms of Shipman's thesis are precisely those of
structural functionalism itself (see also Chapter 1). These have
been marshalled by Kazamias and Schwartz (1973). First there
is an implicit assumption that, since schools exhibit characteristics which meet social needs, and since modernisation is inevitable, so education inevitably moves towards certain characteristics. Using Hempel's (1966) criticism that functional

analysis involves 'the fallacy of affirming the consequent in regard to the premise', Kazamias and Schwartz present Shipman's thesis as follows:

(A)   During 1780–1850 schools functioned adequately i.e. helped maintain social order, in an industrial, specialised and differentiated society.

(B)   Schools function adequately in an urban industrialized society only if men internalise capitalistic values and urban norms.

(C)   Bells, timetables, overt coercion etc. – the traits of the monitorial system would, if present in the schools, satisfy the conditions of socialisation and training.

(D)   Hence during this period these traits were present in schools. (Devised from p. 248)

They then argue that this theory would be valid only if it were possible to show that only the traits of the monitorial system would have satisfied the needs of society for social order – that there were no alternatives. They suggest that Shipman has not demonstrated this. Finally, as Peters (1964) has pointed out, the approach is very much that of a spectator and can be seen to underrate both the concerns of the practitioners and the effects of schooling on those that received it.

A conflict model

Vaughan and Archer (1971) base their model on Weber's thesis that institutional change is caused by the interplay of groups and their ideas in the struggle for domination in society. A dominant group (which unlike Marx's can be either a class *or* an organisation or association), together with its ideology, seeks to maintain its situation in society by controlling other groups and eradicating other ideas by making its own universal. Any universally accepted ideology or ethic can be presumed to be the outcome of past struggles. Other groups may attempt assertion, that is to challenge the existing form of domination. Hence institutional change can be viewed as

ASSERTION	TRANSITION	DOMINATION	ASSERTION
Status group A & its ideas compete with other groups & their ideas	Status group A gains power & seeks to institutionalise its ideas	Status group A becomes dominant & its ideas universal	Status group B & its ideas challenge dominant group A and its ideas

(p. 21)

Vaughan and Archer extend Weber's ideas and apply them to education. They argue that education is never a completely autonomous institution, but is always partly integrated with others. One implication is that the groups that dominate education are never purely educational. At the same time and for the same reason, this dominant group does not have to be the ruling group in society. Educational stability (lack of change) exists when there is no challenge or where the challenge of an asserting group is successfully met by the dominant group. In order to maintain domination, a group must (1) have a *monopoly* in owning or providing facilities; (2) be allied to the *constraints* that ensure the compliance of other groups (such constraints are economic, legal and force); (3) have an *ideology* that justifies its monopoly and constraints in order to gain willing as opposed to forced compliance of other groups. The more integrated education is with the other institutions of society, the more general (not specifically educational) the monopoly and constraints are. The vital aspects in the maintenance of domination are constraints and ideology.

In order to achieve domination, an asserting group has to (1) engage in *instrumental activities*, which devalue the monopoly of the dominant group, for example, by providing an alternative education and/or discovering another source of supply; (2) have *bargaining power* based on two factors, numerical strength and organisation; (3) have an *ideology* that legitimises its claims and activities over those of the dominant group. These are necessary but not sufficient conditions for successful assertion. Vaughan and Archer hypothesise about the likely outcome of confrontation between the factors of domination and assertion. Where these are matched there is organised conflict. When domination is being successfully challenged the first factor to give way is, obviously, ideology, since it no longer provides a universally acceptable legitimisation. Next the power of constraint is weakened since it is no longer seen as legitimate. This stage is reached only if the asserting group is organised into instrumental action. Finally the monopoly of the dominant group is affected by educational change either on its own or together with other institutional changes.

The importance of educational ideology is stressed because apart from its role in domination and assertion it also defines the way in which educational goals are to be achieved. Vaughan and Archer identify three purposes that ideology serves; (1) *legitimation* of the position of the group to its members and the rest of society; (2) *negation* of the sources of legitimation put forward by other groups (an assertion group's ideology automatically has this, but a long-standing dominant group may only develop one when faced by attack); (3) *specification* of a blueprint for educational establishments, for example, their goals, curricula and intakes.

The model at work

Vaughan and Archer are concerned with education in the period 1789–1848 (roughly the same period as that of Shipman) in both England and France. We shall look only at English primary education in that period. Such education as existed in the late eighteenth century was almost entirely under Anglican church control, in either parish or charity schools. There were no constraints because there was no opposition. The period under consideration saw the development of industrialisation and a period of *assertion*. This came initially from two sources in the middle class; (1) dissenters who found Anglican education to be doctrinally unacceptable, preferring their own brand of Christianity, and (2) secularists who pursued morality on philosophic, non-religious lines. Subsequently, towards the end of the period a further assertion was made by elements of the working class. Until the Reform Bill of 1832 the working class had supported the reformist activities of the middle class. The former were seeking political emancipation and the latter to make the workforce docile, both using the same political and educational ideas.

The instrumental activity of the asserting groups was to set up alternative schools to those of the established church. The resources for these schools were provided by voluntary subscriptions and the adoption of the monitorial system. An unintended consequence of the alternative schools was to stimulate the Anglican church into attempts to retain its control over education. Both the Anglicans and the Dissenters, however, refused to allow the state to intervene in education, since neither wanted to integrate the educational with the political institutions, preferring voluntary education related to religion.

Vaughan and Archer illustrate, at some length, both the assertive and defensive ideologies involved. These can be summarised as:

The middle-class assertive ideology

1 *Economic*. This contained two main ideas. (*a*) Education was seen to have a negative role protecting emergent industrialisation by preventing the spread of ideas which would be detrimental to industrial production. There was, then, a need to control the education of industrial workers. (*b*) The alternative view was that the possibility of social conflict would be decreased if basic economic laws were understood; therefore education, by spreading enlightenment, could contribute towards social stability.

2 *Utilitarian*. This ideology separated ethics from religion, and consequently challenged the claimed supremacy of the church. Its objective was the general good of society. Education was viewed as having a role in increasing productivity and morality. The élite were to be motivated by the pleasure derived from promoting the maximum general happiness and the

masses' job was to promote the general good by the pursuit of individual happiness. This suggested separate education for the élite and the masses.

Each of these ideologies provided the specification of separate education along social-class lines. Popular education was seen to need to replace religious with economic indoctrination in order to maintain stability through protecting middle-class property and socialising the working class while increasing their productivity.

The working-class assertive ideology

This stemmed from the French political philosophy of natural rights, which taught that happiness was achieved by freeing individuals from the constraints of society in which inequalities were neither natural nor rational. Education was seen, variously, to function against political and economic indoctrination from other parts of society and also to provide for political and economic emancipation (freedom). In this period, such ideology failed to provide a specification because it suggested *both* that gaining the vote would assure the spread of education *and* that the latter would bring about the former. As Vaughan and Archer point out, 'The divergence between the middle and working class precluded a lasting identification between their educational goals and shaped two distinct bodies of thought' (p. 60).

The defensive ideology of the Anglican domination

The 'looseness' of the Church of England, which can be seen as a necessary result of the Reformation – it allowed a whole range of beliefs to subscribe to it – plus the lack of opposition up to the beginning of the period, meant that it lacked an ideology in regard to education. The ideology that emerged during the period of assertion was that, as the Anglican church represented the supreme moral authority, this rather than any other institution, should assume control and authority over education. Alternatively, and for the same reasons, it was the most desirable moral influence on education, and for moral character training.

Vaughan and Archer conclude that the changes in education during this period were minor and concessionary. The dominant Anglican group maintained its position through voluntarism; 'challenge to the dominant group in England which did not lead to its replacement resulted in certain concessionary forms of educational change, but left structural relations unaltered' (p. 218).

The model's contribution and an evaluation

Again the model presents a picture of education firmly embedded in the institutional structure of society. This time, however, unlike Shipman, Vaughan and Archer see education as being used by groups in a struggle for domination rather than as serving the needs of society. Since the interests of these groups are different there is conflict between them and the educational prescriptions they support. The model stresses the importance of the role of ideology in educational change, which in turn is related to societal change.

Again, too, the criticisms of Vaughan and Archer's thesis is that of conflict theory itself. To display that there was conflict is not to demonstrate that it brought about change. As Cohen (1968) argued, conflict can be seen as a product of change rather than its cause, and, if there is a balance of power in a social situation, conflict can actually obstruct change. In the present case it could be argued that the conflict between the groups may well have impeded governmental involvement in the provision of education. In this respect it is interesting to question why the analysis was discontinued at 1848 rather than 1870, at which time voluntarism was replaced by legislated, rate-supported elementary schools. Kazamias and Schwartz have argued that the conflict may have been both under- and overemphasised. Thus while Vaughan and Archer identified both differences and similarities between the groups' ideologies, the relative strengths are difficult to specify. For example, while there was disagreement between the religious and secularist assertion groups over the religious content of education, there was substantial agreement among them and the dominant group in regard to the monitorial system and the undesirability of state intervention, and little disagreement about the goals of education. Indeed, despite their disagreements the two major factions of Anglicans and Nonconformists shared an image of the educated man – the Christian gentleman versed in the classics. Finally, as is the case in Shipmans' thesis, the present can be seen to underestimate the importance of education as an institution in its own right and in its effects.

A Marxist model

Marxist thought provides a fairly discrete, though related, conflict approach. Because of its contribution and the growing renewal of interest in Marxist sociology within the sociology of education, it calls for separate consideration. An interesting, detailed and recent treatment of American education is that of two economists, Bowles and Gintis (1976). Marxist analysis can be regarded as international in that it is concerned to display how the mode of production – in this case capitalism – determines social relationships in society. Our view of the work concentrates on the more general contributions it makes.

Bowles and Gintis's basic thesis, which they do not expect will surprise many, is that 'the dynamics of the capitalist economy and the pattern of educational change are intimately related' (p. 235). Certainly such a view is familiar to readers of this book, especially since similar ideas were contained in both models reviewed so far. However, they also attempt a tentative identification of the mechanisms that translate economic interests into educational programmes.

Bowles and Gintis consider history from the standpoint of class struggle – how class conflict shifts arenas and the mechanisms developed by the capitalist class to mediate and deflect class conflict. They argue that the economic and educational systems both have fairly distinct and independent characters. The capitalist economy is characterised by incessant change while its educational system is less dynamic, promoting a set of values and supporting an educational élite which reproduces itself and its institutions over time.

The educational system is economically important and contributes to the reproduction of the class system in society by creating within itself a set of social relationships that mirror those in economic life. Nevertheless, because education and the economy have different rates of change – the first operating towards stability and the latter towards rapid change – they always have the possibility of being mismatched with each other, and often are. This is a major cause of educational change. The educational system accommodates to new economic conditions in two ways. First, by what Bowles and Gintis call 'pluralistic accommodation' in which the uncoordinated pursuit by individuals and groups of their interests is mediated through the educational system and results in the reorientation of education, normally along progressive lines – for example, vocationally relevant education. The day-to-day operation of this aspect of education reinforces an image of an open educational system. It is argued that such an image is essential, since education must be seen to be democratic – through local control and public involvement – in order that it is successful in legitimising and reproducing the capitalist order in society. They point out that, whatever appearances are, the process operates in a framework determined by a small number of capitalists who are outside the political arena of society. Second, educational adjustment to changing economic conditions is, at times of historical crises, by 'concrete political struggle along class lines of interest'. The response to popular unrest is typically twofold – the raising of wages and the expansion or reform of education.

The model at work

Given our present concern with British educational history, two very brief illustrations from Bowles and Gintis will suffice, one of American education at a similar developmental stage as dealt with by the other two models, and one recent enough to be familiar. The move towards the capitalist mode of production (industrialisation) in the early nineteenth century was attended by popular labour strikes, and the consequent concession was of higher wages for the organised workers and the consolidation of the common school system. This was a response to the economic need not so much for technically expert labour as for the production of a particular type of person who would willingly and contentedly work in the mode of production being introduced. As was mentioned above, schooling had a vital role in this process through its use of social relationships and structure reflecting that of the economic world. In much the same way, in the 1960s the activities of the civil rights movement and the black urban rebellions were met with attempts to alleviate some of the extremes of black poverty, together with a huge programme of compensatory education designed so that blacks could take better advantage of the schooling provided. In both cases, Bowles and Gintis argue, the capitalist class through the use of power has been able to suppress anti-capitalist alternatives and to impose educational changes which have appeared as reasonable and necessary to most at the same time as supporting the capitalist mode of production.

The model's contribution and an evaluation

Apart from its distinctive language and apparent political character, this model has much in common with the two already considered. The needs of society, class interests and capitalism have a similar ring to them. There is a direct parallel between Shipman's picture of the functional relationship of school and workplace and that of Bowles and Gintis. So there is with Vaughan and Archer's emphasis on group conflict, though Bowles and Gintis see educational change as the result of class conflict, not domination.

The model is distinctive in the extent to which it regards capitalism – as a mode of production – as monolithic, while viewing education as to some degree independent, and giving fairly full range to class conflict. Hence, while education is used by the capitalist class to produce particular types of person to support that mode of production, Bowles and Gintis do not see education as having been imposed upon the working class. Educational change has functioned as a substitute for economic reform, and has played an important role in preserving capitalism by obscuring its contradictions. It has shifted the conflict of capitalism from workplace to school and helped remove political force from the contradictions. Educational reformers have acted as mediators between the classes, though their independence has always been stifled by financial dependence on the business élite to implement reform.

Bowles and Gintis conclude:

> . . . the structure and scope of the modern U.S. educational system cannot be explained without reference to both the demands of working people – for literacy, for the possibility of greater occupational mobility, for financial security, for personal growth, for social respect – and to the imperative of the capitalist class to construct an institution which would both enhance the labor power of working people and help to reproduce the conditions for its exploitation. (p. 240)

Their work presents a clear argument for, and evidence of, the ascendancy of the latter group in educational outcomes.

The often-used criticism of this model – that it displays political bias – is irrelevant to the extent that political bias does not necessarily affect a model's utility, but only for some its acceptability. Leaving that aside, it is clear that the model is cast in much the same mould as other structuralist models. It presents a rather similar picture of educational change and displays the same lack of specificity leading to an inability to clearly identify groups and events involved in processes. Therefore, the comments made throughout this chapter are again applicable.

A general structuralist model

Musgrave (1968; 1970) claims that basically his model is of a stationary Parsonian type, but it has important modifications, incorporating, as will be seen, aspects of a conflict model. Central to the model is the concept of the *definition of the situation*: that is, Acts of Parliament, administrative regulations and official reports, in relation to education. Definitions arise from the forces at work in the institutional sphere of society and derive from the value systems of those groups, persons or interests who bring their power to bear on the formulation of a definition. He dismisses the possibility that Acts of Parliament are merely the imposition of the ideology of the ruling class, arguing that since 1832 there has been enough real power conflict in British society for them to be compromises between conflicting interests within a higher level of consensus of values about the nature of democracy. In Rex's use of the term they represent *truce situations*. A measure of consensus is achieved through negotiation and incorporated into the definition. Such definitions, because they are compromises, contain within them the probability of change – Marx's concept of the seeds of change. When agreement is low or nonexistent, then a change in political power will break the truce and call for a redefinition. If a reasonable level of agreement exists, goals for education arise from the definition and in turn positions and norms are created. Manpower and material resources are then claimed for putting the definition into operation. Administration and co-ordination are undertaken as the system attempts to maintain the pattern set by the definition in two ways, (1) by socialising members to the norms and (2) by attempting to make its product meet the requirements of the definition.

Since, Musgrave argues, the norms and roles of the educational system are rarely laid down very specifically, definitions allow a fairly wide range of behaviours to develop and a tolerance of some tension to exist without the need for a redefinition. This also means that some changes can take place within education – autonomously. Change occurs, then, both from within and without, in the latter case when the definition is the result of a power struggle – a truce situation. Hence a change in the power of the groups involved or a change in the values governing the use of power will lead to a redefinition.

Moves towards a redefinition and new truce situation commence when the strains in the social system or in the institution of education reach a 'threshold' level – when the existing definition is inoperable or unacceptable. The process of educational change is generally in the direction of greater complexity and less specificity. This increases the likelihood of autonomous change within education because individuals are given more scope to perform their roles, and the development of bureaucratic control produces a greater chance of disagreement with the explicit norms. The only reason that education does not fly off into uncontrolled change is that it is interbound with other institutions. He sees a change in the salient (prominent) institutions concerned with education, arguing that religion was salient up to 1860, social class from then till 1944 and the economy since. He also points out that education as an institution can affect the value system of other institutions and cites the development of metallurgy, which arose from pure-science research in universities and owes nothing to the demands of the economy. In writing about the redefinition in, and events leading up to, the 1902 Education Act he comments:

> a new truce situation to meet a changed power situation. The conflict was not over basic values, and was therefore not disruptive. There were, however, large enough differences over goals and, in addition, there were many strains due to the changing position of the main institutions that interlocked with education . . . the point was reached beyond which any further development must lead to a new definition of education. (1968, p. 75)

The model at work

Although Musgrave's work (1968) covers the whole period of English educational history from 1800, given the centrality to his thesis of the definition of the situation and his recognition of only three such major definitions (1870, 1902 and 1944) (p. 4), the period 1870–1902 seems the most suitable for demonstration. Briefly, the 1870 Education Act made elementary schooling to the age of twelve compulsory. In so doing it moved away from the voluntary provision of schools by the churches to a dual system in which the 'state', through local education boards, had power to provide schools where the denominations failed to do so. Musgrave describes the education provided by the Act in elementary schools as a summary version of the three Rs and as education for the working class imposed from above. Secondary education remained the domain of the middle class since it was mainly provided out of their own resources through the payment of fees.

Following the Act a number of strains are identified by Musgrave, within education and other social institutions:

Economy. There were changes in industry that implied the demand for a greater amount of education and training away from the workplace. This was highlighted by the growing successful industrial competition from countries with superior school systems to that of England. Education ceased to be viewed as a luxury.

Political balance of power. The near-universal right for males to vote was achieved in 1884 and the period saw the birth of the Trades Union Congress, Labour Party and Fabian Society. The principle of the public provision of education was accepted and ideas of free secondary education and an end to class segregation in schooling entered the political arena.

Religion declined in importance as a social institution. The churches found it financially difficult to support their part of the dual system, actually going into debt. They also had difficulty in recruiting teachers, even though they trained them, because the maintained schools paid teachers higher salaries and less often demanded extra-curricular duties. Since the principle of state intervention had been accepted, it was, now, further demanded.

Family. There was a rise in the status of women, a decline in the birthrate and measures towards improved child care and welfare. Education, like other child services, was no longer viewed as only or even mainly a family responsibility.

The redefinition, the Education Act of 1902, shaped by these strains moved away from a school system administered predominantly by the denominations towards one run mainly by local education authorities. It included, by way of a tolerant definition, the possibility of a growth in secondary schooling. While Parliament controlled expenditure through the Inspectorate, power in the system shifted towards the administration at L.E.A. level.

The model's contribution and an evaluation

At first glance this model appears to have several distinct advantages over the previous. It recognises both conflict and consensus, it gives credence to the autonomy of education as an institution, allows for societal and political change and sees education as embodied within the institutional structure of society. It even appears to predict when educational redefinition will take place. Closer inspection reveals, however, that these gains are by way of a marked looseness of definition. One can only tell when the strains in society and education reach the threshold – where redefinition is necessary – by the fact that a redefinition has in fact taken place. The latter defines the former. One can only judge the relative strength of strains and conflicts in terms of redefinition. Those that are found in the redefinition can be assumed to have been the strongest. This gives no real indication of the direction of influence. While the demands for secondary education for all were not met in 1902, this could have been due to the relative 'weakness' of strains in this direction, alternatively to the strength of the interest of the middle class in keeping their monopoly in this field, or even to the power of politicians who decided it was desirable not to extend such education to the working class.

An interpretative model?

No model has been constructed from this perspective, and it seems unlikely that one will appear in relation to history as we know it. The work of the ethnomethodologists, in particular, has been very critical of 'official' statistics and recordings of events, seeing them as being divorced from real life (from the viewpoint of the participants). Douglas (1967), for example, expounds 'the dangers involved in constructing theories without a firm foundation of careful descriptions of real-world events' (p. 340). The implication is that careful descriptions arise only from ethnomethodological studies. Existing historical data and statistics are therefore not suitable material for treatment. It is also possible to argue that the concern of interpretative sociologists with the here and now of social reality is ahistorical (as was suggested in Chapter 3). Sharp and Green (1975) have argued that phenomenology 'has no theory of history which transcends the history of individual consciousness' (p. 237).

At the same time it is arguable that work such as that of Keddie (1971, see Chapter 3), in observing the introduction of a new curriculum, will become historical. This work is methodologically only partly removed from that of, say, Shipman, Bolan and Jenkins's (1974) study of the progress of the Keele humanities project. It seems possible, therefore, that given time a model may emerge which could conceivably cast light backwards on to history; alternatively, that the stock of knowledge now being gathered will become acceptable history for this branch of the discipline at a point in the future. In other words, that it needs to create its own historical data.

Overview

A number of considerations have been brought to light in this chapter. The models have been rightly so called since they cannot be seen as theories (not that they are claimed to be such by their authors). They lack definitions specific enough to allow them to be refuted or supported by the evidence presented or even probably by that available. They can, however, be viewed as useful descriptive frameworks on which to hang or rearrange historical facts, and as such should not be undervalued. More important, they can be seen to lay the foundation for, and direction of, more detailed socio-historical research. The complexity of educational provision has been captured in the above accounts. Much of this has been shown as due to the guiding and regulative nature of English educational legislation which left a number of decisions and their implementation to local authorities, voluntary bodies, headteachers, and so on. This goes some way towards explaining why there is not *a* system of education in England and why provision varies (see next chapter). For these two reasons together it can be seen that part of the problem of the models lies with the nature of the historical data available, which have not been collected for the purpose for which they are being used. This is a common enough problem in sociology generally. Since the enterprise is incapable, or rather unable, to produce its own information and data, it must use existing sources. This tends to limit both the production of theories and, more important, the verification of such theories. In the present context it is perhaps particularly noticeable.

In spite of their separate emphases the models have important similarities. Indeed it would seem reasonable to accept them as a package deal. They all adopt a macro, high level of abstraction, approach in which national educational events are recognised as important, as being related to, and having consequences for, other social institutions and society at large. There is some neglect of how these are related, in any meaningful way, to groups of identifiable social beings. All the models see education as one institution among many and as being far from among the most powerful. Education, then, serves society, albeit parts of it differently. Education is regarded as having little control over its own destiny and, with the exceptions of the views of Musgrave and Bowles and Gintis, little autonomy over its own day-to-day running. All the models also recognise both consensus and conflict as part of social reality surrounding education. Indeed, if anything, there is a clear emphasis on the importance of conflict. This seems an inevitable conclusion to draw from history and has been a constant theme among sociologists writing in this field. Ottaway (1953) wrote, 'the education a society provides is determined by the dominant social forces at work in that society' (p. 60), while Bernbaum (1967) concluded, 'Solutions . . . were not achieved by consensus. Debate, argument and conflict between the varied interests resulted in the attainment of truce situations which were determined by the power and resources of the contesting groups' (p. 144).

Accordingly, this chapter reinforces many of the salient and recurrent themes of this book. Education is about socialising and involves domination and conflict. There are a number of variations on this theme which have long historical roots, the major one being social class, which has pervaded education from its birth, was and is the basis for segregation, differentiation and success in education. This has been considered in previous chapters and is specifically pursued in those that follow. The implication here is that education is partly about protecting or furthering the interests of the most powerful groups in society (middle classes) and containing those of the majority. Allied with this is the unresolved question of who should control schools and the resources for education. The uneasy truce between church and government has been largely, but not completely, replaced by one between local authority and government with the possibility, following the publication of the Taylor Report (*A New Partnership for our Schools* 1977), of a further party of parents, teachers and children being involved. The continuation of the religious influence in schools and their curricula (see Chapter 1) probably owes more to the vestiges of the churches' past central involvement in education than any popular acclaim in the present. Finally the controversy over the purposes of education remains a constant theme as it has throughout history. Is it to provide for social stability, class interests, the promotion of individual opportunity? Are these mutually exclusive? Should education be a preparation for life, for occupation, a reflection of effort or the reinforcement of the status of family of origin? Is education vitally linked to the economic wellbeing of society? That there is no agreed answer to these questions once again emphasises debate and conflict. In any case, as has been seen, the putting into educational practice of an idea or ideal is likely to have unintended consequences and to be affected by the interpretations of those in charge of schools.

6

Education and social class

The subject of this chapter – the relationship between education and social class – continues to be a major concern of the sociology of education. Not surprisingly, then, it has been a recurrent theme throughout this book. In this chapter we turn our attention specifically to the relationship between parental social class and the educational achievements of children. A presentation of some of the very substantial evidence of such a relationship is followed by a consideration of some non-school-based explanations that have been put forward. In-school explanations have been dealt with in Chapters 2–4, and it is necessary to appreciate, at the outset, that the separation of the two types of explanation is artificial. Hence the factors already dealt with should be borne in mind while reading this chapter. In the following chapter a view of the relationships between educational achievement and adult social class (occupation and income), and between education and social mobility, completes our consideration of education and social class.

A look at the facts

The interest in the relationship between education and social class is, of course, not only sociological. It has its roots in the whole philosophical and political question of equality (or rather the legitimate criteria for inequality) in education – a question that has characterised much of our educational history.

Although the concept of social class is very complex (a vast literature exists on it), for our present purposes we shall accept the way it has been operationalised for empirical research, 'a grouping of people into categories on the basis of occupation' (Reid 1977a). The main weight of research and concern has been on social class and the passing of terminal educational examinations (mainly O- and A-level G.C.E.). It is possible, however, to trace class differences in participation and performance throughout our educational system. At the pre-school educational stage, children with professionally occupied fathers are twice as likely to attend nursery school than those with unskilled manual fathers (14 per cent compared with 7 per cent), and a bigger difference (18 compared with 7 per cent) exists in attendance at day nurseries or play groups (*General Household Survey* 1972). In each case children from middle-class homes (non-manual) are more likely to attend and working-class (manual) children less likely to attend than the average for all children. Whether, and how, such experience affects subsequent performance at school is not clearly indicated by research. What can be shown, however, is that by the age of seven, in infant or first schools, the differences in performance of the social classes in the essentials of reading and arithmetic are marked (Davie, Butler and Goldstein 1972). Table 6.1 contains figures based on the test scores of some 15,000 children born in a week of 1958 showing that children from social class V are six times more likely to be poor readers than those in class I (see top row of table). The study reveals even greater differences in respect of children who are 'non-readers', social class V being fifteen times more likely than class I to be in that category. The table also shows rather similar differences for mathematics. Note, too, the clear divide between the middle (I, II and III (non-manual)) and the working classes (III (manual) IV and V) and how social class I stands out as being better in terms of performance than the other middle classes while social class V performs correspondingly worse than the other working classes. A rather similar, though older, study displays the progress of children through primary school (Douglas 1964). The particu-

Table 6.1

Reading and arithmetic attainment test scores of seven-year-old
children by fathers' social class (percentages)

	I	II	III (N.M.)	III (M.)	IV	V	All†
			*Social class**				
Grouped Southgate reading-test scores							
0–20	8	15	14	30	37	48	29
21–28	37	39	43	41	38	34	39
29–30	54	47	43	29	25	17	32
Grouped problem arithmetic-test scores							
0–3	12	19	19	30	34	41	29
4–6	38	39	43	42	42	37	41
7–10	50	42	38	28	24	22	31

* For definitions of social-class classification, see Appendix, p. 257
† Of whole sample, including those without father or social-class information
(Derived from Reid 1977a, table 6.1, devised from Davie, Butler and Goldstein
1972, tables A165 and A168)

lar value of this study is that it was longitudinal – it studied the
same children at ages eight and eleven – and used a battery of
tests including intelligence, reading and school-attainment
tests. As table 6.2 reveals, not only is there the expected decline
in average test scores across the social classes at each age (note
that the classification is different from that in table 6.1), but

Table 6.2

Change in the average test scores* of children in each social
class between the ages of eight and eleven years

	Upper middle	Lower middle	Upper working	Lower working
	Social class†			
Average test score at 8	56.64	52.96	49.99	48.05
Average test score at 11	56.99	53.88	50.05	47.55
Change in score	+0.35	+0.92	+0.06	−0.50

* Test scores were standardised so that the average for all children at each age was 50
and the standard deviation was 10
† For definitions of social-class classification, see Appendix, p. 257
(Derived from Douglas 1964, table VI(d))

also that the gap in scores between the classes widens between the two ages. While the two middle classes both show increased scores ($+0.35$ for upper-middle and $+0.92$ for lower-middle), the working classes display a very marginal gain ($+0.06$ for upper-working) and a sizeable loss (-0.50 for lower-working). This is, perhaps, surprising. It could be held that schools ought to operate so that at least initial differences are not heightened, while it could be argued that their purpose should be to equalise differences by improving the performance of weaker pupils.

Chapters 2–4 contained evidence that children from different social classes inhabited different schools and streams, received different teaching and education and that such differentiation affected school performance. These factors are clearly important when viewing the terminal educational achievements of the social classes. So, too, is the question of intelligence or ability (see the discussion below, p. 178). Consequently, although the data in table 6.3 are dated, they are particularly valuable for our purpose since they hold constant the type of school attended and the measured I.Q. ranges of the children studied. The table shows that, other than children of the highest I.Q. range (130 or more) at the O-level stage, differences in achievement existed between middle- and working-class children, in distinct favour of the former. In the middle I.Q. range (115–29) a quarter as many more middle-class children gained five or more O-levels than did the working class, two-thirds as many more gained two A-levels, and more than twice entered degree-level courses. Note, however, that these are not measures of pure achievement. They also involve staying on at school and using educational qualifications to enter higher education rather than employment. Hence part of the difference in A-level success between the classes was due to differences in entry to sixth forms. Even in the highest I.Q. range the percentage of those who actually gained two A-levels and subsequently went to degree courses was 86 per cent for the middle and 60 per cent for the working class. Very similar results were obtained in a study some six years later (*Statistics of Education 1961, Supplement*) which held constant the type of school and the grade of eleven-

Table 6.3
Academic achievement of children born 1940–1, at
maintained grammar schools, by grouped I.Q. scores at age 11
and fathers' social class*, England and Wales (percentages)

I.Q. scores	Achievement	Social class* Non-manual	Manual
130 +	Degree-level course†	37	18
	At least 2 G.C.E. A-levels	43	30
	At least 5 G.C.E. O-levels	73	75
115–29	Degree-level course†	17	8
	At least 2 G.C.E. A-levels	23	14
	At least 5 G.C.E. O-levels	56	45
100–14	Degree-level course†	6	2
	At least 2 G.C.E. A-levels	9	6
	At least 5 G.C.E. O-levels	37	22

* For definition of social-class classification, see Appendix, p. 257
† Figures in this row relate to Great Britain
(Derived from *Higher Education* 1963, appendix 1, part 2, table 5)

plus secondary-school-selection examination. Here, although
the overall achievements at O-level were higher, the social-class
differences remained. These were again revealed in the cohort
from the study mentioned above (Douglas 1964). A follow-up
study, in which ability measured at age fifteen was held constant but not the type of school attended (Douglas, Ross and
Simpson 1968), revealed that the percentage of the top-ability
group who gained five or more O-levels (including at least three
from English language, mathematics, science and a foreign
language) varied from 77 per cent for upper-middle-class children across the classes to 37 per cent for lower-working-class
children.

Post-school education presents the starkest picture of the
relationship between social class and education. The most comprehensive research here was, again, that of the Robbins Report
(*Higher Education* 1963) which surveyed about one in every 200
people born in 1940–1. Table 6.4 shows the highest level of
education they achieved. At every level the percentage of each
social class attaining it declines across the classes from I to IV

Table 6.4

Highest level of education attained by children born in 1940–1, by social class* of father, Great Britain (percentages)

	I	II	III (N.M.)	III (M.)	IV and V	All
Higher education						
Degree-level full-time	33	11	6	2	1	4
Other full-time	12	8	4	2	1	3
Part-time	7	6	3	3	2	4
G.C.E. A-level or S.L.C.†	16	7	7	2	1	3
Other post-school course, or G.C.E. O-level	25	48	51	42	30	40
No post-school course or G.C.E. O-level/S.L.C.†	7	20	29	49	65	47

* For definition of social-class classification, see Appendix, p. 257

† Scottish School-Leaving Certificate

(Derived from *Higher Education* 1963, appendix 1, part 2, section 2, table 2)

and V. In terms of full-time degree-level courses (top row of table), while a third of class I entered such courses, only 1 per cent of classes IV and V did so. In other words, a person from social class I was 33 times more likely to end up on an under-graduate course than someone from classes IV and V. At the other extreme only 7 per cent of social class I failed to gain any educational qualification compared with 65 per cent (nearly two in every three) of classes IV and V. An interesting aspect of this research was that it also looked at the relationship between *mothers'* social class (occupation before marriage) and children's educational achievement, with very similar results to those of father and child. The study did not, however, consider the mothers and fathers together. The evidence we have suggests that any view of the social origins of groups of students in higher or further education reveals an over-representation of the middle classes and an under-representation of the working classes compared to the classes' distribution in society at large. There is, however, one sector of the educational system in which social class appears to have no effect on performance – universities. As has been shown, in spite of the powerful association between class and entry into higher education, studies of university students have failed to show any consistent relationship between their social class and the class of degree they obtain (Brockington and Stein 1963; Kelsall 1963).

There is a certain crudeness in using fathers' occupation as the single criterion of a child's social class. Not only has mothers' social class been shown to be related to educational performance, but we can suspect that fathers and mothers are important in combination. Moreover, it is obvious that aspects of social class beyond occupation have important effects, or are related to, such performance. Particularly important here, and as has been demonstrated in research, is the educational level of parents. Certainly adult social class and occupation are related to educational level (see Chapter 7). In other words occupation is only a shorthand and somewhat vague reference to a large number of factors that can be shown to be related to the educational performance of children. Studies with more information about their subjects reveal interesting insights. One of my own (Reid 1969), for example, identified some sixteen 'family characteristics' related to both educational success and to 'middle-classness'. Detailed analysis revealed a small number of working-class children (defined by father's occupation) who had *more* of these characteristics than many of the 'middle-class' children. They had, for example, middle-class, educated mothers and grandparents and came from educationally responsive and supportive, materially well-off, small families. These children were among the most successful in the whole sample and were the most successful working-class part of it. The reverse was also true: some middle-class children had few of the 'family characteristics' and were not successful. The use of the simple occupational definition of class could be seen to misplace some success and failure. What is being argued, therefore, is that the class chances in education, as outlined above, may in fact be more blatant than they appear. More sophisticated criteria of social class than fathers' occupation might well reveal much greater differences in educational performance between the classes.

Of course the simple facts of the association between parental social class and children's educational performance have always been with us. Generations of teachers have known that middle-class children, variously defined, performed better in school than working-class children. The spate of large-scale investigations of this phenomenon in the late 1950s and early 1960s did no more than accurately describe a known situation. Causal explanations were, as now, much more difficult to provide. It is to these that we now turn.

Towards an explanation

If it could be shown that middle-class children were actually and innately superior in an educational sense, there would be little need for further explanation. Certainly, as we have seen, there is evidence that, in general, middle-class children perform better in school and also on intelligence tests than do working-class children. Since it has already been recognised that educational experience, as well as performance, of the social classes is different, the crucial question is whether or not the classes are innately or genetically of different intelligence. Initial considerations here are what is meant by intelligence, and what is the relationship between that definition and intelligence tests.

Any argument along the lines that middle-class children perform better in school than working-class children because of their superior genetic intelligence rests on a number of questionable assumptions. The first is that the middle class is a readily identifiable group that does not change over time. This is basically untrue, since the middle class has grown over the past fifty years at a rate, and in a manner, that cannot be accounted for by human reproduction (see table 7.9 below). In fact the size and composition of the middle class is determined by the structure of occupations in society and by the occupational definitions used by social scientists to identify it. Further, the composition of the middle class is affected by the movement of persons in and out during a career or between generations (see the section on social mobility in Chapter 7).

Second, the argument would assume that it is possible to distinguish between innate and environmental factors in intelligence. A pertinent question here is where do environmental factors begin to affect, or interact with, the genetic structure of a human? At birth? No, since the environment of the foetus in the womb has already affected its development and is itself related to the incidence of certain characteristics. The moment of conception? What about the preconceptual environment of the sperm and egg? The problem of being unable to distinguish neatly between the innate and the environmental is linked to a third assumption concerning measurement. Obviously intelligence can be recognised only when it is expressed, and in order for that to take place learning must have occurred. Learning is not a spontaneous happening in human beings. Babies are born knowing how to suck but need to be shown where in order to survive. Hence, whenever measurement is made, it must include learning as well as, or rather than, the innate or unlearned. It would appear futile, then, to pursue the separate identification of the two contributory factors, since these are, for such purposes, inseparable. Note that it is not being claimed that innate factors are not involved, merely that they cannot be operationalised. Perhaps intelligence is best viewed as a potential which a baby has along with many others – for example, to reach a certain weight, strength and life expectancy. Whether these potentialities are realised, or rather to what extent they are, depends on environmental factors. If the baby is kept in a box, has its feet bound up, lives in an unhealthy environment or is fed incorrectly its performance will be affected. The same is true of intelligence.

A further assumption is that intelligence tests measure a general capacity rather than something that is culturally produced or learned. Yet the great strength of intelligence tests is their reasonably good prediction of educational performance; this could, obviously, mean that they measure the same thing or aspects of it. Verbal tests clearly depend on a knowledge of, and ability to use, language, which is of course learned and varies culturally. Thus the fact that urban children perform better in such tests than rural children (or white than black) probably points to environmental rather than innate differences. A further consideration here is that most tests have, for convenience, been standardised on urban school populations, and it would be easy to produce a test based on rural phenomena which would leave urban children baffled! Non-verbal tests work on the assumption that all children have the same familiarity with the manipulation of shapes, figures and blocks etc. – more than a bold claim. Finally, test performance is normally dependent to some extent on speed, and can to an extent be improved by learning and practice.

It could be that real intelligence (not necessarily that which intelligence tests test) is randomly distributed through society but that its application and expression in the form which shows up on tests is not. It is worth bearing in mind that psychologists tell us that intelligence, like many other genetic characteristics, returns towards the mean over generations. Very intelligent parents generally have children who are intelligent but not aggressively so – their I.Q. will be closer to the average for the population than that of the parents; similarly, but in the opposite direction, for the children of parents with low, but normal, intelligence.

The intention here is not to imply that psychologists are unimpressed with the interplay between innate and environmental factors. A very interesting exposure of the importance of the environment on intelligence is that of Hebb (1949), who cites an experiment with white rats from the same litter bred from the same stock – that is, their heredity had been held constant – which were exposed to widely different environments. One group was put at birth into stimulating cages, full of things to do, the others into non-stimulating, plain cages. On maturity both groups were put into maze-solving situations (a common end for psychologists' rats!). The first group, as might be expected, performed much better than did the second. The experimenters then gave all the rats maze-learning instruction. Not only did the first group learn more quickly than the second, but the latter group never managed to match the performance of the first group. From the same stock, then, were produced 'intelligent' and 'unintelligent' rats. While there are dangers in translating 'facts' from rats to human beings, the possible relationship is there. Indeed the initial differences can be accepted in the human case.

A further consideration must be of the whole concept of intelligence and ability in terms of its psychological as opposed to its everyday meaning. While it is true that the psychological view of intelligence – that it is measurable and fairly constant over time – has become part of the way we think of intelligence, this is a comparatively recent concept. In previous centuries the word 'intelligence' was used in a different sense – surviving today only in the armed forces – as knowledge. In times past, for example, people went to university to 'increase their intellig-ence' rather than as now 'because they are intelligent'. This is closer to how in everyday situations we 'recognise' intelligence – through people's actions and the display of their knowledge and/or experience. A university professor with an incredibly high I.Q. can look pretty unintelligent alongside a mechanic with a low I.Q. at 3.00 a.m. in front of a broken-down motor car! I used to sit in awe of the 'intelligence' of some of my university tutors as they dealt brilliantly with difficult ques-tions in class. After a few years of teaching I realised my awe was of their experience, not their intelligence. Having been struck dumb by a question, I found an answer so that next time around it was a different story. Similarly I may now appear more intelligent than when I started to teach, not for any change in my basic ability but because of the opportunities and time I have had to acquire knowledge together with an ability to display it. These experiences enable me, in some situations, to appear more intelligent than I would do otherwise.

Probably the most telling criticism that can be made in the present discussion is that even where 'ability' or intelligence is held constant social-class differences are still apparent and there-fore remain to be explained. Unfortunately sociological explanations of this are far from watertight. There are, however, three areas of inquiry which have been seen to have some

potential as explanations. None of these is complete in itself –
they are developing – and each ought to be viewed as contributing towards a full explanation in conjunction with in-school
explanations. If the approach to an explanation appears complex, that should not be surprising, since so is the problem. If it
were not so the problem would either not exist or would have
been solved by the efforts of teachers, educationists, politicians
and social scientists.

Language

This is the best-known and least understood – or most mis-
understood – approach of the three. Although in many people's
minds the explanation of differing social-class educational
achievements via language is synonymous with the name of
Bernstein, it has a long history and involves a number of
researchers and commentators not all of whom are sociologists.
We shall concentrate on Bernstein's work because it is pre-
eminently a classical sociological approach. His work covers
nearly two decades and a large number of publications. Commentators have variously described Bernstein as being ambigu-
ous, modifying his views or merely developing his ideas. At the
same time it is true that his ideas have been misrepresented and
oversimplified. Oversimplification is obviously a danger in our
present treatment. Our consideration will be of a fairly recent
statement (Bernstein 1971; Hymes and Gumperz 1971). Bernstein's major papers have been usefully published together
(Bernstein 1971 and 1973).

Bernstein's writings and research are an attempt to relate the
social structure to educational achievement via language. An
early realisation of the difficulty of communicating with
working-class children in formal classroom language, and the
greater discrepancy between working-class scores on verbal and
non-verbal I.Q. tests than middle-class, appear to have given
rise to his concept of two linguistic codes – the *restricted* and the
elaborated. Put as simply as possible, the restricted code is a form

of speech that can be predicted by an observer; is basically simple, involving a limited range of alternatives; is descriptive and narrative rather than analytical and abstract; relies on a common understanding between speaker and listener; some of its meaning is implicit; and the manner and circumstance of speech are of importance as well as its content. In contrast, the elaborated code is more difficult to predict; is more complex, involving a wide range of alternatives; is analytical and abstract; does not rely on a common understanding of meaning; its meaning is explicit; and extra-verbal factors are of little importance.

Bernstein's thesis is that these codes are the products of distinctive social situations associated with social-class differences. In the case of the working class, he maintains that if the factors of similarity of occupation, status and residence, strong communal bonds, work relationships, little individual decision making in work, poor homes and little intellectual stimulus all come together, 'it is plausible to assume that such a social setting will generate a particular form of communication which will shape the intellectual, social and effective orientation of the children' (1973, p. 165). The resulting communication or code he declares will 'emphasize verbally the communal rather than the abstract, substance rather than the elaboration of processes, the here and now rather than the explanation of motives and intentions, and positional rather than people orientated forms of social control' (1973, p. 165). Readers will recognise that he is referring to the restricted code and appreciate that the contrasting work, life and social situation of the middle class, by the same reasoning, give rise to the elaborated code. It is important to understand that Bernstein is *not* saying either that the codes are mutually exclusive or that they are the exclusive property of one social class. The restricted code arises wherever the culture of a group emphasizes *we* rather than *I* and occurs to reinforce social relationships and create social solidarity. Hence, it is characteristic of many groups such as prisoners, adolescents, members of the armed forces, friends, and husband and wife. The elaborated code, in contrast, is found where the culture emphasizes *I* rather than *we*, whenever, that is, common identity and understanding cannot be anticipated. In general terms, then, *all* people have access to restricted codes, but parts of the working class do not have the same access to an elaborated code as do the middle class. As a simple illustration I may, according to the argument, switch from a restricted code over breakfast with my family to the elaborated with, say, my students at work; whereas, if I worked at a local factory or coal mine among people I had grown up with, I might stay within a restricted code. To recap, the linguistic codes exist to reinforce the social relationships of a group or situation, and they are related to that group's position within the social structure.

Bernstein does not rest his case on social class, stating that 'as the connection between social class and linguistic codes is too imprecise' (p. 176) it is necessary to make a further consideration, that of family role systems. He distinguishes between *positional families* in which decisions are made according to the formal status of a person's role (father, mother, child). Such a family system gives rise to 'closed' communication which is less likely to encourage the verbalisation of individuals' differences, intentions and motives since these are prescribed by the family. Social control relies upon the relative power of the people involved rather than on speech. On the other hand, *person-orientated families* occur where decisions are made on the grounds of the psychological and individual differences of members rather than their formal status. This involves 'open' communication which is likely to encourage discussion rather than legislation and to support expression of the individual differences of members. Social control, here, will be through verbal elaboration. These ideas provide a complex theory involving a number of variables which can come together in any combination and in varying degrees. Bernstein maintains, however, that access to the codes is broadly related to social class – that is, there is a relationship between the working class, positional family and the restricted code; between the middle class, person-orientated families and the elaborated code. The theory allows for exceptions and variation. Some working-class families in non-traditional settings (through rehousing, employment, and so on) who move towards person-orientated family systems may also display movement towards the elaborated code. However, as Bernstein states, the literature strongly suggests that the traditional working-class family is of the positional type and that while the conditions now exist for more individualisation of relationships it is not possible to claim that working-class culture has been eroded and replaced by middle-class culture.

Two further considerations should be made. The codes reflect and in turn support differing views of the world. The restricted code is related to a view of the world as something which has to be responded to in which the subject (person) is passive. The elaborated code relates to a view of the world as something capable of being manipulated, where the subject is active. These can be seen as being related to social-class differences in work situations and to have consequences for attitudes towards, and the use of education (see also the next section). Second, as Bernstein stresses, the codes are concerned with performance and *not* competency – that is, language use and not knowledge. Lawton (1968) found that in interview situations as opposed to writing and discussion groups, working-class boys used language inclined more towards the elaborated code. This suggests that they were not ignorant of the code but rather that in more usual school situations it was not their normal linguistic performance.

The relationship between the codes and school performance is probably best summed up by Bernstein's own words:

It happens, however, that this communication code [restricted] directs the child to orders of learning and relevance that are not in harmony with those required by the school. Where the child is sensitive to the communication system of the school and thus to its orders of learning and relation, then the experience of school for this child is one of symbolic and social development; where the child is not sensitive . . . then this child's experience . . . becomes one of symbolic and social change. In the first case we have an elaboration of social identity; in the second case, a change of social identity. Thus between the school and community of the working-class child, there may exist a cultural discontinuity based upon two radically different systems of communication. (p. 166)

Bernstein's work and ideas have attracted a large number of criticisms. Our concern will be with two, which, in fact, can be seen to add to the potential of explanation that the thesis contains.

The inferiority of the restricted code

Many commentators have claimed that Bernstein's work has contributed to the view that lower-class language and thought suffers from verbal deprivation and that these are inferior, illogical and limited in comparision with those of the middle class. Edwards (1976) has argued that Bernstein has wanted it both ways – that at the same time as rejecting such criticisms he claims a profound educational disadvantage for restricted code users. Before commenting on the criticism it is as well to look in more detail at its substance. One of the best-known rejectors of the superiority of standard over non-standard English is Labov (1969). His account is very detailed but his ideas are easily illustrated by two pieces of recorded speech. The first is by Larry who is a loud and rough black gang member who is asked what colour God is.

LARRY. He'd be white, man.
INTERVIEWER. Why?
LARRY. Why? I'll tell you why. 'Cause the average whitey out here got everything, you dig? And the nigger ain't got shit, y'know? Y'understan'? So – um – in order for *that* to happen, you know it ain't no black God that's doin' that bullshit.

The second is of a college-educated upper-middle-class black who is asked whether dreams come true.

> CHARLES. Well, I even heard my parents say that there is such a thing as something in dreams. Some things like that, and sometimes dreams do come true. I have personally never had a dream come true. I've never dreamt that somebody was dying and they actually died, (Mhm) or that I was going to have ten dollars the next day and somehow I got ten dollars in my pocket. (Mhm) I don't particularly believe in that, I don't think it's true.

As Labov points out, and as will be obvious to readers, Larry's statement is a complex of ideas, orderly and effectively presented, even though its style may be unfamiliar and far removed from that of Charles. The latter's statement is much simpler but the language more conventional. In fact the full text (the above is only the first third) reveals that Charles uses words unnecessarily (verbosely), some modifying and qualifying, others repeating or padding the main argument. Our reaction to the two speeches is by way of a 'firmly fixed social convention' of preferences for one over the other. Of course we have no way of knowing how typical these two speakers are of their peers, but we do now have the suggestion that language codes or forms can be viewed both as inferior or superior to each other, depending on whether content or style is being considered. Certainly we must be impressed that they are different, as both Bernstein and Labov are. It is, however, fairly apparent that whether or not one code or form is intrinsically superior to the other is quite superfluous to the argument here because of the importance of the social setting of language use. As Labov writes, 'The initial impression of him [Charles] as a good speaker is simply our long conditioned reaction to middle class verbosity.' If, then, teachers and the educational system recognise standard English or the elaborated code as the superior or the only acceptable form of expression, it follows that, in this situation non-standard English or the restricted code is inferior or not acceptable. In fact we can be assured that this is how teachers in general react, and indeed as we saw above (p. 141) they even have preferences for accents. Hence Bernstein has a defensible position – the restricted code is different rather than deficient in itself – and there is no real conflict between his and Labov's views. The value of Labov's discussion is that it illustrates the dangers of assuming too much or too little about the thought, ideas and ability of a person from the 'appearance' of his language.

It is now possible to turn this criticism of Bernstein around – instead of seeing his thesis as a criticism of the restricted code, to view it as one of schools and education. This is precisely what he has done by criticising compensatory education (1969). 'If the culture of the teacher is to become part of the consciousness of the child, then the culture of the child must first be in the consciousness of the teacher'; or, as the Department of Education and Science (*A Language for Life* 1975) would have it, the teacher 'should start where the child is and should accept the language he brings to school'. However attractive the possibility of explaining the differing social-class educational achievements along these lines may be, the reality is that the research has yet to be done. Understandably, though unfortunately for our purposes, Bernstein's research team's efforts have been directed towards investigating the part played by the family and socialisation in the development of the codes. The extent to which teachers and schools use the elaborated code, and the consequent processes whereby restricted code users fare badly – which would demand intensive classroom observation – has yet to be demonstrated on any scale.

The definition of social class
Bernstein's work contains no clear or precise definition of the term social class. While he shares this in common with many other users of the term in the sociology of education, it remains an unfortunate omission. In many instances, he is careful to describe restricted code users as 'lower-working-class' or as inhabiting 'traditional working-class areas', and his treatment

of the elaborated code users suggests the upper and educated end of the middle class. This, of course, leaves the majority of society outside the clear class categories of code users. While, as we saw in the first section of this chapter, the two groups he identifies are the polar ends of the scales of social and educational achievement, such a treatment limits the explanatory power of his thesis. An explanation of the variable achievements of the large soft-centre of the social structure calls for developments in the definition of social classes and their relationship to the codes. This crudeness is conceded by Bernstein, and as we have seen he adds the further factors of the orientation of the family role system, the mode of social control and the resultant linguistic relationship. However, these do not provide a very useful operationalisation, since the measurement of such factors, if possible, would be laborious in the extreme. We return to these questions in the final chapter.

To conclude, what Bernstein has provided is an intriguing and plausible association of factors which, while holding out the possibility of helping to explain the relationship between social class and education, awaits demonstration.

Values, attitudes, interests and aspirations

Unlike the last, this area has no central British representative in the sociology of education, the work being somewhat fragmentary. As was discussed in Chapter 2, a common sociological, and everyday, assumption is that a person's behaviour is affected by the values he holds relating to the situation in question. Such values are not invented by the individual but are clearly related to the social reality in which he is brought up and lives. In that chapter it was also argued that groups inhabiting the same position in a social structure or system share a common culture or subculture – a sort of corporate kit for survival in, and to cope with, social life. Clearly, as the work of Bernstein has shown, social classes can be viewed as subcultures. Squibb (1973) has displayed how important it is to view subcultures in relation to each other. In other words, to see how, together, the various cultures in a society tend to give cohesion and stability to the social structure as a whole. Culture – through values – defines and legitimises both one's own group's position, behaviour and relationship and that of others (this has been discussed with respect to education, in Chapter 4 and pp. 227–32 below). Squibb further reminds us that the history or past experience of a group is a vital consideration in understanding its culture. A change in circumstances does not necessarily bring about a change in values or attitudes, while the latter may only be explicable in terms of the past. In the educational context, then, it can be suspected that social-class differences in social and educational experience – past, present and anticipated – may be associated with differing values. Indeed we witness such throughout this book. That social-class differences in values exist is not in question. What must be discussed is whether such differences can be related to differing educational achievement, and, more important, whether they have any explanatory power.

It is possible to differentiate between *manifest values* – those relating directly to education – and *latent values* – those relating to areas which have only a tenuous or indirect relationship with education. Similarly the literature deals with parental and child values. While parental values are the most researched – note the similarity here with the greater research on teachers than pupils in Chapters 2 and 3 – they are clearly more problematic. In asserting the effect of values on behaviour we are assuming rather than demonstrating an influence, while probably ignoring intervening variables; in imputing effects of parental values on children's behaviour we are compounding that assumption. Further, there are quite severe methodological problems involved in identifying and measuring values, problems that much of the research has ignored or made light of. Similarly, as the title of this section indicates, it is concerned with a whole variety of factors which can only be very loosely referred to as values – though the term is used here for the sake of brevity.

Manifest values

There exists a substantial body of research to show that parents of children who are successful in school take a greater interest in their education, visit school more often, provide greater encouragement, value education more highly, want them to have a better and longer education and have higher occupational aspirations, than do parents of less successful children. Such findings have a long and consistent history in the literature. To quote an influential large-scale government research (*Children and their Primary Schools* 1967):

. . . associations were found between social class and the responsibility and initiative taken by parents over their children's education, in the interest shown and support given by fathers over their education and upbringing, in the time and attention parents devoted to their children's development and in their interest in and knowledge of the work their children were doing at school. In respect of each of these factors the home situation was likely to be more favourable the higher the social class of the home. (Para. 4.9, Appendix 3)

In relating such factors to school performance the report concludes: 'The variation in parental attitudes can account for more of the variation in children's school achievement than either the variation in home circumstances or variation in schools' (Para. 6(A), Appendix 4).

Now since social class has been shown to relate to educational achievement, if achievement is related to certain parental values, then a potentially powerful explanation could have been identified. To work it would demand that the relationship was direct and causal, as follows:

Parental values $+ \rightarrow$ child's educational achievements $+$
Parental values $- \rightarrow$ child's educational achievements $-$

The value of this explanation would be that it might explain achievement variation not only between the social classes but also within them. Success at school would be due to having certain values, lack of success to being without them. Such a view would, however, include a failure to see that the holding of values is a process. Values arise from cultural settings but they are also dynamic, being shaped and affected through experience, in this case by the child's educational experience. Bynner (1972), in her follow-up study to *Children and their Primary Schools*, shows that the marked social-class difference in aspiration is dependent partly on the fact that more middle-class children than working-class get into secondary schools which provide an opportunity for further education – since differences in parental aspirations are of the same order across the types of schools as they are across the social classes. Barker Lunn (1970) has demonstrated that streaming can affect parental aspirations in both directions, upwards for working-class parents with children of above-average ability and downwards for middle-class parents of average-ability children. Finlayson (1971) has challenged the suggestion in *Children and their Primary Schools* that because parental attitudes were a better predictor of achievement than home circumstances there was hope that unfavourable attitudes might be affected, leading to an improvement in children's achievement. He sees a dynamic between the normative (initial parental attitudes) and the informational (feedback from the school). As parents gain more information, so their attitudes and aspirations 'get more realistic' – that is, more closely related to the child's actual performance. This appears a plausible explanation of the survey's finding that the strength of the relationship between parental attitudes and child's achievement was greater among children at the top end of primary schools than among those in infant schools.

Such concerns call for further research that is more sophisticated in a number of directions, mainly, in being more detailed and truly longitudinal. On the parental side an obvious lack is our knowledge of their educational experience, both direct and indirect. We can suspect that people's valuation of education is related to their assumptions about its utility to them, their observations of its utility to others, and their anticipation of its value to their children. We also need more information about children's actual educational experience. Together with this we require an exploration of the mechanisms whereby experience and values are articulated and communicated and their relative effects on the people concerned – all this over the time span of a child's career in school. Such gaps in knowledge (and there are others) serve as a caution to the utility of most research to date based as it is on answers to bland questions – the answers to which may be socially affected – and other gross assumptions.

Precisely the same observations can be made about the research findings on children's manifest values concerning education. Briefly, these present much the same picture and have been illustrated earlier in this book. Children who were successful, or in the process of being successful, in school, have been shown to value education more highly, be in greater accord with the school's regime and teachers' values, more diligent in study and behaviour and have higher educational and occupational aspirations, than their less successful peers. Here again we may question the methods and collection of this information and the causal direction of values. Are values the cause of achievement or the effect of it? At the moment it is only safe to accept that they are associated.

Latent values

These are more general, perhaps more basic, values which are assumed to be culturally distributed and related to educational achievement. A commonly used conceptualisation is that of Kluckhohn and Strodbeck (1961) who suggested five value orientations. Three of these have been used to investigate both parents' and children's values and relate them to educational performance. They are:

ACTIVITY	passive ————	active
TIME	present ————	future
RELATIONS WITH OTHERS	familistic ———	individualistic

The right-hand column is that which, it is argued, corresponds to the middle class's value orientation and therefore to the assumption that such values are of benefit in educational situations. Value orientation is measured by questionnaires containing a number of statements to which people respond on a 5- or 6-point scale ('strongly agree' to 'strongly disagree', sometimes with a 'no view' category). Here are some examples:

ACTIVITY 'You must accept life as it is for there is nothing much you can do to alter things.' (disagreement equals active orientation)

TIME 'You have to give up having a good time now to do well later on.' (agreement equals future orientation)

RELATIONS WITH OTHERS 'Keeping in contact with friends and relations is more important than moving up in the world.' (disagreement equals individualistic orientation)

British studies have not been consistent in their findings. Sugarman (1966) investigated boys in four London secondary schools (see also p. 57 above). Other than in the grammar school he found high scores on the three value orientations (that is in the middle-class direction) related to school achievement (holding I.Q. constant) and teacher-rated conduct. Interestingly enough there was no significant relationship between the boys' values and their fathers' social class. Within each social class, however, the underachievers (relative to their I.Q.) were more often low value scorers and overachievers were more often high scorers. This fact was most striking in the working classes. In other words, Sugarman suggests, these values are middle class in the sense that they separated out those boys who were bound, via school achievement, for middle-class jobs. Banks and Finlayson (1973), in their Liverpool study of grammar and academic-stream comprehensive pupils, found little relationship between these values and achievement. They suggest this could be because the measure is too crude to allow differentiation between relatively high achievers or that a questionnaire is the wrong instrument with which to tap these areas. Sugarman rightly claims that he has an association – between values and achievement – rather than a causal relationship, and suggests three possibilities

1 Achievement and conduct affects values.
2 Values affect achievement and conduct.
3 All three may be related to a further factor.

He supports the third from his study and identifies the further factor as the 'intellectual quality' of the home (defined on p. 58 above). He reckons that it is the home that principally affects values, which in turn affect school achievement and conduct, though he also mentions the intervening factors of school and peer group.

Craft (1974) used these value orientations in Dublin, with the parents of a group of children, of whom half had left school at the minimum age and half had stayed on. The two groups were matched for ability, family size and sex, and all were working class and Catholic. Those who stayed on had parents with higher value scores. Particularly important was the *time* orientation and mother's as opposed to father's values. Father low and mother high was much more likely to be associated with staying on than the reverse and in many cases was as effective as when they were both high. The scores similarly predicted the length of further and higher education.

Swift (1967) was concerned to relate parental-mobility ideologies with children's performance in the eleven-plus selection examination, and his subjects were followed up to the age of sixteen by the author (Reid 1969). Swift's contribution to the concern of this whole chapter is his insistence that a variable related to success should be shown to operate within each social class, since this avoids merely remeasuring middle-class attributes. He interviewed the parents of 132 children before the eleven-plus examination and operationalised mobility ideology in three ways.

Parents' social horizons
Parents were asked what jobs they would like their children to have. Parents, both working- and middle-class, of children who were successful at eleven and sixteen chose middle-class jobs. 'Successful' working-class parents' choices were more like those of the middle class than of working-class parents of unsuccessful

children, though their choices included 'lower'-middle-class jobs not considered by middle-class parents. Of course it is likely that parental choice was affected by parents' knowledge of their child's performance at school to the age of ten.

Parents' social-class identification

Parents with successful children were much more likely to see themselves as middle class than parents of the unsuccessful (at eleven and sixteen). Successful parents who identified with the working class were more likely to see themselves as upper as opposed to lower working class.

Fathers' mobility pessimism

This was measured by responses to questions like 'It is said that Britain is a land of opportunity and that people get pretty much what they are worth. Do you think this is true?' A negative answer was seen as pessimistic. In both social classes, fathers of high pessimism were significantly more likely to have successful children at eleven, though this relationship was not true in the working class at sixteen. Since mobility pessimism was much more characteristic of the working than middle class, Swift argued that it operated in different ways. In the working class the most pessimistic fathers had successful children while in the middle class lack of pessimism resulted in failure. Swift argues that its different operation is the result of intervening and contaminating variables in the social situation. Of course, the effect of latent values can only be appreciated when viewed in relationship to those of the school and education. As Bourdieu (1974) has pointed out, it is because schools are a conservative force that education continues to reward mainly only those with a particular cultural heritage.

The educationally supportive home and environment

The sort of evidence critically reviewed so far in this chapter can be seen to have broader implications. Simply, it forms part of the argument that the cultural and familial settings of some children, particularly but not only middle class, provide for, or assist, them to take advantage of the educational system. Successful children, in the educational sense, can be seen as being variously socially equipped; for example, their language, values and attitudes are similar to those of the school, they are motivated to achieve and are well supported in their efforts. Other children do not have these 'advantages' and, it can be argued (see below), are at a disadvantage. In other words, it is a part of the long history of attempts to identify factors of the successful family in the educational sense. It is interesting to note that the early research here was concerned with poverty and the material conditions and situations of families. Further, it must be remembered that, while it may be out of research 'fashion', poverty, both real and relative, remains a factor in people's lifestyles and lifechances in the seventies. There are those who would argue that it is not over-cynical to claim that factors like poverty, overcrowding, slums, and so on, became unpopular because, while their cure was obvious, society was unwilling to undertake it — much easier, they would argue, for society to concentrate research and effort on fairly nebulous factors which are difficult enough to describe and investigate let alone act upon.

To be reasonable, however, it is true that the imprecision of predictions about educational outcomes based on any or all of these familial or cultural factors is likely to stem from one or more of the following:

1 The lack of anything approaching complete knowledge of any real family social situations
2 An inability to identify, investigate or to measure the factors involved
3 A failure to appreciate the complex interrelationships, compensations and contradictions, between the factors.

All of these call for more, and more sophisticated, research.

Cultural deficit or cultural difference?

Surprisingly — even terrifyingly — given the cautions dealt with so far, this type of evidence has given rise among some teachers and educators to the opinion that the unsuccessful in school are culturally deficient; that, for example, working-class and minority groups' cultures are deficient in that they produce children who are incapable of, or handicapped in, becoming educated. As has been suggested, cultures are 'produced', exist in relation to given social situations and cannot be viewed as deficient with respect to those situations. To use a very extreme example, think about the likely features of the culture of the poor unemployed in a slum ghetto and then that of a rich middle-class academic ghetto in a residential college. While both are well related to their circumstances, neither would be much use in the other. They are clearly different but the differences are only really apparent and become crucial when they enter a common arena where one is recognised and rewarded more than the other – adults in court or children in school. If, in such arenas, the first culture is seen as deficient, it smacks of middle-class imperialism. Refusing to recognise cultures as deficient but accepting that they are different is no mere tinkering around with words because of the implications. First, deficiency implies inferiority and consequently lack of respect or understanding. After reading this book readers might like to ponder on whether the fact that working-class parents have lower aspirations than middle-class parents for children of the same ability is due to cultural deficiency or whether it is not rather due to reasonable expectations arising from both social classes' knowledge of the social system in which they live. In other words, both are realistic and understandable in terms of cultural differences related to differing positions in the social structure. Second, deficiency can imply educational responses aimed at making up what is assumed to be lacking, or, more extremely and disastrously, can lead to the acceptance that such a lack indicates the relatively ineducability of such children and consequently the avoidance of serious concern. On the other hand, recognising cultural differences could entail attempting to accommodate these in a real and meaningful sense in the organisation, teaching and curriculum of schools. Nevertheless, given that schooling and examinations represent in large measure the dominant culture of society, working-class culture can contextually be viewed as relatively deficient to the extent that it is not as directly related to these particular institutions as middle-class culture.

Educational ecology and the allocation of resources

Explanations of differing social-class attainment which depend on the idea of cultural or child deficits tend to assume that educational provision is similar in all sections of our society. Actually we have had knowledge for some time that quite large variations exist. Indeed, these are almost inherent, given the decentralised nature of our school system, which even after local government reorganisation involves 104 local authorities in England and Wales. The government revealed that poor areas had poor schools (*Half Our Future* 1963). Douglas (1964) found that the provision of selective secondary-school places varied among the regions of Britain from between 10 and 30 per cent of the relevant age group. Examination of the variations between local authorities at that time revealed an even bigger spread from 8 to over 40 per cent. It can be suspected that the introduction of comprehensive schools has done little other than hide such differences, especially since probably only 20 per cent of secondary school children attend real comprehensive schools in the strict definition of the term (Benn 1975). Recent official figures state that some 68 per cent of maintained secondary schools, catering for 76 per cent of pupils, are comprehensive (*Statistics of Education 1976*). It is pointed out, however, that this category includes many types of school and that 'many newly reorganised schools will, in practice, still be in transition'. Douglas concluded that the differences in the provision of grammar-school places did not reflect real differences either in the ability of the children – according to his tests, 18 per cent of children in Wales and the South region of England should have had places, when in fact the figures were 29 and 13 per cent – or in the availability of private schools. So where one lives affects what type of school one attends, which, together with the variation within the type of school, affects one's educational experience and its outcome.

As readers might expect, such differences are not chance happenings, or at least can be related to other factors. The exploration, if not the explanation, of such has become known as educational ecology – the study of education and its provision in relationship to its environment. Surprisingly, this is a comparatively recent development in the sociology of education. Douglas, Ross and Simpson (1968), working with a large national sample, found that 38 per cent of those living in Scotland attended selective schools as compared with 30 per cent in England and Wales. South of the line from the Bristol Channel to the Wash was an area where 30 per cent attended such schools, while to the north of the line the figure was 18 per cent. This provision was found to be related to educational attainment, though if social class was held constant the results were similar – suggesting that there were more working-class children in the North (see below and Reid 1977a). However, they found that working-class children in the South, with its superior selective-school provision, had higher reading scores than those in the North; 4 per cent more obtained selective education, they were more likely to stay on at school, and at each level of measured ability attained slightly higher grades in public examinations.

This suggestion that there are two parts to our society was acutely and extensively viewed by Taylor and Ayres (1969). Using a wide range of available official data, their book draws a number of stark comparisons between the North and South of England, or what Taylor (1971) called 'the education split'. They argue that the educational opportunity provided for a child and his ability to take it up depend on a number of non-educational factors in the environment. These can be summarised as follows.

Environmental factors of the family

The north (the North-West, Yorkshire and Humberside and North regions of England) had higher rates of adult mortality, sickness and injury and, therefore, more one-parent families and families with chronically sick parents. There were fewer doctors and dentists in relation to population than in the South, and its babies and children had poorer health. Its houses were older, more overcrowded, more often lacking in basic amenities and surrounded by greater dereliction. The Southern regions, with the exception of the South-West, had higher family incomes than the Northern. The standards of adult education varied similarly: in Tyneside 37 mothers in every 1,000 had received sixth form education, but in Greater London the figure was 136; in Featherstone (Yorkshire) only 17 out of each 1,000 mothers had left education at age seventeen to nineteen, whereas in Hampstead (London) it was 170 per 1,000. The South was distinguished from the North in that the proportion of women so educated exceeded that of the men.

Social structure and career opportunities

The North had a higher proportion of the semi- and unskilled and a lower proportion of professional and managerial workers than the South. It had higher rates of unemployment and greater dependency on single industries. Job opportunities and high incomes were more limited in the North, leading to migration of the skilled and ambitious to the South. These factors were also seen as important in affecting parental and child attitudes towards extended education.

Local-authority income and provision

A measure of the wealth of an authority is its rate income per child. This is computed by dividing the amount of money raised by a penny on the rates by the number of children in an authority. Comparison of these figures showed that the poverty of the North was mirrored by the prosperity of the South. Of local authorities in the North-West region 17 of the 23 were below the national average, as were 12 of the 15 in the Yorkshire and Humberside region, compared with 22 of the 23 authorities in the South-East region which were *above* the national average. In spite of the government's attempts to help poor authorities, by rate support grants, Taylor and Ayres maintain that they lacked the resources to provide an average educational service, and at the same time they were those authorities which, in terms of need, should have provided a higher level. Much educational expenditure is determined by national scales – for example, teachers' salaries, students' grants, debt charges, and the like. Expenditure that is not so determined is economised on by poorer authorities – such as repairs, maintenance, minor improvements, books and learning equipment. The same authorities tended to have more than their fair share of old schools because school-building policy had been for 'roofs over heads' and these areas have had shrinking school populations. Consequently the paucity of school buildings was related to old and overcrowded homes.

Educational outcomes

In the North a smaller percentage than the national average stayed at school beyond the minimum age, while in the South the percentage was higher. The percentage of school-leavers with two or more G.C.E. A-levels in the North was just short of the national average, while that in the South was above. A smaller percentage of those in the North entered university and a slightly higher one went to colleges of education. In the North, university students were more likely to attend technological universities (reflecting their A-level choices) and less likely to go to Oxford or Cambridge than those in the South.

So far our discussion in this section has, once more, led us to see that the social structure is mirrored in the educational system. It has, however, been at a fairly descriptive level. An attempt to put this thinking into a theoretical structure has been made by Byrne and Williamson (1972) and developed by Byrne, Williamson and Fletcher (1975). Underlying what they call a 'socio-spatial model of educational attainment' are three propositions, two of which follow Weber's concept of social class (see also pp. 153, 227–8).

1 Social classes are viewed as relationships between groups that are differently placed in terms of the rewards in society.

2 Relationships between the social classes are those of control and domination via power. They vary from direct control to the manipulation of symbols, concepts and ideas.

3 The rewards which the social classes have are spatially distributed (as demonstrated by Taylor and Ayres) and can be viewed as reflecting the distribution of income in society. Income here is very broadly defined, including, for example, educational provision.

What they are saying is that educational attainment is a product of the distribution of power and resources in society rather than the distribution of intelligence. They identify the following as the most important factors:

1 social-class background
2 local environmental factors
3 local-authority policy
4 local-authority resources
5 local-authority provision

and they set out to relate these to educational attainment.

In their analysis of eleven local authorities in the North-East of England they found two tendencies (their later work using the same techniques revealed a similar overall pattern, though identifying six types of local authority; see Byrne, Williamson and Fletcher 1975).

1 Those areas with the highest proportion of the lower social classes had the smallest resources (penny rate per pupil) but spent proportionately more on education (reflecting policy decisions) and spent it preferentially on the primary as opposed to the secondary sector of the education.

2 Those areas with the highest proportion of the higher social classes had the highest resources but spent proportionately less on education and spent it preferentially on the secondary as opposed to the primary sector.

Type 1 areas have what Byrne and Williamson call an anti-élitist policy, spending more on that sector which benefits the entire school population (primary). Type 2 areas, they say, have élitist policy and spend on the sector which benefits a minority (secondary). This is reflected by the fact that type 1 authorities have less overcrowding in primary schools than type 2. More important, the two types of authority are related to educational outcomes. Staying on at school to sixteen (minimum school-leaving age was then fifteen) was related to local-authority resources and the proportion of high social class but negatively related to the proportion of low social class. The authors conclude that social-class factors are most important here while resources and policy play a mediating role. Social-class factors are less importantly related to staying on into the sixth form and entering higher and further education. Here resources and policy play the largest part, so that type 2 authorities have higher rates of staying-on and entry to university and 'higher-grade' further education. Type 1 authorities have lower rates of staying-on, and those pupils who do tend to go for teacher training and 'lower-grade' further education.

The importance of the role of policy decisions by local authorities in the type and extent of educational provision has been supported by other work. For example, Boaden (1971), in analysing authorities' educational spending, found that their total expenditure was related both to need (the number of children in the educational system) and the political disposition of the authorities' council. Labour-controlled councils spent more on education whatever the need. Since Labour control reflected the local social structure, and since school provision goes across class boundaries, the social-class composition of an area is more important in determining the *direction* (say towards comprehensivisation) rather than the overall level of spending. An interesting example of how legislation designed to help equalise educational opportunity can go wrong, and its benefits be unequally distributed, is provided by Reddin (1972). Educational maintenance allowances were introduced to enable, or help, children of poor parents to stay at school beyond the minimum age. In 1970 some 20,000 children (4 per cent of the age group still at school) received an average of £72. If the original recommendations are updated to 1972, the figures suggest that this was less than half what they should have received. The qualifying parental income for the awards was not only lower than that for university grants but in some areas so low that the employed poor were virtually excluded, though most local authorities viewed the unemployed as qualifying. The total cost of the awards was £1.4 million, compared with £16 million spent by local authorities on boarding children in independent and direct-grant schools. The local-authority variations were gross. Durham gave 14 per cent of its children an average of £94 while Swansea gave 1 per cent £42. Clearly, local-authority policy in respect to E.M.A.s is the most important factor in deciding what resources are available. In individual terms, place of residence could determine whether or not a pupil had the opportunity to remain at school or not. Since the qualifying income for an E.M.A. could well be lower than that for grants for higher education (most of which are not given at the discretion of the local authority), policy decisions here may be the crucial factor in access to higher education as well as to the sixth form.

So far the studies mentioned have involved comparing large geographical areas, within which one can expect considerable variation. King (1974) investigated a single local authority in the South of England to explore the relationship between educational provision and attainment. His findings were rather different from what one might have expected, given those of Byrne and Williamson. Schools serving working-class areas showed lower attainment than the middle-class ones, but had better provision in terms of more favourable pupil–teacher ratios, greater C.S.E. examination opportunities, and their staffs were more stable than those of the middle-class schools. It is not easy to reconcile these two sets of findings, though they are not necessarily contradictory. They could both be right if, for example, King's authority was a rare exception. As King points out, this type of research is in an early stage of development and is using global and rather crude variables. On the one hand, both studies have used the social class of economically active males in the area rather than that of the pupils' parents. On the other, they have both treated provision as being the global property of the local authority or the school rather than of individual pupils. In order to further our knowledge in this area we need more sophisticated studies, and especially some investigations of the resources received by different types of pupils within schools. Here our actual knowledge, as opposed to our assumptions, is extremely limited. It may be that the deployment of staff, facilities and the curriculum means that costs per pupil decline with ability down to, but not including, the remedial level, which in turn reflects social-class differences; but this has yet to be demonstrated (see the discussion in Chapter 4).

The approach discussed in this section is new, it offers the possibility of an advance in our understanding of social class and education, and represents a further development of the structuralist perspective in the sociology of education.

Models of educational attainment

The contents of this chapter can be seen to advance a number of explanatory models (after Byrne and Williamson). Its initial concern was to illustrate the differing social-class educational attainments.

$$\text{Social class} \longrightarrow \text{attainment}$$

OR
$$\text{Middle class} \longrightarrow \text{attainment } +$$
$$\text{Working class} \longrightarrow \text{attainment } -$$

Explanations of this relationship have been sought by attempting to establish intermediate variables.

$$\text{Social class} \longrightarrow \begin{array}{c} \text{familial,} \\ \text{socio-cultural} \\ \text{variables} \end{array} \longrightarrow \text{attainment}$$

Some work in the field has suggested either that the social classes are related to differing familial, socio-cultural variables (for example Bernstein) or that such variables may operate in differing ways in each social class (for example Swift). Hence, their model is:

Middle class   ⟶   familial,   ⟶   attainment +
Working class   ⟶   socio-cultural ⟶ attainment −
                                    variables

These considerations led some researchers to attempt to lose social class, as in Wiseman's work for the Plowden Committee.

      Familial, socio-   + ⟶ attainment +
      cultural variables   − ⟶ attainment −

However, the coincidence of social class and the identified variables still has to be recognised. A change in emphasis, though with the coincidence clearly in mind, was that of Taylor and Ayres.

                      + ⟶   +

Material environment   attainment

                     − ⟶   −

The contribution of Byrne and Williamson was more complex, stressing social class, educational resources and policy.

High social class ⟶ greater ⟶ élitist ⟶ +
                     RESOURCES → **POLICY** ⟶ **ATTAINMENT**
Low social class ⟶ less ⟶ anti-élitist ⟶ −

While such presentations may help to clarify the approaches, they are also oversimplifications in that most of the studies either contained or allowed for aspects of the others. Further, as we have found, each and any are only partial explanations. Indeed the overriding impression is that even together they do not go very far towards actually explaining how social class and educational attainment are related, but are rather indications or promises of such.

Any final model or conclusion must remain tentative and open. Further it must take account of those factors associated with the processes of schooling that have been discussed in previous chapters. A total explanation would also have to include more individual factors. While such factors have not been seen as part of the sociology of education, they have a clear importance in an educational sense.

7

Education, occupation and mobility

Introduction

This chapter traces the consequences of educational experience and achievement in their most obvious form, in life after school. While education appears to be about a whole variety of things in life – according to some people, it's about everything – a very important factor is that of occupational preparation. A common selling line of teachers is to tell pupils that they should work hard and get on in school in order to get a job which pays well, has security, offers prospects and is generally worthwhile. Apart from the fact that it is true, it is a strange sales line. It could mean that the intrinsic appeal of the curriculum is so limited that it needs the additional motivation of long-term gains to be at all palatable; or that the message has elements of moral deferred gratification in it – he who forgoes present pleasure in order to succeed at school will be rewarded in his occupational life. Parents and pupils often have a similar faith (positive or negative) in the educational system, while politicians support immense budgets in the belief that the long-term health of the economy and politics depends on education.

The importance of occupation in our society goes far beyond the type of job a person does. As I concluded in a review of the data on social differences:

> We can state that middle-class people [those who have non-manual jobs], in comparison with the working class [those with manual jobs], enjoy better health; live longer; live in

superior homes, with more amenities; have more money to spend; work shorter hours; receive different and longer education, and are educationally more successful; marry later in life; rear fewer children; attend church more frequently; belong to clubs more often; have different tastes in the media and the arts; are politically more involved – to mention only a few examples. (Reid 1977a, p. 234)

In other words occupation and hence to some extent education is about life chances and lifestyle. This must be viewed in a cultural value set which clearly suggests that the middle-class (non-manual) way of life is superior to, and more desirable than, working-class. Although this, being a value judgement, is open to debate, it appears to be at the base of many assumptions within education and people's attitudes towards it. We can also expect that variations within the classes are as great as those between them; within the working class skilled jobs and in the middle class professional jobs are likely to be most highly sought after. This is one way in which the belief in the importance of education for occupational placement is constantly witnessed, and its importance is seen too in ideas of democracy, equality and opportunity. A cosy, and for society useful, view of our society is that jobs, lifestyles, and so on, are open (available) to all providing they are capable and/or have the qualifications. In this way education becomes a major legitimiser, not only in the sense that this person has job A because he has X qualifications but also in that, since all have access to education, so too they all have access to all occupations. The over-simple assumptions here will already be clear to readers (particularly from Chapters 4 and 6) and are again examined in this chapter with regard to the role(s) of education in relation to occupation.

Our first concern is to establish the extent and nature, mainly in quantitative terms, of the relationship between educational qualification, occupation and income, and to explore something of the explanation of that relationship. Our second concern is related to the first and to the content of the last chapter. Since, as has been seen, there exists a relationship between parental social class and children's educational performance, the other side of this relationship is now explored. What is the role of education in affecting the relationship between parent's and child's occupation, and what is its role in job-changing in adult life?

Education, occupation and income

As has been suggested, an important, though by no means the only, role of education is to equip a person for his occupational role in society. In other words the educational system can be seen as having to provide suitable candidates for the occupational structure of society. While such relationships may seem obvious to most readers, it is necessary to establish their existence and to explore something of their nature and extent. The first step is to look at the available data in four areas.

Education and occupation
Clearly everybody accepts that some occupations are open only to people who have particular educational qualifications, especially, for example, the professions (doctors, chemists, accountants, and so on). However, the present concern is with the complete and general picture. The most extensive data on this are provided by the census. Table 7.1 is based on a 10 per cent sample (one and a half million) of males who were economically active in 1961 (the 1971 figures have yet to be published). The educational measure is the age at which they left full-time education, so it tells us nothing much about what type of education they received, its outcome, of part-time, or courses for the mature. The occupations have been grouped into six categories called by the Registrar General socio-economic groups, which are listed in the Appendix (for further details see *Classification of Occupations* 1960 or Reid 1977a). The table reveals that the overall tendency is that the 'higher' the occupation the longer the time spent in education. The most marked

Table 7.1
Terminal educational age of economically active males by
occupational group, England and Wales 1961 (percentages*)

Terminal education age	*Occupational category* †						
	1	2	3	4	5	6	**All**
Under 15 years	13	47	42	68	72	86	60
15 years	9	14	18	24	21	11	21
16 years	20	17	20	6	4	2	10
17–19 years	21	15	13	2	2	0.5	6
20 years and over	37	7	7	0.6	0.5	0.2	4

* Percentages over 1 rounded
† For definition, see Appendix, p. 257
(Derived from Reid 1977a, table 6.1, devised from *Education Tables* (10 % sample)
1966, Census 1961, table 3)

differences are to be found among those who left education at
sixteen years old or later. We can assume that these completed
at least secondary or selective school courses. Of all those
surveyed some 20 per cent finished their education at sixteen or
over. The figures vary: for professional workers it was 78 per
cent, for employers, managers and intermediate and junior
non-manual workers it was around 40 per cent; for skilled and
semiskilled manual workers about 7 per cent; and for the
unskilled manual workers just below 3 per cent. One problem
to be borne in mind (also for tables 7.2 and 7.3) is that the
survey covered people aged between fifteen and sixty-five and
that, therefore, their educational experience spans some fifty
years or so. In that period the statutory minimum school-
leaving age was raised to fourteen in 1921 and to fifteen in
1947. Hence while table 7.1 shows that over all 60 per cent left
education under fifteen years of age; this varied over the age
groups. Of those aged between fifteen and twenty-four years
only 7 per cent had left school by that age; for those aged
between twenty-five and fourty-four it was 58 per cent and for
those over forty-five it was 80 per cent. The changes in the
educational and occupational structure are dealt with below
(pp. 217–21).

A view of the actual educational qualifications held by people
in the same occupational categories is given in table 7.2 for

males, and in table 7.3 for females. The tables reveal a rather similar pattern: the higher the occupational category the smaller the percentage of persons without formal educational qualifications and the larger with such qualifications. Generally speaking, the holders of higher-education qualifications (the top two rows) are almost exclusively employed in non-manual occupations. In comparing the two tables stark differences can be noted between the sexes in respect of both educational qualifications and occupations. The overall relevant figures are reproduced in table 7.4. At the extremes this table shows that 5 per cent of the males and 0.6 per cent of females had professional occupations, and 6 per cent of males and 9 per cent of females had unskilled manual jobs; 5 per cent of males were graduates compared to 2 per cent of females, while 57 per cent of males and 66 per cent of females had no formal educational qualifications.

Apart from confirming that over all there is a relationship between education and occupation, the data presented so far also reveal inconsistencies. With respect to males some 3 per cent of professional workers have no educational qualifications and 13 per cent left school before the age of fifteen (note that eleven years separate the two studies). This is, of course, related to changing methods of entry into professional jobs. Many of the older members will have been articled and therefore taken their qualification away from full-time education, and some will belong to professions that have only recently demanded educational qualifications for entry. At the opposite end a few (0.2 per cent) unskilled manual workers held degrees and left full-time education at the age of twenty or over. The conclusion must be that while there is a very strong relationship between education and occupation it is not absolute. For example, not all those with higher-education qualifications work as professionals, employers or managers, nor are these jobs undertaken exclusively by the holders of such qualifications. This must be due to changes in the occupational structure and educational opportunities over time, and to the importance of factors other than education in getting and keeping a job.

Table 7.2

Educational qualification and occupational category of males,
Great Britain 1972 (percentages)*

	Occupational category†						
	1	2	3	4	5	6	All
1 Degree or equivalent	53	8	7	0.3	0.1	0.2	5
2 Higher education below degree	20	10	12	2	0.5	—	5
3 G.C.E. A-level or equivalent	10	9	10	4	2	1	6
4 G.C.E. O-level or equivalent, or C.S.E. Grade 1	7	20	20	12	6	3	13
5 C.S.E. other grades/commercial/apprenticeship	1	8	8	16	7	4	10
6 Foreign and other	5	4	4	3	3	1	3
7 None	3	41	39	63	81	90	57
Social class of sample	*5*	*14*	*19*	*41*	*16*	*6*	*100*

* Percentages over 1 rounded
† For definition, see Appendix, p. 257
(Derived from Reid 1977a, table 6.2, devised from *General Household Survey 1972* 1975, table 4.7)

Table 7.3

Educational qualification and occupational category of
females, Great Britain 1972 (percentages)*

	Occupational category†						
	1	2	3	4	5	6	All
1 Degree or equivalent	(21)	4	3	0.5	0.1	—	2
2 Higher education below degree	(1)	11	11	0.7	0.4	—	6
3 G.C.E. A-level or equivalent	(2)	3	3	2	0.5	—	2
4 G.C.E. O-level or equivalent, or C.S.E. Grade 1	(4)	11	19	8	5	1	12
5 C.S.E. other grades/commercial/apprenticeship	(1)	8	14	8	4	2	9
6 Foreign and other	(2)	5	4	2	2	0.4	3
7 None	(3)	60	46	79	88	96	66
Social class of sample	*0.6*	*4*	*50*	*8*	*28*	*9*	*100*

* Percentages over 1 rounded
† For definition, see Appendix, p. 257
( ) = Actual numbers too small for conversion to percentages
(Derived from Reid 1977a, table 6.3, devised from *General Household Survey 1972* 1975, table 4.7)

Table 7.4

Differences between education and occupation of males and females, Great Britain (percentages)

Educational qualification*	1	2	3	4	5	6	7
Male	5	5	6	13	10	3	57
Female	2	6	2	12	9	3	66
Occupational group†	1	2	3	4	5	6	
Male	5	14	19	41	16	6	
Female	0.6	4	50	8	28	9	

* For definition, see table 7.2, left-hand column
† For definition, see Appendix, p. 257
(Devised from *General Household Survey 1972* 1975, table 4.7)

Education and income

In all societies that have them occupations are differently rewarded, and so we would expect, from the last section, that education via occupation would be related to income. In our society there are large variations in income within the same occupations. Schoolteachers (other than deputies and head-teachers), for example, could earn between £2,565 and £6,252 per year in 1976, and similar differences occur in many jobs. It is, then, useful and interesting to look in a general and direct way at education and income. Table 7.5 shows the median earnings in 1972 of holders of various educational qualifications by age groups. It reveals that the higher the qualifications the higher the earnings. From the age group thirty to thirty-nine upwards there is a clear separation of level of earnings by qualification; those with degrees or equivalents earn over £3,000, those with other higher-education qualifications range up to £2,500, while those with no qualifications remain below £1,500. Although the figures are based on age groups composed of different people, the lines in table 7.5 suggest that people with any sort of higher-education qualifications have incremental earnings – they rise with age – while the earnings of those without any educational qualifications decline with age.

The clearest evidence of the effect of education on income is to be seen in table 7.6, which shows the percentage of males (the top half) and females (the lower half) with given qualifications

Table 7.5

Median annual earnings of males in full-time employment* by educational qualification and age†, Great Britain

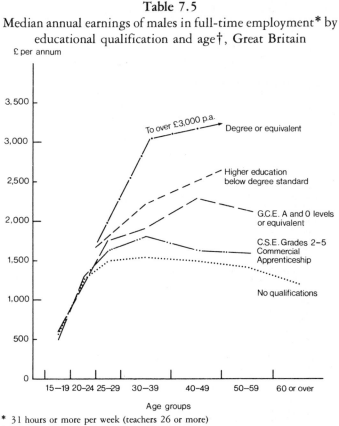

£ per annum

* 31 hours or more per week (teachers 26 or more)
† Base for some ages too small to indicate earnings
(Derived from *General Household Survey 1972* 1975, figure 4.2)

who earned certain incomes, in 1973. The effect is very clear: whereas 44 per cent of males with degrees or equivalents earned more than £3,000 per year, only 1.7 per cent of those without educational qualifications earned as much. Notice, too, that some of the lines cross. This shows that at the lower levels of earnings males without qualifications earned more than those with G.C.E. O-levels and equivalents; for example, 11.5 per

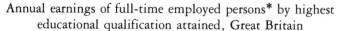

Table 7.6
Annual earnings of full-time employed persons* by highest educational qualification attained, Great Britain

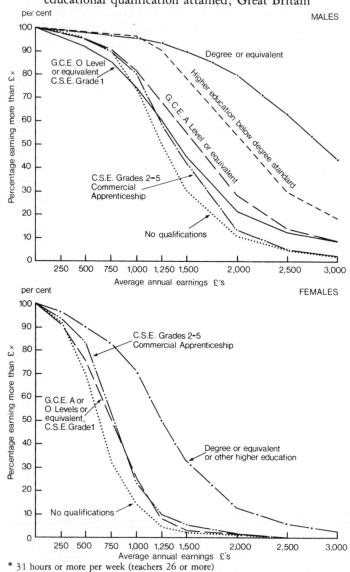

* 31 hours or more per week (teachers 26 or more)

(Derived from *General Household Survey Introductory Report* 1973, figure 7.3)

cent of the former compared with 17 per cent of the latter earned less than £1,000 per year. The lower part of the figure shows a similar relationship between education and income for females. More strikingly, however, the whole figure displays that, regardless of education, females earned very considerably less than males. Only 2 per cent of female degree holders earned over £3,000 per year together with 0.1 per cent of those without qualifications (male figures were 44 and 1.7 per cent respectively). Over all, whereas 75 per cent of males earned more than £1,000 per year, only 19 per cent of women did. As in the last section, then, it can be seen that there is a strong, but not complete, relationship. Not all holders of educational qualifications earn more than those without, nor were all the high-income earners holders of qualifications. Blaug (1970) states that relationships between education and income have been demonstrated in thirty countries.

It is now necessary to place both education and occupation into a historical perspective, since these, and the relationship between them, are essentially dynamic.

Changes in the educational attainment of the population

The history of education in Britain, as elsewhere, has been one of increasing provision and attainment. For the present discussion a useful indicator of change is the percentage of the relevant age group which enters forms of higher education. Table 7.7a shows that over all the increase in this figure was of the order of 1200 per cent between 1900 and 1973/4 – from 1.2 to 14 per cent of the age group. While university and teacher-training increases have been dramatic other forms of post-school education have shown considerable increases, particularly since the mid-1950s and the development of polytechnics. Table 7.7b shows this growth between 1962 and 1973/4 by sex (this was discussed above, p. 112). Of course, other measures of educational attainment are of value, particularly school-based achievement. There are problems here, mainly because of changes in the examinations themselves from School-Leaving Certificate to General Certificate of Education and the parallel

Table 7.7a
Percentage of the age group* entering higher education 1900–1973/4, Great Britain

	1900	1938	1957	1962	1973/4
University	0.8	1.7	3.9	4.0	5.5†
Teacher training	0.4	0.7	2.2	2.5	2.4†
Further education⁺	—	0.3	0.9	2.0	N.A.
All full-time	1.2	2.7	7.0	8.5	14.0

*Figures for 1900–1962 are for *all* entrants, 1973/4 figures for 'university' and 'teacher training' are for school-leavers, and for 'all full-time' are for entrants under 21 only
† England and Wales only
⁺ Advanced further education only
(Derived from (1) figures other than 1973/4 from *Higher Education* 1963, table 4; (2) from *Statistics of Education 1974, Vol. 2*, table B and *Higher Education into the 1990s* (1978)

Table 7.7b
Percentage of school-leavers by sex entering full-time education in 1962/3 and 1973/4*

	1962/3		1973/4	
	Men	Women	Men	Women
University	4.7	2.0	6.9	4.2
Teacher training	0.8	2.9	0.9	3.9
Further education†	7.6	10.7	9.1	14.9
All full-time	13.1	15.6	16.9	23.0

* Destination on leaving school, England and Wales
† All full-time further education
(Derived from *Statistics of Education 1963, Part 3*, table A; *Statistics of Education 1974, Vol. 2*, table B)

introduction of the Certificate of Secondary Education. Further, not only has the access to sit examinations been changed by the introduction of free secondary education in 1944 and comprehensive schools, but also by changes in the underlying philosophy – that secondary modern children should sit examinations and from entering only for a full range of subjects to taking a few or even only one. Given these strictures, probably the most illustrative figures for our purposes are the changes in attainment of school-leavers since the introduction of G.C.E. and C.S.E., given in table 7.8a. As can be seen, the percentage of the relevant age group gaining five or more O-levels rose from

11 to 23 per cent between 1954/5 and 1971/2, while those gaining one or more A-levels rose from 6 to 16 per cent, and remained at about that level. The combined effect of the introduction of C.S.E. and the raising of the school-leaving age (1972/3) was that the percentage leaving without any qualifications was 67 per cent in 1963/4, 43 per cent in 1971/2 and only 21 per cent in 1973/4 (see table 7.8b). Basically the message, is

Table 7.8a

Percentage* of the relevant age groups gaining given educational qualifications from schools, England and Wales

Boys and girls	1954/5	1958/9	1963/4	1968/9	1971/2	1974/5
1 or more G.C.E. A-levels	6	7	10	15	16	15
5 or more G.C.E. O-levels†	11	14	17	21	23	22
Boys						
1 or more G.C.E. A-levels	7	9	11	16	17	16
5 or more G.C.E. O-levels†	11	15	17	22	23	22
Girls						
1 or more G.C.E. A-levels	4	6	8	13	15	14
5 or more G.C.E. O-levels†	11	14	16	21	23	23

* All percentages rounded
† Including C.S.E. Grade 1, for 1968/9 onwards
(Derived from *Statistics of Education 1964, Vol. 3*, table 21; *Statistics of Education 1974 and 75, Vol. 2*, table 22

Table 7.8b

Percentage* of school-leavers with given educational qualifications 1963/4 to 1973/4, England and Wales

	1963/4	1968/9	1971/2	1973/4
3 or more G.C.E. A-levels	6	8	8	8
2 G.C.E. A-levels	3	4	5	4
1 G.C.E. A-level	2	4	4	3
5 or more G.C.E. O-levels only †	8	8	9	9
1–4 G.C.E O-levels only⁺	15	18	19	24
1 or more C.S.E. Grades 2–5	—	11	13	30
No qualifications	67	47	43	21

* All percentages rounded
† With *no* A-level passes
⁺ Includes C.S.E. Grade 1 other than for 1963/4
(Derived from *Statistics of Education 1974, Vol. 2*, table i)

clear, an increasing proportion of the population is achieving educational qualifications. We are as a society becoming more and more qualified if not educated.

Changes in the structure of occupations

Over the same period there has been a considerable change in the occupational structure of our society. Table 7.9 compares the structure of 1911 with that of 1966. The most noticeable feature is that, whereas there has been a decline in employers and proprietors of nearly 50 per cent (from 6.7 to 3.4 per cent) and of manual workers from almost 75 per cent to some 58 per cent, the proportion of white-collar workers has increased by more than 100 per cent (from 18.7 to 38.3 per cent). The implication is that the resultant structure contains a very much larger proportion of occupations for which educational qualifications are necessary. The middle of the table reveals that the greatest rate of growth within the white-collar section has been in higher professionals, clerks and lesser professionals and tech-

Table 7.9
Changes in the structure of occupations between 1911 and 1966
(percentages)

All occupations	1911	1966
Employers and proprietors	6.7	3.4
White-collar workers	18.7	38.3
Manual workers	74.6	58.3
White-collar workers		
Managers and administrators	3.4	6.1
Higher professionals	1.0	3.4
Lesser professionals/technicians	3.1	6.5
Foremen and inspectors	1.3	3.0
Clerks	4.5	13.2
Salesmen and shop assistants	5.4	6.1
Manual workers		
Skilled manual	30.5	23.7
Semi-skilled manual	34.4	26.1
Unskilled manual	9.6	8.5

(Derived from Halsey 1972, table 4.1)

nicians, whereas the proportion of salesmen and shop assistants has remained relatively stable. The remaining occupations, while displaying increases, are more difficult to relate directly to education. Managers and particularly foremen and inspectors may, for example, be more dependent on experience and skill than on educational qualification. Over the period reviewed the major shift has been towards more non-manual (white-collar) and fewer manual occupations.

Having reviewed the four pieces of evidence above, we are left with two basic questions to pursue:

1 On what basis can we explain the fact that better-educated people have different jobs and higher incomes than those who are less well educated or are without educational qualifications?
2 On what basis can we explain the combination of rising educational attainment and a changing occupational structure in our society? Second, what is the relationship between them and which causes what?

In a sense the two questions are really one. They relate to the fundamental relationship of education and the social structure (society). In attempting an answer to them we shall not be able to differentiate neatly between them.

One further factor, which it is difficult to substantiate in quantitative terms for Britain, is the extent to which employers have increased their demands for educational qualifications from prospective employees. At a descriptive level one can instance such changes as, for example, the moves towards all graduate entry into various professions (engineering, accountancy, the law and teaching etc.), and the growing number of advertisements for routine clerical/office and manual jobs which demand G.C.E. or C.S.E. qualifications. What is lacking is the sort of research that exists in America where a study in 1937–8 (Bell 1940) and one in 1967 (Collins 1969) showed that, of employers of professional workers, 52 per cent required college degrees in 1937 and 70 per cent in 1967, together with a further 5 per cent who required postgraduate degrees. The changes in requirements for skilled manual workers were from 11 per cent for high-school diplomas to 28 per cent for high-school diplomas and 10 per cent for vocational training after high school. In all the cases cited it would be difficult to distinguish the basis on which employers raised the educational levels demanded. The obvious possibilities are:

1 Because the skills or educational requirements of the job had increased.
2 Employers, realising that there were more people around with educational qualifications, decided they would like to have some.
3 Employers had a wish to restrict the number of entrants to, or the number of applicants for, jobs and hence raised the standards they demanded.
4 Employers found that the performance level of their normal recruitment had dropped, and hoped to regain it by raising educational demands.

A good treatment of the whole area, for the purposes of this book, is that by Collins (1971) who set out to compare the structural-functional and the conflict theoretical explanations of what he called educational stratification. Though our concern is Britain and his America, Collins's paper provides the basis for the discussion that follows. It begins with a presentation and appraisal of the structural-functional approach to the problem.

The technical-function theory of education
The theory was developed by Clark (1962) and can be identified by three propositions.

1 The skill requirements of jobs increases with technological change in industrialised societies. This results in two changes:

(*a*) The percentage of low-skilled jobs declines; the percentage of highly skilled jobs increases
(*b*) Some jobs increase their demands of skill.

Examples of (*b*) would be those whose jobs are affected by the introduction of advanced technology, possibly for example, bank clerks by computers.

2 Education provides people with *either*

(*a*) specific skills for jobs *or*

(*b*) general capacities for jobs.

3 Therefore the educational requirements for jobs rise and an increasing proportion of the population spends longer on education and achieves qualifications.

These ideas are based on the structural-functional theory of social stratification (for details see Davis and Moore in Bendix and Lipset (1967) which also contains a critique by Tumin). Briefly this can be stated as:

1 Occupations require varying forms of skill.

2 People with appropriate skills must be recruited for them.

3 Differential rewards exist to motivate people with the appropriate skills to take up particular occupations and to keep them there.

4 By implication the education system functions to help this process.

Collins puts Clark's propositions to the test of evidence and finds them unconvincing. Since we again lack British evidence we shall rely on the American in respect of proposition 1.

Proposition 1(a)

A study by Fogler and Nam (1964) suggests that only 15 per cent of the increase in the educational level of the American workforce can be attributed to changes in the occupational structure. The bulk of the increase took place within existing jobs.

Proposition 1(b)

According to a United States Department of Labour study, between 1950 and 1960 the educational level of the workforce increased in excess of that plausibly necessary for the changing requirements due to the growth of skills demanded by occupations. It further stated that 'over'-education for jobs was found particularly among male graduates and female high-school graduates. That is, they often worked in jobs that did not require so high a level of education.

Proposition 2
This can be stated in two ways:

1 *Better-educated employees are more productive.* At a simple level and providing there was perfect competition between them (that they were interchangeable), the fact that, as we have seen, educated labour is paid more highly than raw labour would mean that they are more productive. Such higher productivity would explain their higher income. Of course this argument is circular, and in any case Blaug (1972) has argued that the competition is far from perfect (see (*b*) below). The evidence is of two types, indirect and direct.

(*a*) *Indirect evidence*

(i) *The national-growth approach.* Here calculations are made about national growth and the part played by the capital and labour used in its production. What is left unexplained by these two factors is attributed to changes in the educational levels of the workforce. It can be argued that such a claim is largely arbitrary because it leaves out a number of other factors such as changes in technology, in organisation and in cultural values which are also likely to affect production.

(ii) *Cross-cultural approaches.* Generally speaking, those countries with the highest economic levels also have the highest educational levels, an interesting exception being India where the overproduction of graduates leads not only to their unemployment but apparently does little to enhance the country's economic wellbeing. In any case it begs the question of the direction of causality. Hoselitz (1965) suggests that the very wide variations between societies of similar economic situation

in the percentage of population at any given level of education
indicate that these can only be explained in terms of political (as
opposed to economic) demands for education. These can run
counter to the economic needs of societies.

(iii) *Time-lag approaches*. It has been established that the
'take-off' stage in a society's move from an agrarian to an
industrial economic base is achieved when between 30 and 50
per cent of the seven to fourteen-year-olds are in school. Similarly, economic developments are predicted to be related to
further educational achievements. Peaslee (1969) has shown
that, in studies involving thirty-seven countries, these predictions are far from clearly supported. The establishment of secondary schools appears related to economic advance in only twelve
of the countries. While university development is so related in
twenty-one of the countries, the exceptions – America, Russia,
Japan, France and Sweden, for example – rather make a mockery
of the theory.

(*b*) *Direct evidence*. Berg (1970) has reviewed what evidence of
this type exists, relating productivity to the educational levels
of factory workers, store clerks, technicians, secretaries, in-
surance salesmen, research scientists, the military and civil ser-
vants. Berg concludes that the evidence actually shows a negative relationship between educational level and productivity.
Layard, Sargan, Ager and Jones (1971) compared sixty-eight
British companies in the electrical industry, matched for the
type of product they produced. Assuming that they operated
with similar capital and labour ratio, they related their educational structure (broken down into graduates, professionally
trained, H.N.C. and O.N.C. holders) to

(i) profit rates
(ii) sales per unit of capital
(iii) rates of growth of sales
(iv) higher outputs per unit of labour
(v) lower unit costs

None of these was found to be statistically related. While not
actually claiming to refute the assumption that educated labour

is more productive, Layard suggests that the evidence might shake our faith in the economic explanation. Berg (1970) also reports a negative relationship between educational level and job satisfaction – the more educated are also the more dissatisfied.

2 *Are vocational skills learnt in the educational system or elsewhere?* Collins suggests that most manual workers acquire their skills on the job or casually. He reports that Duncan (1964) noticed that school-leavers who had attended vocational schools in America were more likely to be unemployed than those who had dropped out (failed to graduate) from high-schools.

With regard to non-manual occupations, there are further difficulties in evaluation. Some professions do show a relationship between educational level and the level of professional responsibility; Perrucci and Perrucci (1970) proved this in the case of engineers in America. The same study found, however, that 40 per cent of practising engineers in the 1950s were without college degrees, suggesting that all the necessary skills could be learnt on the job. In our country it is of interest to note that most firms who recruit graduates run subsequent training schemes for them, and vocationally specific degree courses are in the minority. A fairly recent innovation – sandwich degree courses, designed to provide industrial experience and direction – have not always been seen as having equivalent status, or even utility, as more traditional and 'academic' degrees.

Collins continues his argument by claiming that the 'demands' of an occupation are not fixed but are the result of behaviour (or negotiation) between employer and employees. In order to gain and hold a job, an employee must display that amount of productive or other skill that the employer can or does demand of him. Both sides can be seen to refrain from giving or demanding. Employers' strategies are geared towards gaining satisfactory rather than optimum performance and they make changes only when performance falls below fairly low standards. Workers, on the other hand, are protected from having to give their all by trade-union agreements, informal organisation, and standards. In the same way, ascriptive factors remain of considerable importance in industrialised society. The business élite in America is predominantly Protestant, white, male and upper-middle class. Likewise we noted in Chapter 4 that the élite of our society was composed, to a large extent, of products of the public schools recruited almost exclusively from the upper section of our social structure. Within a traditional structural-functionalist framework such relationships would be viewed as a residual happening, but there is little evidence to show that any major change is taking place. One hypothesis put forward by Collins is that the prime basis of selection is the ascribed group, technical skills being a secondary consideration. Education is a mark of membership of a particular group. Hence the institution of examinations for posts in the civil service (in 1870, before which posts were bought) was the result of a struggle between the upper-middle educated classes and the traditional aristocracy.

Having provided what should be seen as a substantial critique of technical-function theory, Collins proposes an alternative.

A *conflict theory of educational stratification*
This rests on two ideas developed from the work of Weber.

1 *Status groups*. Weber argued that the basic units of society were associational groups who shared a common culture (language, tastes, manners, opinions, leisure, and so on) and a sense of status equality. They distinguish themselves from other groups by way of moral (social) evaluation and exclude those who do not possess the 'in-group' culture. Weber did not claim that such groups had distinct boundaries, but that there were three main determinants:

(*a*) economic situation, or class
(*b*) differences in power
(*c*) cultural conditions such as race, religion, area, intellectual/aesthetic culture etc.

2 *Struggle for advantage*. Weber saw this as a struggle over socially scarce goods like wealth, power and prestige, taking place on the basis of groups rather than individuals. Those

holding power in society or in an organisation – called here the élite – have an interest in maintaining their advantage. This they pursue by attempting to recruit into the élite group people who are similar to those already there, and to recruit for the non-élite (or workforce), wherever possible, people having a respect for the élite's cultural superiority.

Education is viewed as status culture, and the main function of schools, colleges, and so on, is the teaching of particular status cultures. Hence any failure to teach technical knowledge and specific skills is not important, since vocabulary, inflexion, tastes, values, manners, emphasis on sociability and athletics are not extraneous but core factors of a particular status culture. Here readers will recognise that some of these factors, in a different context, were discussed in previous chapters of this book (see Chapters 2 and 4). Education is, then, viewed as a labelling process allowing the ready identification and recruitment of suitable élite and employees.

General evidence of the utility of the conflict theory can be seen in the following terms:

1 That distinctions exist between status-group cultures (presumably such evidence as social-class differences, see Reid 1977a)
2 That status groups occupy different positions in the occupational structure and in organisations (as is suggested by such data as those in tables 7.2, 7.3 and 4.2)
3 That there exists a struggle for power between status groups (industrial and political strife)

That employers use educational experience and qualifications to recruit members of different status groups for managerial and production jobs demands evidence that:

1 Schools either educate pupils into élite culture or into a respect for it. This was discussed in Chapters 2 and 4 where it was suggested that only the academically able and public schools explored the whole nature of education and that schools elicited a full response only from such pupils.

2 Employers use education as a means of selecting cultural attributes.

In support of his second point Collins quotes research to show that employers see education as a screening device enabling them to choose employees with desirable (middle-class) character traits. This was seen as particularly important in white-collar jobs because such employees were most visible to the public. In much the same way Berg (1970) argues that employers have beliefs that education provides evidence of ability to get on with others, to make the most of opportunities and of greater potential for learning and promotion. At the same time he reveals that virtually no employers collect data to examine these beliefs. Lydall (1968) takes a somewhat different line, though with the same consequences. He argues that employers are unaware of precisely what requirements they have of employees, but that experience tells them that those with given levels of education usually have what they want: in other words, that educational level predicts a higher level of performance without necessarily contributing to it. On the other hand, for students, educational qualifications mean a meal ticket to top table. This he claims could explain why earnings and educational level are related and why qualifications are often not suited to jobs. If education does function in this way – screening and selecting for employers – then its net contribution to national output might well be negative. Greater educational provision may well only serve to increase the competition for certain jobs. In economic terms the educated may well exploit the uneducated because they are paid more than they contribute (echoes here of their role in schools, see Chapter 4).

A survey of the recruitment strategies of large organisations (Gorden and Howell 1959) showed that degrees were regarded as important qualifications for trainee managers – not on account of ability or technical skill but because they were assumed to indicate motivation and social experience. Being a graduate of a business school was seen as important, in spite of the employers' wide scepticism of the course's utility, because it showed commitment to a career in business. Collins's own study of some 309 organisations showed that those most concerned with having normative control over their employees tended to emphasise educational qualifications most highly. These organisations were concerned with financial, professional, governmental and public services as opposed to manufacturing, construction and trade. Interestingly enough, the stress on education was true only for the white-collar workers.

Collins predicts that education is most important when two conditions are found together:

1 The type of education most closely reflects the membership of a particular status group
2 The same status group controls the employment.

This rather neatly encapsulates the British public school and Oxford and Cambridge universities with respect to the concerns identified (see table 4.2 above). He also demonstrates that large firms are predominantly manned by personnel recruited from the American equivalents (private schools and the Ivy League colleges). Minority-group members worked in smaller businesses. Technological change affected demands for educational qualifications only in the smaller, localised firms. A study of nationally prominent American businessmen found that the most highly educated were not working in rapidly developing enterprises but in financial and utility companies. Since the highly qualified businessmen tended to have social origins in the upper middle class, it appears to be indicated that education is more a correlate of their social origins than a determinant of their success.

Collins's concept of education as 'status culture' goes some way to explaining the lack of correspondence between educational achievement and occupational placement; the relationship between education, occupation and income; and the fact that educational and occupational opportunities appear to be stratified in a rather similar way to the social stratification of society. Certainly it casts doubt on the usefulness of seeing education and occupation as essentially linked in the purely technical sense, allowing for, if not explaining the lack of direct correlation between the two. The relationship between education, occupation and income must be viewed as being mediated by the social and power structure and relations of society. Not only has this to be seen in the differing opportunities and access to education and occupation but also, as Young (1971) has pointed out, in terms of the control of knowledge. It is necessary to see that what is commonly accepted as knowledge or education is both defined and stratified culturally. Young has characterised 'high-status' knowledge as being abstract, highly literate, individualistic and unrelated to non-school knowledge. The persistence of, and high rewards for, such knowledge occur not because of their necessary utility or superiority 'but because they are the conscious or unconscious cultural choices which accord with the values and beliefs of dominant groups at a particular time' (p. 38). To which we might add, they can be viewed as being in such groups' best interests, given their relationship to, and control of, the educational institutions that provide such knowledge and the occupational, social and political structures that reward it.

Very similar conclusions are reached by Bowles and Gintis (1976), who put forward the thesis that schooling, by reproducing in school the social relationships of economic life, provides for the development of types of people attuned to work contentedly in the capitalist mode of production rather than people with technical expertise. The educational system is, for them, one form of legitimation of inequality in capitalist society. In reviewing the relationship between education and income and the role of the educational system, they write:

. . . our argument suggests . . . that the mental-skill demands of work are sufficiently limited, the skills produced by our educational system sufficiently varied, and the possibilities for acquiring additional skills on the job sufficiently great so that skill differences among individuals who are acceptable for a given job on the basis of other criteria including race, sex, personality and credentials are of little

> economic import . . . Education reproduces inequality by
> justifying privilege and attributing poverty to personal fail-
> ure. (p. 114)

Education, they argue, reproduces inequality along what is
apparently objective merit — school performance — but the
justification of inequality is largely symbolic because the transmission of social and economic status is mainly by non-
cognitive mechanisms. Hence different levels of education
recruit from different sections of the social structure, socialise in
different ways, and subsequently feed their products into different levels of the occupational structure. They point out that
among American whites about a third of the correlation between school and economic attainment can be accounted for by
socio-economic background. Children from the poorest tenth of
American families had a third of the likelihood of ending up
economically well off than children from the wealthiest tenth,
even when their educational achievements and childhood I.Q.s
were identical. They further identify four sets of non-cognitive
worker traits — work-related personality characteristics, modes
of self-presentation, racial, sexual and ethnic characteristics,
and credentials — which are involved in the association between
educational level and economic success.

Education and social mobility

Having established a relationship between education and occupation and explored something of its explanation, we now turn
our attention to social mobility. Many people change their
occupations during their working life. For most this change is
from employment in one place or firm to another with little or
no change in the job they do. Sociologists refer to this as
horizontal social mobility; it will not be a concern of this section.
For others, however, the change is dramatic — for example
errand boy to peer, miner to academic or the other way round.
When the change involves moving up or down across the social

classes during one's working career, it is known as *intragenerational* social mobility. Finally, the most researched form of social mobility concerns the relationship between parental and child's occupation – called *intergenerational* social mobility. It is a sociological convention to view such mobility with respect to males only.

Problems arise in measuring social mobility. Has the son of a clerical worker who becomes first a teacher and then a university professor been either, or both, intra- and intergenerationally mobile? The normal way of measuring social mobility is to identify movement across the manual/non-manual occupational divide. This line is used because, generally speaking,

1 non-manual occupations have more prestige and are better paid than manual (especially when income over working life is compared);
2 non-manual occupations require a higher level of education, which it is assumed implies both status and a set of values;
3 non-manual workers, even those in routine jobs, tend to identify with, and exhibit the characteristics of, the middle rather than the working class;
4 it is a comparatively simple, easily collected measure which has become a sociological convention.

It should be appreciated that such measurement is crude, misses subtle mobility, as suggested above, and recognises short-term and relatively unimportant movements, say from small shopkeeper to skilled operative and back again. A further problem in the measurement of intergenerational mobility centres upon how and when one records the occupations of father and son. Ideally it should be either at the same age, or stage of career, of each, but studies often fail to achieve this. In any case it is also true that the status of some occupations changes over time, as do occupational opportunities. Interestingly enough, the literature is more concerned with upward than downward mobility (see pp. 243–4). The factors involved in social mobility can be seen to fall into two categories.

Structural factors

1 A growth in middle-class (non-manual) jobs and a decline in manual jobs (see table 7.9).
2 Up to the present there has been an inverse relationship between fertility and social class so that the middle classes have not reproduced themselves, hence creating vacancies for recruits from the working classes.
3 Historically there has been some decline in the importance of inherited status or ascribed factors on occupational placement, and growth in the importance of achieved factors.

Such structural factors indicate that opportunities exist for upward social mobility. What they do not explain is why the opportunities are taken, or why some working-class people are socially mobile while others are not. To understand this consideration must be made of

Non-structural factors

While sociologists have recognised the importance of non-structural factors, they have not been very active in identifying or exploring them. Veblen argued that a person's own social self-esteem was based on cues he received from others and that there was a general tendency for people to want to improve upon even a favourable self-esteem. Psychologists and social psychologists inform us that people vary in their need to achieve or to improve their and other people's opinions of themselves. McClelland laid the framework for what is known as n'ach (need for achievement) which can be measured by several tests. For people who score highly on these tests, the prospect of success is greater than their fear of failure, and they strive and enter competitive situations more frequently than others. Stacey (1965) (who also provides a useful review of the literature, 1969) conducted a British study in which he found that men and women who had been upwardly socially mobile had higher n'ach scores than those who were stationary, who in turn scored higher than those who were downwardly mobile. In a study partly by the author (Reid and Cohen 1973) it was discovered that, among college of education students who qualified to read for degrees (B.Ed.), it was those with the highest n'ach who did so, those with lower scores opting for the certificate course. Other studies have suggested that intelligence is a factor in social mobility (Anderson, Brown and Bowman 1952). Obviously structural and non-structural factors combine to create mobility. I use the term (which is my own) 'gluckenspiel' to refer to this in relation to upward mobility. 'Gluck' consists, mainly, of being in the right place at the right time, while 'spiel' is the ability to take advantage of the 'gluck'. Most successful people's careers contain incidents of this nature.

The main consideration in this chapter is, however, the role of education in social mobility. There seems to be some general agreement that education now plays an important if not a crucial role in occupational placement and consequently in social mobility. Floud (1950) writing in the early days of the tripartite, post-1944 Education Act, system said 'The importance of formal educational qualifications in industry has continuously increased over the last fifty years, and there is little doubt that educational opportunity has largely ousted the accumulation of small capital as the principal means of advancement' (p. 118). Notice that this statement is qualified by the words 'little doubt' and 'largely ousted'. An inherent danger in analysing the role of education in most situations is to overemphasise its importance. Before turning to some of the specific evidence, we can gain a general picture by building a hypothetical model in which a number of unrealistic assumptions are made. To do this we shall borrow from economics their concept of 'perfect'. Simply, this is an abstraction in which intervening real-life variables – like individual differences, luck and choice – are ignored and the relationship between two factors is seen as direct. Hence, in the present case, we shall initially accept that educational qualifications are directly related to occupation, that *all* those without qualifications get type A jobs, those with one to four O-levels get type B, and so on. In other words, regardless of all other factors (background situation, personality, opportunity), education determines social status or occupation – the relationship is 'perfect'. A model of education and social mobility would rest on three assumptions:

1 'perfect' educational opportunity
2 'perfect' entry into occupations via educational qualifications
3 'perfect' promotion via educational qualifications.

Put as boldly as this, the reality of education is underlined as a social phenomenon and as but one factor in any life situation or chance. It starkly reveals, in the light of our previous considerations, the absurdity of attempting to isolate the effect of education outside its social context. The three assumptions above need to be seriously questioned if not rejected.

Educational opportunity

As we have seen in Chapter 6 and elsewhere in this book, such opportunity is very far from 'perfect'. Opportunity is affected by educational provision which varies geographically and hence socially; economically, in respect of 'public' schools; by the way in which schools operate; and in variations among pupils in respect of a complexity of factors that can be referred to under the heading of social class. The weight of evidence reviewed clearly points to the fact that the educational system tends to reproduce the existing social structure rather than to change it dramatically. Of course this is a general view and does not deny the experience of many individuals for whom education has provided mobility from very poor backgrounds to highly paid occupations, but these are exceptions. Even if there was perfect educational opportunity, it would be only the first step towards education being the major factor in social placement and mobility.

Occupational entry

Already in this chapter it has been seen that the relationship between educational qualifications and occupation, while apparent, is not 'perfect'. Not all highly qualified people were engaged in 'appropriate' occupations and vice versa. The gaining and use of qualifications can be seen as commonly related to aspirations. Douglas, Ross and Simpson (1968) showed that, while 79 per cent of high-ability boys from the upper middle class were expected by their parents to enter the professions, this was true of only 39 per cent of lower-manual boys of the same ability. Maxwell (1969), in a similar Scottish study, concludes

But with the world before them, what appears to govern the future careers of these young people? The underlying influence seems to be social class. With all the surface variations, the basic relations are those which relate social class to the use of the educational opportunities available. Pupils of high ability leave school and close the avenue to further formal qualifications, and pupils of average ability persist, and enter the professions. Intellectual ability and personal preference come into it, but the relationship between fathers' occupational class and the critical decision is very strong. Social class also tends to determine the employment chosen where choice is relatively wide. Sons tend to follow their fathers. (pp. 97–8)

Occupational entry is not only affected by individual subjective factors but also by structural barriers. In Chapter 4 it was suggested that some occupations might be relatively closed to applicants other than those from 'public ' schools and/or Oxford and Cambridge. These factors can be suspected to operate at a more general level, for example Lee (1968) suggests 'For those who pass successfully through the hurdles at 11+, 16+ and onward, there probably exists a final barrier upon entry to the labour market at which influence, breeding and background still bestow an advantage' (p. 309). The main structural barrier, however, is the available stock of job opportunities. This varies considerably from area to area. The South-East region has a larger proportion of non-manual occupations than other parts of Britain. In some areas the decision to enter such a job may entail moving to another part of the country; this has been true, for example, of Wales in respect of schoolteachers. Indeed, social mobility generally implies some geographical mobility. The present state of unemployment, especially among school-leavers and newly trained teachers and graduates, often means a choice between no job or one which, in different conditions, would be considered unsuitable. Similarly, if the educational system produces more people with specific qualifications than the labour market can use, then the relationship between qualifications and occupation will be weakened (see also p. 107 above).

Aspects of educational opportunity and occupational entry also operate together. Since there are relationships both between father's occupation and son's education and between educational achievement and occupation we can anticipate that the typical pattern will be one of similarity between father and son, particularly in respect of occupational groups as broad as social classes.

Occupational promotion

Although evidence is more than limited, it seems probable that, however important educational qualifications are for entry into an occupation, their importance in the process of gaining promotion is likely to be overshadowed by other factors. This is mainly due to the fact that promotion is dependent on length of service, on the job performance or on some combination of the two. Individual and personality factors are likely to become more important – how well one 'fits in', how ambitious one is, the opportunities that exist for promotion, and so on. An illuminating study in this area is that of Perrucci (1961) who examined the social origins and job positions of a large sample of American engineering graduates. He found that fathers' social class was related to sons' careers – despite the fact that all had similar qualifications. Engineers from professional homes were more frequently found in the top jobs (presidents and vice-presidents of engineering concerns) than were those from unskilled homes who more often had lower-category jobs (design and project engineers). In reviewing the careers of graduates between 1911 and 1950, Perrucci argues that the opportunities for social mobility among graduate engineers have diminished over time. In this case, as in many others reviewed in this book,

the effects of education are mediated by other social factors —
here, once again, social class.

Turning to more specific evidence on the role of education in
social mobility, one is struck by the lack of British material.
The major work, that of Glass (1954), is now a classic, and a
modern counterpart has yet to be published. A conclusion of the
Glass study was that grammar schools were the major factor in
social mobility. Attendance at such a school made for a high
relationship between father and son's occupations in the middle
class, since it lessened the likelihood, or distance, of occupational descent. In the working class it greatly increased the
likelihood, or distance, of occupational ascent. Since, as we have
seen (p. 116), middle-class children had a much greater chance
of attending grammar schools than working-class children, the
net result was to modify rather than destroy the general relationship between father and son's occupation. In reworking the
Glass data Anderson (1961) concludes that sons with low educational achievement lost status in relation to their fathers less
often, and sons with high achievements rose less often, than
would be expected if education was the sole criterion. In regard
to American data he argues that a comparison of the actual data
with two possible models —

1 where education and occupation were randomly related
2 where the relationship between the two was direct and
   maximal
— suggests that reality is nearer the first than the second.

Within education, ability is of obvious importance, and Anderson, Brown and Bowman (1952) found that 80 per cent of
working-class boys (in their sample) with I.Q.s in the top third
of scores were upwardly mobile while only 16 per cent of
upper-class boys with I.Q.s in the lower third remained in that
class. Once again I.Q. was related to original social class and, in
particular, to small families, and eldest and only children were
overrepresented in the highest I.Q. group. Small working-class

families could be instrumental in producing socially mobile individuals — 'such' children might be better materially supported within limited means, and the relatively increased involvement of such children with adults probably heightens verbal ability and n'ach. Thompson (1971) has proposed two alternative emphases in the explanation of why some working-class males are upwardly mobile while others are not. The first she calls *objective* — that the barriers to mobility are greater for some parts of the working class than others. The second is *subjective* — that values and the desire for mobility may vary within the working class. She recognises, of course, that the two may go hand in hand. Her findings, based on British data, were that the educational aspirations of the boys' parents (subjective) were more important than the material condition of the home (objective), but that both these were overshadowed by the type of secondary school attended, grammar school boys tending to be more mobile than secondary modern boys. This re-emphasised the point made by Glass (see above). What implications for social mobility the disappearance of grammar schools has or will have remains to be seen.

An attempt to view both educational opportunity and social mobility in a dynamic framework was made by Little and Westergaard (1964). They present evidence to show that over the first half of this century class differentials in education have slightly diminished; in other words, more working-class children are gaining educational qualifications. At the same time, they conclude that there has been a removal of alternative routes (not involving education) into middle-class jobs. The net result is an unchanging frequency of intergenerational social mobility with the implication that the nature of the route has changed towards education. Their evidence of growing educational selectivity in middle-class jobs comes from studies of people's educational and social backgrounds. For example, Clark (1966) showed in his samples that the proportion of managers with extended education had grown over time and that there had been a slight net drop in the number of managers with working-class backgrounds. Lee (1968) has disagreed, however, arguing that the composition of an occupation should not be confused with opportunities to enter it. He suggests that the situation is static, that the chances of working-class persons without education entering such jobs have never been good, and such chances may, in the future, diminish. What emerges clearly from these researches is that there is no clear evidence that upward social mobility is on the increase, in spite of very real increases in educational provision, if not opportunity. Further, that education is but one factor in social mobility (as it is in occupational placement), mainly because preparation for occupation is but one function of education and because of the existence and importance of extra-educational factors in the process.

A rather fascinating further insight into the limitations of social mobility has been made by Noble (1975). In reviewing studies of the upwardly mobile, he shows that the mothers of many had previously been downwardly mobile (the so-called 'sunken middle class'). He estimates that for some 40 per cent of those moving from the working to the middle class the move represents a return, over three generations, to a previous family social status.

While the relationship between fathers' occupation and children's educational achievements has been well charted (Chapter 6), we have only limited knowledge of the amount and extent of intragenerational mobility and the role of education (particularly part-time and technical) in it. A valuable view of intragenerational mobility, albeit over just a ten-year period, is given by Harris and Clausen (1967). Table 7.10 compares the social class of some 4,062 males in 1953 with their class in 1963. As can be seen, movement took place in both directions. In class III non-manual, 12 per cent moved up, while 12 per cent moved down into manual occupations; in class III manual, 9 per cent moved upwards and 13 per cent downwards. Generally, however, the crossings of the manual/non-manual line (the normal indication of social mobility) was less common; over all, around $2\frac{1}{2}$ per cent of non-manual workers became manual and 7 per cent of manual workers became non-manual. This clearly indicates a net upward movement which could well have been more

Table 7.10

Male social mobility during a decade

(Social class of men in 1963 compared with that in 1953)

(percentages)

Social class 1953*	Social class 1963					
	I	II	III (N.M.)	III (M.)	IV	V
I	94	2	3	—	1	—
II	†	86	7	3	3	†
III (N.M.)	2	10	76	5	6	1
III (M.)	1	4	4	78	10	3
IV	—	4	3	14	73	6
V	—	1	1	10	20	68

* For definitions, see Appendix, p. 257

† Less than 0.5 per cent

(Derived from Harris and Clausen 1967, table 52)

pronounced if the data referred to men's working careers rather than a decade. The study also reveals that such mobility mainly involved changing employer. Much of this movement can be attributed to structural changes and redefinition of employment and opportunities. It is not possible to say how typical this decade was in the changing composition of the labour force, or what proportion moved because they gained educational quali- fications. Certainly through the sixties there was an expansion of part-time and technical education. The opportunities for, say, day-release students to gain Ordinary and Higher National Certificates or Diplomas and to enter into middle management may well have been enhanced by the increased provision of such courses, providing vacancies existed which were not filled by other recruits. Similarly the arrival of the Open University provided a further possibility for social mobility via education. Although the bulk of its students have, to date, been those who already had educational qualifications (mainly certificated teachers, many of whom had already been intergenerationally mobile), the open-entry policy — no previous qualifications necessary — certainly provides an avenue. Such developments point up the need to consider the role of *all* types of educational provision, not just full-time schooling, higher and further

education. Obviously, too, intragenerational mobility is intimately related to intergenerational mobility and can be viewed
as somewhat independent of full-time educational opportunity.

In the face of our consideration of the evidence (or lack of it) so
far, it is quite in order to ask why there is so much concern with
education, social mobility and their relationship. It appears that
much is due to what can be termed the *mobility myth*. Social
mobility is seen as a necessary characteristic of industrialised
society, both economically – changing technology and production demand a redefinition of occupations – and culturally –
democracy has a value set aiming towards an open, meritocratic
society. Educational qualifications can be viewed as a relatively
neutral criterion for occupational entry once educational opportunity has been extended, even minimally, to the whole of
society. The functions of the educational system are to provide
people with the qualifications and aspirations to meet society's
occupational needs. Built into the system is the assumption that
people will, or should, want to be upwardly mobile. Underlying such reasoning is, then, the belief that social mobility is a
desirable characteristic of society and that the educational system exists to promote and facilitate it. Given these assumptions, the educational system is viewed and evaluated in terms
of how it facilitates mobility rather than how it obstructs it.
This is precisely how education is sold to consumers, pupils and
parents alike: educational opportunity equals occupational
opportunity. If approached from this stance, research, writings
and thinking about the role of education in social mobility are
likely to result in its overemphasis and glamourisation. At the
same time this approach can provide society with a useful
supporting belief in the openness of society through the educational system. One effect of the evidence reviewed in this book
ought to be to suggest that such views are worth questioning.
As has been seen, educational opportunity and achievement are
strongly related to ascribed social factors, and social mobility is
not so great as to suggest an open society that in any real way
approaches a meritocracy: that is, as Young (1958) stated, a
society in which intelligence + effort = merit. It would be

equally justifiable to cast aside the 'mobility myth' and to view the educational system as obstructing social mobility, limiting educational opportunity and achievement, and contributing to the closedness of our society. That this has not been done on any scale again underlines the fact that the sociology of education, like education itself, operates within a set of cultural values. To work from such an assumption could well prove no more useful, but its consideration should lead readers to be wary. In particular, it emphasises that our educational system works in both directions, leading to both an open and a closed society. As has been seen in Chapter 6 and elsewhere in this book, it does not so operate indiscriminately. In general terms, it appears to follow the Biblical edict regarding the social structure: 'For the man who has will be given more, till he has enough and to spare' (Matthew 13:12).

8

The sociology of education

In the first chapter of this book it was argued that it was possible to talk of sociologies of education. These were identified by reference to the theoretical perspectives used in the discipline. In subsequent chapters the separateness of these sociologies was, as far as possible, sustained. At the same time, as will have been obvious to readers, and was intimated in the text, there were clear needs and tendencies to bring them together. In spite of differences, these sociologies share fundamental similarities that go far beyond the simple fact that they have a common subject matter – schooling and education. The concern of this chapter is to explore the extent to which the evidence reviewed indicates that there is one sociology of education. Therefore it discusses the relationships between the perspectives in the sociology of education and explores the nature and extent of the knowledge provided, both as a sociology and as an explanation of educational phenomena.

In the following treatment there is no extensive review of the contents of previous chapters, but rather a concentration on general concerns raised in those chapters, in order that readers may reflect upon what they have read and return to evaluate it within a fresh and systematic framework. This same framework may be found useful in approaching further reading in the sociology of education.

Complementary perspectives

The concern of this section is only with the two major perspectives within the sociology of education — structuralist and interpretative. At the same time the discussion is applicable to the subtypes within these two — consensus and conflict in the structuralist perspective and symbolic interactionism and phenomenology in the interpretative perspective. As has been seen, the major perspectives have not been used to the same extent in the investigation of all the topics reviewed. In the later chapters, concerned with the 'macro' aspects of education and society, for instance, most of the knowledge stemmed from structuralistic perspectives. Even there, though, the relevance and potential utility of interpretative approaches were recognised. Most strikingly, however, the complementary nature of the perspectives was displayed in the consideration of the school. In Chapters 2 and 3 we saw that the sociology of education ranged from the application of general theories of the social system, through participant studies of schools, to detailed observation of classrooms. This range also displayed a variety in the extent of its subject matter — from schools in general to specific groups in a classroom. The major contribution of interpretative studies was a deepening rather than a broadening of our knowledge of the social processes of education. Indeed, many of the factors previously identified were 'rediscovered', like social class, sex, the centrality of the teacher, the dominance of institutional requirements in teaching and learning, the cultural definition and role of education, and so on. What was provided was an exposure of the depth of detail and subtlety of the social processes which had not previously been demonstrated.

While the two perspectives can be seen as setting out from separate starting points — the macro and micro — they also quickly appear to be questioning, and indeed contributing to, each other. The establishment and investigation of patterns or generalisations cannot really begin, and certainly not progress, without knowledge of specific situations and events. Conversely the intimate study of a single classroom leads rapidly to questions of how what is observed is affected by, and relates to, the institution in which the class is situated, the biographies of those involved and the social and educational system of which they are part. It is quite futile not to appreciate the complementary nature of the perspectives. It is like attempting to teach with no knowledge of the subject, the organisation of the school, pupils or the examination and occupational system, or designing a curriculum without knowledge of teaching, classroom practice and children's abilities.

By analogy, the present scene in the sociology of education can be likened to two groups exploring a mountain. One, the structuralists, have started from the top and are working down. The other, interpretative sociologists, have started at the bottom and are working up. Eventually they must meet. What should be clear is that they are both on the same mountain and are both exploring it. What can be suggested is that for people interested in the mountain as a whole the two routes are both necessary and complementary. Most sociologists are hopeful that when two groups meet they will be able to share their knowledge and provide a complete picture. Like most analogies this one has its limitations. Throughout this book the difference between the perspectives has been taken to be only one of emphasis. In sociology it is impossible to generalise without some knowledge of the specific (and vice versa), if only because of the clear involvement in both elements by virtue of one's social experience.

Any refusal to accept the complementary nature of the perspectives and any claim for the separateness or the superiority of one ought to be recognised as products of the institutionalisation of knowledge in our society. Academic life displays a distinct tendency to compartmentalise knowledge. The pursuit and teaching of knowledge tend to be individual and limited by time, resources and people's career concerns. This situation appears to encourage limited approaches and to lead to their vigorous presentation and defence. They ought to be recognised as such by all real students of education. Indeed, as has been seen, such approaches appear to be a passing phase in the sociology of education. Researchers in the field are now joining many teachers of the discipline in beginning to span the perspectives. In Chapter 3 we viewed the work of Sharp and Green (1975) who, having begun with a phenomenological study of three classrooms, ended up with a markedly structuralist consideration. On the other hand, as was seen in Chapter 6, Reynolds's (1976) study commenced with a traditional quantitative structuralist analysis of schools but moved towards the micro in terms of the observation and identification of qualitative differences in social relationships within schools. This, once more, clearly suggests that the discipline fully embraces all its perspectives, as indeed do the theoretical writings of Spencer, Weber and Parsons.

In spite, then, of appearances and some sociologists' claims for sociologies of education, it is asserted that the contents of this book clearly display a single discipline of the sociology of education. The evidence suggests that, although the different theoretical perspectives of the discipline may be functional (see p. 249), their autonomy is artificial, and in no way can they be seen to amount to distinct disciplines within the sociology of education. They are united by both their complementary nature and the common approach they share towards the explanation of educational phenomena. This latter point is taken up on pp. 252–6 below, but first we consider further the present state of the sociology of education.

A developing discipline

British sociology of education has had a short history characterised by very rapid and considerable growth in size and complexity. This development, as was seen in Chapter 1, was intimately related to the growth of higher education and particularly of teacher education in the 1960s and early 1970s. The history of the discipline can be viewed in terms of three overlapping and presently concurrent phases. The first was marked by the predominance of structural functionalism; the second, which can be dated at around 1970, by the emergence and establishment of the interpretative perspectives; and the last characterised by attempts at a new synthesis commenced in the mid-seventies. Any apparent conflict between the perspectives could then be accounted for by the youth and vigour of the discipline along with that of its practitioners, as well as institutional factors outlined above. What must be appreciated is that these phases were only a question of emphasis; each contained elements of the other, but none was truly comprehensive.

Another view is that the development of new or conflicting theoretical perspectives is essential to the development of any discipline (Kuhn 1962). It can be argued, for instance, that so long as the sociology of education had a single perspective – that of structural functionalism – and its practitioners worked within it, seeing educational phenomena in the same way, the discipline would not have progressed. The impetus for development came from those who brought fresh perspectives to the sociology of education. It is difficult to accept or reject Kuhn's idea because of our knowledge of the discipline. In one sense the argument relies on the fact that structural functionalism was a single and limited approach, a fact we have questioned by challenging its strawman characterisation (p. 9) and by demonstrating something of its variety and scope. It is certainly possible to see that towards the end of the 1960s research was being conducted which had changed level in comparison with earlier large-scale demographic-type studies. For example, participatory studies of schools were undertaken (Hargreaves 1967; Lacey 1970; King 1969). We cannot be certain whether the contemporary micro study of classrooms would be the same if the interpretative perspectives had not emerged. What did happen, however, was a major reorientation of much research and teaching in the sociology of education. It is also true that the knowledge emanating from such studies was vital to the whole discipline. The protagonists of the interpretative perspectives agree that their investigations have only just begun and call for much more, better and more extensive research to be carried out.

Before that phase was properly established and explored, however, a further shift in the discipline, towards a synthesis of the perspectives, can be detected (Sharp and Green 1975; Open University Course E 202). Such moves led Hargreaves to pose the serious question to a recent conference of sociologists of education, 'Whatever happened to symbolic interaction?' (Hargreaves 1978). He expressed a concern, shared by many others, about the dangers of rapid fashion changes in the discipline. Hardly has one settled in when a new shift in fashion detracts from the proper investigation and development of current models. He considers an important role of interpretative sociology to be the provision of a critical challenge to structuralism, which should lead to the development of the latter. Indeed his concept of the perspectives' complementary nature is towards the theoretical. Each one produces problems the other ought to attempt to solve within itself. At the general level, for instance, interpretative sociology of education ought to help correct the tendency of structuralism to 'oversimplify, underestimate or ignore the complexity of the detailed operation of the relevant factors in actual social settings'. Clearly the converse can also be easily argued. Hargreaves is calling, quite rightly, for a greater discourse and mutual use of both or all perspectives.

While there are tendencies towards a new synthesis, it may be more appropriate, given the institutional structure within which the discipline operates, and the needs of the sociology of education rather than sociology *per se*, to hope for new co-operation and co-ordination. Instead of continuing with small-scale, single-perspective studies, what is called for are larger-scale multi-perspective approaches on a systematic basis (Reid 1978). A co-ordinated attack on a specific area, say the classroom, by a group of sociologists is likely to be a great improvement upon the present rather fragmentary studies. Such an approach, using the full range of available theory and methodology, could well make significant contributions to both sociology and education.

It is interesting that the suggestions of Hargreaves and myself have institutional as well as theoretical implications, in calling for new attitudes towards sociological knowledge and research and for greater unification of the discipline. As we have seen, there exist institutional obstructions to such a development. It would be particularly ironic if sociologists, who by definition are students of institutions, were unable to come to grips with those they themselves inhabit and to an extent have created.

The same perspective – of a developing discipline – needs to be applied to what we have recognised as shortcomings in the sociology of education. One recognition was that knowledge in some areas is selective, limited and also affected by rapid changes in our society. A minor example is that the studies of secondary schools in current use were nearly all made before the raising of the school-leaving age to sixteen and mostly in grammar and secondary modern schools. Similarly the discipline often has to rely on knowledge and data collected by non-sociological agencies. For example, census figures relating to occupied males in a school's catchment area may have to be used to indicate the social backgrounds of pupils. It has further been recognised that sometimes there is a lack of, or vagueness in, the definition of terms – or even the simultaneous use of a variety of definitions. The lack of an agreed conceptual language can be confusing to beginning students and even some sociologists! A prime example here is social class. In spite of its almost constant use, not only is it very rarely explicitly defined but it is not uncommon to find data from different sources presented together without distinction or for the definition apparently to shift from context to context. Again this problem is related to the divorce in the sociology of education between conceptualisation and operationalisation. In social class the first is normally very complex and multidimensional and the latter based simply on occupation. At the same time these aspects of the discipline can be seen as functional in the same way as its theoretical perspectives. Several definitions encourage or at least do not hinder a full exploration of phenomena.

The intention, in raising these concerns, is not, of course, to overemphasize the limitations and problems of the sociology of education in particular. Precisely these concerns abound in all other disciplines, including the 'pure' sciences. It is a conviction of the author, however, that these considerations ought to be borne in mind by anyone approaching the discipline, not only to assist understanding and appreciation but also because a critical audience is a contribution to any discipline.

What is the sociology of education?

In view of our considerations so far, this is a perfectly reasonable question to ask. Apart from the title of a book or article or its author's claim, how does one recognise the sociology of education? It has always been impracticable to identify a discipline in terms of what it studies. In the present case schools and education are the subject matter of a large number of disciplines including psychology, history, philosophy, economics, politics and education or pedagogy itself, to mention only the obvious. Schools and education are also popular and controversial topics which attract a great deal of more general writing and discussion. Disciplines can only be properly distinguished by the approach they adopt to their subject matter.

The sociology of education is, then, best seen as a particular approach to the explanation of educational phenomena – an approach distinguished by the fact that it is sociological. Sociology is by definition concerned with the social. One way of appreciating this is to think in terms of levels of abstraction. Man can be viewed at a variety of such levels – as a chemical, physical or biological entity, as a discrete individual in the psychological or theological sense or, from the sociological viewpoint, as a social being – a part of a social situation or system. Hence sociology is not particularly concerned with individuals but with *people*. People are essentially social beings: in very many senses they do not exist other than in a social setting, nor can they be seen as other than products or outcomes of social experiences. Sociologists do not ignore the non-social aspects of man but in referring to these they use knowledge from other disciplines. What is peculiar about the sociology of education is that ultimately it approaches education at a level of abstraction which is essentially concerned with the social institutions of education, from peer groups through classes and schools to the system of education, with institutional compositions, structures, procedures, ideologies and functioning (workings and outcomes), and with interrelationships between education and other institutions.

In this book the sociology of education has been shown to have three further basic characteristics in its approach. Here these are presented as a set of reasonable expectations or criteria of recognition for the discipline.

1 *Theoretical*. The word is used here in a general sense to suggest that the sociology of education goes beyond pure description. It is concerned with explanations of educational phenomena which are couched in terms other than the characteristics of the phenomena being explored. One simple clear example, abundantly illustrated in this book, is the way in which factors from the social structure are seen as important in explaining what goes on in classrooms and schools.

2 *Empirical*. Sociology of education, in all its forms, depends on observation of one type or another. The variety is considerable – from information from existing sources, through data collected from questionnaires, tests and interviews (sometimes treated statistically), to various forms of direct and indirect observation and experimentation through change or comparison. The importance of empirical investigation is that such knowledge can be checked by further observation, either of the same type (replication) or using other methods. In this way the knowledge gained is both developmental and accumulative.

3 *Objective*. Sociology of education is more than merely a single individual's reflection upon, or reaction to, a social situation or knowledge. Of course, it has to be appreciated that facts never speak for themselves, presentation implies interpre-

tation, and consequently objectivity is only relative. However, an expectation of the discipline must be some degree of objectivity. This is attained either by sociologists viewing phenomena from a variety of perspectives, a proper use of their data, or by their being explicit about the perspectives, values and evidence they use. In any case a measure of objectivity, or at least opportunity for appraisal, is afforded by subscription to the first two tenets – theory and empiricism.

In so defining the sociology of education a clear statement is being made that the discipline is directly and substantially part of sociology *per se*. As has been argued and demonstrated in this book, there are two main implications. On the one hand, the sociology of education is affected by the interests, content and direction of sociology itself and, on the other, it makes considerable contributions to it. This relationship is intimate and has no predominant direction, as Gouldner (1956) has argued: 'Any metaphor which conceives of applied social science as the off-spring, and of the basic discipline as the parent is misleading. It obscures the point that the applied sciences often contribute as much to pure science as they receive from it.' The subject matter of the sociology of education and the fact that the discipline is mainly practised in teacher education also indicate that it has contributions to make at a more pragmatic level. This is not to imply that the discipline is or necessarily will be about providing specific prescriptions or answers to practical teaching, classroom or school problems. Indeed none of the other contributory disciplines to education addresses itself to such direct problems. What the sociology of education does provide is both a unique picture and a questioning analysis of education. This is precisely the value of the discipline. Its role is educative rather than prescriptive or directly utiliarian, in that it enables disciplined thinking about education in a separate and different way. Its prime contribution is its singular insistence on viewing schools and education as pre-eminently social. Such a view is in contrast to, and corrective of, both common everyday inclinations of the public, professionals and policy makers and of other disciplines in education, particularly the psychology of education.

The influence of the sociology of education can be recognised in educational-policy documents. Compare the following examples:

> Intellectual development during childhood appears to progress as if it were governed by a single central factor, usually known as 'general intelligence', which may be broadly described as innate all-round intellectual ability . . . We were informed that, with few exceptions, it is possible at a very early age to predict with some degree of accuracy the ultimate level of a child's intellectual powers . . . (*Secondary Education* 1938, pp. 123–4)

> The numbers who are capable of benefiting from higher education are a function not only of heredity but also of a host of other influences varying with standards of educational provision, family incomes and attitudes and the education received by previous generations. (*Higher Education* 1963, chapter 6, p. 54)

In the first quotation the singular contribution is that of psychology. The pupil is seen as an individual with a given innate potential. In the second quotation (some twenty-five years on) there is a clear if not predominant sociological consideration. The pupil is seen as a person whose potential is related to social factors.

At the more general level, the sociology of education has contributed a demonstration of the relationship of teachers, pupils and their activities with society and of how the social structure enters and affects the social reality of the classroom. Alongside, there has been an exposure of the social definition and functions of education on time scales and to extents which are not immediately apparent to practitioners. The sociology of education provides an invaluable opportunity for exploring and considering these areas. More recently, as Hargreaves (1978) has pointed out, there has been an exploration of the 'common sense' knowledge of classroom members and the extent to which teachers' classroom skills depend upon their tacit knowledge of the classroom. He claims that the development of a language to describe this knowledge can 'enrich the working vocabulary of teachers and teacher-trainers', giving rise to the discussion, communication and learning of these skills.

The value of the sociology of education is that it provides a unique conceptual framework, language and knowledge of education. Basically it provides a view of education as a social process and institution, which is invaluable, since education is essentially if not obviously a social phenomenon. Consequently the sociology of education is a vital discipline for all those who wish to understand or who are involved with schools and education.

Appendix

Key to social-class classifications used in the tables to the text

Social class refers to the grouping of people into categories on the basis of occupation.

Tables 6.1, 6.3, 6.4 and 7.10 use the Registrar General's social-class classification devised for census purposes, which is as follows:

Social class	*Descriptive definition*	*Examples of occupations included*
I	Professional etc.	Accountant, architect, chemist, clergyman, doctor, lawyer, surveyor, university teacher
II	Intermediate	Aircraft pilot or engineer, chiropodist, farmer, manager, Member of Parliament, nurse, police or fire-brigade officer, schoolteacher
III	Skilled non-manual	Clerical worker, draughtsman, sales representative, secretary, shop assistant, telephone supervisor, waiter
III	Skilled manual	Bus driver, butcher, bricklayer, carpenter, cook, electrician, miner (underground), railway guard, upholsterer

| IV | Partly skilled | Agricultural worker, barman, bus conductor, fisherman, machine sewer, packer, postman, telephone operator |
| V | Unskilled | Kitchen hand, labourer, lorry driver's mate, messenger, office cleaner, railway porter, stevedore, window cleaner |

Tables 7.1, 7.2, 7.3 and 7.4 use a similar Registrar General's scale devised from his socio-economic groups.

Socio-economic class	Descriptive definition
1	Professional
2	Employers and managers
3	Intermediate and junior non-manual
4	Skilled manual (with own account non-professional)
5	Semi-skilled manual and personal service
6	Unskilled manual

Table 6.2 uses a scale devised for the National Survey of Health and Development. It combines father's occupation with the educational and social background of the father and mother as follows:

Social class	Descriptive definition
(U.M.) Upper middle class	Father has non-manual occupation and (a) both parents had secondary-school education and middle-class upbringing (i.e. had father with non-manual occupation) or (b) both parents had secondary-school education, and one parent had middle-class upbringing – or (c) both parents had middle-class upbringing and one parent had secondary-school education

(L.M.) Lower middle class	All other fathers with non-manual occupations
(U.W.) Upper manual working class	Father has manual occupation and (a) either or both parents had secondary-school education and/or (b) either or both parents had middle-class upbringing
(L.W.) Lower manual working class	Father has manual occupation and (a) both parents had elementary-school education only and (b) both parents had working-class upbringing (i.e. had father with manual occupation)

Bibliography and Author index

All these sources are followed by page references to show where they are mentioned or discussed in this book. Works are referenced, wherever possible, by author(s)/editor(s) and otherwise by their title. Where articles have been reproduced in readers which are listed this is indicated.

Her Majesty's Stationery Office has been abbreviated to H.M.S.O., National Foundation for Educational Research to N.F.E.R., and Office of Population Censuses and Surveys to O.P.C.S.

A Language for Life (1975) (The Bullock Report) Department of Education and Science. London: H.M.S.O. 188.

A New Partnership for our Schools (1977) (The Taylor Report) Department of Education and Science and Welsh Office. London: H.M.S.O. 169.

ANDERSON, C. A. (1961) 'A Skeptical Note on the Relation of Vertical Mobility to Education'. *American Journal of Sociology* 66 No. 6, 560–70. Reproduced in Halsey, Floud and Anderson 1961. 239.

ANDERSON, C. A., BROWN, J. C., and BOWMAN, M. J. (1952) 'Intelligence and Occupational Mobility'. *Journal of Political Economy* 60 No. 3, 218–39. 235.

ASHLEY, B. J., COHEN, H. S., and SLATTER, R. G. (1969) *An Introduction to the Sociology of Education*. London: Macmillan. 8.

A.T.C.D.E. (1969) *Sociology in the Education of Teachers*. London: Association of Teachers in Colleges and Departments of Education.

BANKS, O. (1968, 1971, 1976) *The Sociology of Education.* London: Batsford. 8, 21, 50, 62, 66.

BANKS, O., and FINLAYSON, D. (1973) *Success and Failure in the Secondary School.* London: Methuen. 194.

BARKER LUNN, J. C. (1970) *Streaming in the Primary School.* Slough: N.F.E.R. 39, 125–31, 139–40, 192.

BARNES, D. (1969) *Language in the Secondary School*, in Barnes, Britton and Rosen 1969. 94.

BARNES, D., BRITTON, J., and ROSEN, H. (1969) *Language, the Learner and the School.* Harmondsworth: Penguin.

BARTON, L., and MEIGHAN, R. (1978) *Sociological Interpretations of Schooling and Classrooms.* Driffield: Nafferton.

BECKER, H. S. (1952) 'Social Class Variation in Pupil-Teacher Relationships'. *Journal of Educational Sociology* 25 No. 8, 451–65. Reproduced in Bell and Stub 1968 and Cosin, Dale, Esland and Swift 1971. 50.

BELL, H. M. (1940) *Matching Youth and Jobs.* Washington: American Council on Education. 221.

BELL, R. R., and STUB, H. R. (1968) *The Sociology of Education: A Sourcebook.* Homewood: Dorsey Press.

BENDIX, R., and LIPSET, S. M. (1967) *Class, Status and Power.* London: Routledge and Kegan Paul. 223.

BENN, C. (1975) *We Must Choose Which We Want.* London: National Union of Teachers and Campaign for Comprehensive Education. 199.

BENN, C., and SIMON, B. (1972) *Half Way There.* 2nd ed. Harmondsworth: Penguin. 37, 111.

BERG, I. (1970 and 1973) *Education and Jobs.* Baltimore: Penguin; Harmondsworth: Penguin. 225–6, 229.

BERG, L. (1968) *Risinghill: Death of a Comprehensive School.* Harmondsworth: Penguin. 110.

BERNBAUM, G. (1967) *Social Change and the Schools 1918–44.* London: Routledge and Kegan Paul. 169.

BERNSTEIN, B. (1969) 'A Critique of the Concept of Compensatory Education'. Paper given at the Work Conference of the Teachers' College, Columbia University, New York. Reproduced in Bernstein 1971 and 1973. 188.

BERNSTEIN, B. (1971) 'A Socio-Linguistic Approach to Socialisation: with some Reference to Educability', in Hymes and Gumperz 1971 and Bernstein 1971 and 1973. 182–9.

BERNSTEIN, B. (1971 and 1973) *Class, Codes and Control.* London: Routledge and Kegan Paul; St Albans: Granada (Paladin). 182–9.

BERNSTEIN, B. (1974) 'Sociology and the Sociology of Education: A Brief Account', in Rex 1974. 6, 21.

BLAU, P. M. (1956) *Bureaucracy in Modern Society.* New York: Random House. 66.

BLAUG, M. (1970) *An Introduction to the Economics of Education.* Harmondsworth: Penguin. 217.

BLAUG, M. (1972) 'The Correlation between Education and Earnings: What Does it Signify?' *Higher Education* 1 No. 1, 53–76. 224.

BLUMER, H. (1965) 'Sociological Implications of the Thought of G. H. Mead'. *American Journal of Sociology* 71 No. 4, 535–44. Reproduced in Cosin, Dale, Esland and Swift 1971 and Wallace 1969. 13.

BOADEN M. (1971) *Urban Policy-Making: Influences on County Boroughs in England and Wales.* Cambridge: Cambridge University Press. 204.

BOOCOCK, S. S. (1973) 'The School as a Social Environment for Learning: Social Organisation and Micro-Social Process in Education'. *Sociology of Education* 46 No. 1. 15–50. 57.

BOURDIEU, P. (1974) 'The School as a Conservative Force: Scholastic and Cultural Inequalities.' in Eggleston, 1974. 196.

BOWLES, S., and GINTIS, H. (1976) *Schooling in Capitalist America.* London: Routledge and Kegan Paul. 159–62, 231–2.

BOYD, D. (1973) *Elites and their Education.* Slough: N.F.E.R. 118.

BROCKINGTON, F., and STEIN, Z. (1963) 'Admission, Achievement and Social Class'. *Universities Quarterly* 18 No. 1, 52–73. 177.

BROPHY, J. E., and GOOD, T. L. (1974) *Teacher-Student Relationships.* New York: Holt, Rinehart and Winston. 133, 135.

BROWN, R. (1973) *Knowledge, Education, and Cultural Change.* London: Tavistock. 22.

BURT, C. (1961) 'The Gifted Child'. *British Journal of Statistical Psychology* 14 No. 2, 123–39. 120.

BUSH, R. M. (1954) *The Teacher–Pupil Relationship.* Englewood Cliffs, New Jersey: Prentice-Hall. 38.

BYNNER, J., CASHDAN, A., and COMMINGS, B. (1972) *Attitudes, Learning Problems.* Course E281, Unit 15, Appendix B. Bletchley: the Open University Press. 141.

BYNNER, J. M. (1972) *Parents' Attitudes to Education*. O.P.C.S. Social Surveys Division. London: H.M.S.O. 192.

BYRNE, D. S., and WILLIAMSON, W. (1972) 'Some Intra-Regional Variations in Educational Provision and their Bearing upon Educational Attainment – the Case of the North-East'. *Sociology* 6 No. 1, 71–87. Reproduced in Eggleston 1974. 202–4.

BYRNE, D. S., WILLIAMSON, W., and FLETCHER, B. (1975) *The Poverty of Education*. London: Martin Robertson. 202.

CHANAN, G., and DELAMONT, S. (1975) *Frontiers of Classroom Research*. Slough: N.F.E.R.

Children and their Primary Schools (1967) (The Plowden Report.) Department of Education and Science. London: H.M.S.O. 37, 39, 191.

CLARK, B. R. (1962) *Educating the Expert Society*. San Francisco: Chandler. 222.

CLARK, D. G. (1966) *The Industrial Manager – his Background and Career Pattern*. London: Business Publications. 240.

Classification of Occupations (1960) O.P.C.S. London: H.M.S.O. 210.

COHEN, P. S. (1968) *Modern Social Theory*. London: Heinemann. 6, 10, 43, 15.

COLEMAN, J. S. (1961) *The Adolescent Society*. Glencoe: Free Press. 55–7.

COLEMAN, J. S. (1965) *Adolescents and their Schools*. New York: Basic Books. 55.

COLLINS, R. (1969) 'Education and Employment'. Unpublished Ph.D., University of California at Berkeley. 221.

COLLINS, R. (1971) 'Functional and Conflict Theories of Educational Stratification'. *American Sociological Review* 36 No. 6, 1002–18. 107, 222–31.

Consultative Committee on the Primary School (1931) (The Hadow Report) Board of Education. London: H.M.S.O. 124.

CORWIN, R. G. (1965) *A Sociology of Education*. New York: Appleton-Century. 17, 18.

COSER, L. A. (1956) *The Functions of Social Conflict*. Glencoe: Free Press. 12.

COSIN, B. R., DALE, I. R., ESLAND, G. M., and SWIFT, D. F. (1971) *School and Society*. London: Routledge and Kegan Paul; Open University Press. 8, 23.

CRAFT, M. (1974) 'Talent, Family Values and Education in Ireland', in Eggleston 1974. 195.

CROWL, T. K., and MACGINITIE, W. H. (1974) 'The Influence of Students' Speech Characteristics on Teacher's Evaluations of Oral Answers'. *Journal of Educational Psychology* 66 No. 3, 304–8. 141.

DAHLKE, H. O. (1958) *Values in Culture and Classroom.* New York: Harper. 46, 49.

DAHRENDORF, R. (1959) *Class and Class Conflict in Industrial Society.* London: Routledge and Kegan Paul. 11, 44.

DALE, R., ESLAND, G., and MACDONALD, M. (1976) *Schooling and Capitalism.* London: Routledge and Kegan Paul. 23.

DANIELS, J. C. (1961) 'The Effects of Streaming in the Primary School'. *British Journal of Educational Psychology* 31 No. 1, 69–78. 125.

DATTA, L., SCHAEFER, E., and DAVIS, M. (1968) 'Sex and Scholastic Aptitude as Variables in Teachers' Ratings of the Adjustment and Classroom Behavior of Negro and other Seventh-Grade Students'. *Journal of Educational Psychology* 59 No. 2, 94–101. 135.

DAVIE, R., BUTLER, M., and GOLDSTEIN, H. (1972) *From Birth to Seven.* London: Longman. 172–3.

DAVIES, B. (1973) 'On the Contribution of Organisational Analysis to the Study of Educational Institutions', in Brown 1973. 60, 66, 69.

DAVIS, K. (1949) *Human Society.* New York: Macmillan. 1.

DAWE, A. (1970) 'The Two Sociologies'. *British Journal of Sociology* 11 No. 2, 207–18. 7.

DELAMONT, S. (1976a) *Interaction in the Classroom.* London: Methuen. 78, 94, 97, 135.

DELAMONT, S. (1976b) 'Beyond Flanders Fields', in Stubbs and Delamont 1976. 97.

DELAMONT, S., and HAMILTON, D. (1974) 'Classroom Research: A Cautionary Tale'. *Research in Education* 11 No. 1, 1–16. Reproduced in Stubbs and Delamont 1976. 74.

DENT, H. C. (1944) 7th ed. (1958) *The Education Act 1944.* London: University of London Press. 31.

DOUGLAS, J. D. (1967) *The Social Meaning of Suicide.* Princeton: Princeton University Press. 167.

DOUGLAS, J. D. (1971) *Understanding Everyday Life: Toward the Reconstruction of Sociological Knowledge.* London: Routledge and Kegan Paul. 15.

DOUGLAS, J. W. B. (1964) *The Home and the School*. London: MacGibbon and Kee. 126, 135, 138–9, 172–5, 199.

DOUGLAS, J. W. B., and CHERRY, N. (1977) 'Does Sex Make any Difference?' *The Times Educational Supplement*, 9.12.77, 16–18. 112.

DOUGLAS, J. W. B., ROSS, J. M., and SIMPSON, H. R. (1968) *All Our Future*. London: Peter Davies. 119, 175, 199, 237.

DUNCAN, B. (1964) 'Dropouts and the Unemployed'. *Journal of Political Economy* 73 (April), 121–34. 226.

DURKHEIM, E. (1952) *Suicide* (1897). London: Routledge and Kegan Paul. 105.

DURKHEIM, E. (1956) *Education and Sociology* (1922). New York: Free Press. 106, 107, 108.

EDUCATION SURVEY 21 (1975) *Curricular Differences for Boys and Girls*. Department of Education and Science. London: H.M.S.O. 112.

Education Tables (10% Sample) (1966) Census 1961, England and Wales, O.P.C.S. London: H.M.S.O. 211

EDWARDS, A. D. (1976) *Language in Culture and Class*. London: Heinemann. 186.

EGGLESTON, J. (1974) *Contemporary Research in the Sociology of Education*. London: Methuen.

ELLIS, D., MCCREADY, D., and MORGAN, C. (1969) 'Sociology Main Courses in Colleges of Education', in A.T.C.D.E. 1969. 21.

Equality of Educational Opportunity (1966) (The Coleman Report) U.S. Department of Health, Education and Welfare. Washington: U.S. Government Printing Office. 37.

ETZIONI, A. (1962) *Readings on Modern Organisations*. New York: Holt, Rinehart and Winston.

ETZIONI, A. (1964) *Modern Organisations*. Englewood Cliffs, New Jersey: Prentice-Hall. 62.

ETZIONI, A. (1969) *The Semi-Professions and their Organisation*. Glencoe: Free Press. 71.

EVE, R. A. (1975) 'Adolescent Culture: Convenient Myth or Social Reality. A Comparison of Students and their Teachers'. *Sociology of Education* 48 No. 2, 152–67. 57.

FERRI, E. (1971) *Streaming: 2 Years Later*. Slough: N.F.E.R. 126.

FESBACH, N. (1969) 'Student Teacher Preferences for Elementary School Pupils Varying in Personality Characteristics' *Journal of Educational Psychology* 60 No. 2, 126–32. 140.

15–18 (1960) (The Crowther Report) Central Advisory Council for Education, Ministry of Education. London: H.M.S.O. 115.

FINLAYSON, D. S. (1971) 'Parental Aspirations and the Educational Achievement of Children'. *Educational Research* 14 No. 1, 61–4. 192.

FLOUD, J. (1950) 'Educational Opportunity and Social Mobility', in *The Year Book of Education 1950.* London: Evans. 121, 235.

FLOUD, J., and HALSEY, A. H. (1958) 'The Sociology of Education. A Trend Report and Bibliography'. *Current Sociology* 3 No. 3, 66.

FLOUD, J., HALSEY, A. H., and MARTIN, F. M. (1956) *Social Class and Educational Opportunity.* London: Heinemann. 21.

FOGLER, J. K., and NAM, C. B. (1964) 'Trends in Education in Relation to the Occupational Structure'. *Sociology of Education* 38 No. 1, 19–33. 223.

FORD, J. (1969) *Social Class and the Comprehensive School.* London: Routledge and Kegan Paul. 39, 129.

FRIEDENBURG, E. Z. (1963) 'The School as a Social Environment', in *College Admissions 10: The Behavioral Sciences and Education.* New York: College Entrance Examination Board. Reproduced in Bell and Stub 1968. 38.

FUCHS, E. (1968) 'How Teachers Learn to Help Children Fail'. *Transactions*, September, 45–9. Reproduced in Keddie 1973, 87, 143.

FURLONG, V. (1976) 'Interaction Sets in the Classroom: Towards a Study of Pupil Knowledge', in Stubbs and Delamont 1976. Reproduced in Hammersley and Woods 1976. 77.

GANNAWAY, H. (1976) 'Making Sense of School', in Stubbs and Delamont 1976. 78.

GARFINKEL, H. (1967) *Studies in Ethnomethodology.* Englewood Cliffs, New Jersey: Prentice-Hall. 15.

General Household Survey Introductory Report (1973) O.P.C.S. Social Surveys Division. London: H.M.S.O. 216.

General Household Survey 1972 (1975) O.P.C.S. Social Surveys Division. London: H.M.S.O. 117, 172, 213–15.

GETZELS, J. W., and THELEN, H. A. (1960) 'The Classroom as a Unique Social System', in *The Dynamics of Instructional Groups.* National Society for the Study of Education Yearbook. Chicago: University of Chicago Press. 43.

GLASER, B. G., and STRAUSS, A. L. (1967) *The Discovery of Grounded Theory*. Chicago: Aldine. 66.

GLASER, B. G., and STRAUSS, A. L. (1968) *Time for Dying*. Chicago: Aldine. 66.

GLASS, D. V. (1954) *Social Mobility in Britain*. London: Routledge and Kegan Paul. 21, 239.

GOFFMAN, E. (1962) 'The Characteristics of Total Institutions', in Etzioni 1962. 121.

GOODACRE, E. J. (1967) *Reading in Infant Classes*. Slough: N.F.E.R. 134.

GOODACRE, E. J. (1968) *Teachers and Their Pupils' Home Backgrounds*. Slough: N.F.E.R. 134, 136–8, 143.

GORBUTT, D. (1972) 'The New Sociology of Education'. *Education for Teaching* 89, 3–11, Reproduced in Reid and Wormald 1974. 27, 66.

GORDEN, R. A., and HOWELL, J. E. (1959) *Higher Education for Business*. New York: Columbia University Press. 229.

GOULD, J. (1977) 'Scholarship, or Propaganda?' *The Times Educational Supplement* 4.2.1977, 20. 23.

GOULD, J. (1977 *The Attack on Higher Education*. Institute for the Study of Conflict Ltd. 23.

GOULDNER, A. W. (1956) 'Explorations in Applied Social Science'. *Social Problems* 3 No. 3, 169–81. 254.

GOULDNER, A. W. (1973) *For Sociology*. Harmondsworth: Penguin. 25.

GREER, B. (1968) 'Teaching', in Sills 1968. Reproduced in Cosin, Dale, Esland and Swift 1971. 41.

Half our Future (1963) (The Newsom Report) Central Advisory Council for Education (England) Report, Ministry of Education. London: H.M.S.O. 37, 39, 106, 199.

HALSEY, A. H. (1972) *Trends in British Society Since 1900*. London: Macmillan. 220.

HALSEY, A. H., FLOUD, J., and ANDERSON, C. A. (1961)*Education, Economy and Society*. Glencoe: Free Press. 8, 21.

HAMMERSLEY, M. (1974) 'The Organisation of Pupil Participation'. *Sociological Review* 22 No. 3, 355–68. 95.

HAMMERSLEY, M. (1976) 'The Mobilisation of Pupil Attention', in Hammersley and Woods 1976. 99.

HAMMERSLEY, M., and WOODS, P. (1976) *The Process of Schooling*. London: Routledge and Kegan Paul. 8, 23.

HARARI, H., and McDAVID, J. W. (1973) 'Name Stereo-Types and Teacher Expectations'. *Journal of Educational Psychology* 65 No. 2, 222–5. 141.

HARGREAVES, D. H. (1967) *Social Relations in a Secondary School*. London: Routledge and Kegan Paul. 39, 53, 60, 108, 129, 249.

HARGREAVES, D. H. (1972) *Interpersonal Relationships and Education*. London: Routledge and Kegan Paul. 61, 70.

HARGREAVES, D. H. (1976) 'Reactions to Labelling', in Hammersley and Woods 1976. 84.

HARGREAVES, D. H. (1978) 'Whatever Happened to Symbolic Interactionism?', in Barton and Meighan 1978. 250, 256.

HARGREAVES, D. H., HESTER, S. K., and MELLOR, F. J. (1975) *Deviance in Classrooms*. London: Routledge and Kegan Paul. 81–4.

HARRIS, A. I., and CLAUSEN, R. (1967) *Labour Mobility in Great Britain*. O.P.C.S. Social Surveys Division. London: H.M.S.O. 241–2.

HAVIGHURST, R. J., and NEUGARTEN, B. L. (1967) *Society and Education*. 3rd ed. Boston: Allyn and Bacon. 49.

HEBB, D. O. (1949) *Organisation of Behavior*. New York: Wiley. 180.

HEMPEL, C. G. (1966) *Aspects of Scientific Explanations*. New York: Free Press. 152.

HERRIOT, R. E., and ST JOHN, W. H. (1966) *Social Class and the Urban School*. New York: Wiley. 38.

Higher Education (1963) (The Robbins Report) Command Paper 2154. London: H.M.S.O. 175–6, 218, 255.

Higher Education into the 1990s: A Discussion Document (1978) Department of Education and Science and the Scottish Education Department. London: H.M.S.O. 218.

HILLMAN, K. G. (1969) 'Student Valuation of Academic Achievement'. *Sociological Quarterly* 10 No. 3, 384–91. 56.

HILSUM, S., and CANE, B. S. (1971) *The Teacher's Day*. Slough: N.F.E.R. 42.

HOPPER, E. (1971) *Readings in the Theory of Educational Systems*. London: Hutchinson. 106.

HORTON, J. (1966) 'Order and Conflict Theories of Social Problems'. *American Journal of Sociology* 11 No. 6, 701–13. 7.

HOSELITZ, B. F. (1965) 'Investment in Education and its Political Impact', in Coleman, J. S. (1965b) *Education and Political Development*. Princeton: Princeton University Press. 224.

HYMES, D., and GUMPERZ, J. J. (1971) *Directions in Socio-Linguistics*. New York: Holt, Rinehart and Winston.

JACKSON, B. (1964) *Streaming: An Education System in Miniature*. London: Routledge and Kegan Paul. 37, 124, 125.

JACKSON, B., and MARSDEN, D. (1962 and 1966) *Education and the Working Class*. London: Routledge and Kegan Paul. Rev. ed. (1966) Harmondsworth: Penguin. 52, 109.

JACKSON, P. W. (1968) *Life in Classrooms*. New York: Holt, Rinehart and Winston. 26, 139.

KALTON, G. (1966) *The Public Schools*. London: Longman. 119.

KANDEL, D. B., and LESSER, G. S. (1969) 'Parental and Peer Influences on Educational Plans of Adolescents'. *American Sociological Review* 34 No. 2, 213–38. 56.

KATZ, M. (1973) 'Attitudinal Modernity, Classroom Power and Status Characteristics: An Investigation'. Paper presented to American Educational Research Association. 135.

KAZAMIAS, A. M., and SCHWARTZ, K. (1973) 'Sociological Theories and Educational Change'. *Comparative Education Review* 17 No. 2, 245–54. 152–3, 158.

KEDDIE, N. (1971) 'Classroom Knowledge', in Young 1971. 47, 85–8, 140, 143, 167.

KEDDIE, N. (1973) *Tinker, Tailor . . . The Myth of Cultural Deprivation*. Harmondsworth: Penguin.

KELSALL, R. K. (1963) 'Survey of all Graduates'. *Sociological Review Monographs, No. 7*. 177.

KING, R. (1969) *Values and Involvement in a Grammar School*. London: Routledge and Kegan Paul. 108, 129, 249.

KING, R. (1974) 'Social Class, Educational Attainment and Provision. L.E.A. Case Study'. *Policy and Politics* 2 No. 3, 195–207. 205.

KLUCKHOHN, F. R., and STRODBECK, F. L. (1961) *Variations in Value Orientations*. Illinois: Row Peterson. 193–4.

KRAUSS, I. (1964) 'Sources of Educational Aspiration Among the Working Class Youth'. *American Sociological Review* 29 No. 5, 867–85.

KUHN, T. S. (1962) *The Structure of Scientific Revolutions*. Chicago: University of Chicago Press. 249.

LABOV, W. (1969) 'The Logic of Non-Standard English'. *Georgetown Monographs on Language and Linguistics* 22, 1–31. Reproduced in Keddie 1973. 186.

LACEY, C. (1970) *Hightown Grammar*. Manchester: Manchester University Press. 108, 129, 249.

LACEY, C. (1974) 'Destreaming in a "Pressured" Academic Environment', in Eggleston 1974, 129.

LAMBERT, R., with MILLAM, S. (1968) *The Hothouse Society*. London: Weidenfeld and Nicolson. 60.

LARSON, L. E. (1972) 'The Influence of Parents and Peers During Adolescence'. *Journal of Marriage and the Family* 34 No. 1, 67–74. 56.

LAYARD, P. R. G., SARGAN, J. D., AGER, M. E., and JONES, D. J. (1971) *Qualified Manpower and Economic Performance*. Harmondsworth: Penguin. 225.

LAWSON, J., and SILVER, H. (1973) *A Social History of Education in England*. London: Methuen. 147.

LAWTON, D. (1968) *Social Class, Language and Education*. London: Routledge and Kegan Paul. 185.

LAZERFIELD, P. F., SEWELL, W. H., and WILENSKY, H. L. (1968) *The Uses of Sociology*. London: Weidenfeld and Nicolson.

LEE, D. J. (1968) 'Class Differentials in Educational Opportunity and Promotion from the Ranks'. *Sociology* 2 No. 2, 293–312. 237, 240.

LEE, H. (1927) *The Status of Educational Sociology in Normal Schools, Teachers Colleges and Universities*. New York: New York University Press. 17.

LEVITAS, M. (1974) *Marxist Perspectives in the Sociology of Education*. London: Routledge and Kegan Paul. 39.

LITTLE, A. (1975) 'The Educational Achievement of Ethnic Minority Children in London Schools', in Verma and Bagley 1975. 112.

LITTLE, A., and WESTERGAARD, J. (1964) 'The Trend of Class Differentials in Educational Opportunity in England and Wales'. *British Journal of Sociology* 15 No. 4, 301–15. 240.

LORTIE, D. C. (1969) 'The Balance of Control and Autonomy in Elementary Teaching', in Etzioni 1969. 72.

LYDALL, H. (1968) *The Structure of Earnings*. London: Oxford University Press. 229.

McCREADY, D. (1972) *Guide to Social Science Courses*. London: Association of Teachers in Colleges and Departments of Education. 27.

McDILL, E. L., MEYERS, E. D. and RIGSBY, L. C. (1967) 'Institutional Effects on the Academic Behavior of High-School Students'. *Sociology of Education* 40 No. 3, 181–99. 56.

McLEISH, J. (1970) *Student's Attitudes and College Environments*. Cambridge: Cambridge Institute of Education. 25.

McNAMARA, D. R. (1972) 'Sociology of Education and the Education of Teachers'. *British Journal of Educational Studies* 20 No. 2, 137–47. Reproduced in Reid and Wormald 1974. 27.

MACIVER, R. M., and PAGE, C. H. (1950) *Society*. London: Macmillan. 1.

MANNHEIM, K., and STEWART, W. A. C. (1962) *An Introduction to the Sociology of Education*. London: Routledge and Kegan Paul. 16.

MARSDEN, D. (1971) *Politicians, Comprehensives and Equality*. Fabian Society Tract 411. London: Gollancz. 122.

MASTERS, P. L., and HOCKEY, S. W. (1963) 'Natural Reserves of Ability – Some Evidence from Independent Schools', *The Times Educational Supplement* 17.5.1963, 1061. 118.

MAXWELL, J. (1969) *Sixteen Years On*. London: London University Press. 237.

MENNELL, S. (1974) *Sociological Theory: Uses and Unities*. London: Nelson. 6, 14, 15.

MERTON, R. K. (1957) *Social Theory and Social Structure*. Glencoe: Free Press. 51, 53, 105.

MILNER, D. (1975) *Children and Race*. Harmondsworth: Penguin. 113.

MURDOCK, G., and PHELPS, G. (1972) 'Youth Culture and the School Revisited'. *British Journal of Sociology* 23 No. 4, 478–82. 59.

MUSGRAVE, P. W. (1965 and 1972) *The Sociology of Education*. London: Methuen. 21.

MUSGRAVE, P. W. (1968) *Society and Education in England Since 1800*. London: Methuen. 44, 163–6.

MUSGRAVE, P. W. (1970) 'A Model for the Analysis of the Development of the English Educational System from 1860'. *Transactions of the Sixth World Congress of Sociology* 4, 65–82. Reproduced in Musgrave 1970. 44, 163–6.

MUSGRAVE, P. W. (1970) *Sociology, History and Education*. London: Methuen. 44, 163–6.

NASH, R. (1971) 'Camouflage in the Classroom'. *New Society* 17 No. 447, 667–9. Reproduced in Eggleston 1974.

NASH, R. (1973) *Classrooms Observed*. London: Routledge and Kegan Paul. 80, 134, 140.

NASH, R. (1974) 'Pupils' Expectations for their Teachers'. *Research in Education* 12, 47–61. Reproduced in Stubbs and Delamont 1976. 77.

NOBLE, T. (1975) *Modern Britain: Structure and Change*. London: Batsford. 241.

Organisation of Secondary Education (1965) Circular 10/65, Department of Education and Science. London: H.M.S.O. 37, 122.

OTTAWAY, A. K. C. (1953) *Education and Society*. London: Routledge and Kegan Paul. 1, 169.

PALLISTER, R., and WILSON, J. (1970) 'Parents' Attitudes to Education'. *Educational Research* 13 No. 1, 56–66. 37, 106.

PARSONS, T. (1942) 'Age and Sex in the Social Structure of the United States'. *American Sociological Review* 7 No. 5, 604–16. Reproduced in Parsons 1964. 54.

PARSONS, T. (1949) *Essays in Sociological Theory*. New York: Free Press. 10.

PARSONS, T. (1951) *The Social System*. New York: Free Press. 10.

PARSONS, T. (1959) 'The School Class as a Social System'. *Harvard Educational Review* 29 No. 4, 297–318. Reproduced in Halsey, Floud and Anderson 1961 and Bell and Stub 1968. 35–9, 46.

PARSONS, T. (1960) *Structure and Process in Modern Societies*. Glencoe: Free Press. 62.

PARSONS, T. (1964) *Essays in Sociological Theory*. New York: Free Press.

PARTRIDGE, J. (1966 and 1968) *Life in a Secondary Modern School*. London: Gollancz. Rev. ed. (1968) Harmondsworth: Penguin. 129.

PAVALKO, R. M. (1968) *Sociology of Education*. Illinois: Peacock.

PEASLEE, A. L. (1969) 'Education's Role in Development'. *Economic Development and Cultural Change* 17 (April), 293–318. 225.

PERRUCCI, R. (1961) 'The Significance of Intra-generational Mobility: Some Methodological and Theoretical Notes, together with a Case Study of Engineers.' *American Sociological Review* 2 No. 2, 874–83. 238.

PERRUCCI, C. C., and PERRUCCI, R. (1970) 'Social Origins, Educational Contexts and Career Mobility'. *American Sociological Review* 35 No. 3, 451–63. 226.

PETERS, R. S. (1964) *Education as Initiation.* London: Harrap. 153.

POLK, K., and PINK, W. (1970) 'Youth Culture and the School. A Replication'. *British Journal of Sociology* 22 No. 2, 160–71. 59.

Public Schools Commission: First Report (1968) Department of Education and Science. London: H.M.S.O. 117, 118, 119, 120.

PUNNETT, R. M. (1971) *British Government and Politics.* London: Heinemann. 118.

REDDIN, M. (1972) 'Which L.E.A.s help Children Stay on at School?' *Where* 72, 250–2. 204.

REID, I. (1969) 'An Analysis of Social Factors in Children's Educational Experience and Achievements Between 10 and 17 years of Age in two Local Education Authority Areas'. Unpublished M.A. Thesis, University of Liverpool. 177, 195–6.

REID, I. (1975) 'Some Reflections on Sociology in Colleges of Education'. *Educational Studies* 1 No. 1, 9–14. 21, 27.

REID, I. (1977a) *Social Class Differences in Britain.* London: Open Books. 24, 105, 172–3, 200, 208–9, 228.

REID, I. (1977b) 'Some Views of Sunday School Teachers'. *Learning for Living* 17 No. 2, 79–81. 41.

REID, I. (1978) 'Past and Present Trends in the Sociology of Education: A Plea for a Return to Educational Sociology', in Barton and Meighan 1978. 250.

REID, I., and COHEN, L. (1973) 'Achievement Orientation, Intellectual Achievement Responsibility and Choice Between Degree and Certificate Courses in Colleges of Education'. *British Journal of Educational Psychology* 42 No. 1, 63–6. 235.

REID, I., and WORMALD, E. (1974) *Sociology and Teacher Education.* London: A.T.C.D.E. 21, 26.

REX, J. (1974) *Approaches to Sociology.* London: Routledge and Kegan Paul.

REYNOLDS, D. (1976) 'The Delinquent School', in Hammersley and Woods 1976. 101, 248.

RICHARDSON, E. (1973) *The Environment of Learning.* London: Heinemann. 46.

Rist, R. C. (1970) 'Student, Social Class and Teacher Expectation'. *Harvard Educational Review* 40 No. 3, 411–51. 46–7, 134.

Rosenthal, R., and Jacobson, L. (1968) *Pygmalion in the Classroom*. New York: Holt, Rinehart and Winston. 140.

Rubovits, P. M. and Maehr, M. L. (1973) 'Pygmalion Black and White'. *Journal of Personality and Social Psychology* 25 No. 2, 210–8. 135.

Secondary Education (1938) (The Spens Report) Board of Education, London: H.M.S.O. 255.

Sharp, R., and Green, A. (1975) *Education and Social Control*. London: Routledge and Kegan Paul. 88–92, 167, 248, 250.

Sharpe, S. (1976) *Just Like A Girl*. Harmondsworth: Penguin. 111.

Shipman, M. D. (1968 and 1975) *Sociology of the School*. London: Longmans. 8, 22, 41, 44, 63.

Shipman, M. D. (1969) 'Commentary', in A.T.C.D.E. 1969. 21.

Shipman, M. D. (1971) *Education and Modernisation*. London: Faber. 147–53.

Shipman, M. D. (1974) 'Reflections on Early Courses', in Reid and Wormald 1974. 21.

Shipman, M. D., Bolan, D., and Jenkins, D. R. (1974) *Inside a Curriculum Project: A Case Study into the Process of Curriculum Change*. London: Methuen. 167.

Sills, D. L. (1968) *International Encyclopedia of Social Science*. New York: Macmillan.

Silver, H. (1973) *Equal Opportunity in Education*. London: Methuen. 115.

Sinclair, J. M., and Coulthard, R. M. (1974) *Towards an Analysis of Discourse: The English Used by Teachers and Pupils*. London: Oxford University Press. 96.

Soloff, S. (1973) 'The Effect of Non-content Factors on the Grading of Essays'. *Graduate Research in Education and Related Disciplines* 6 No. 2, 44–54. 142.

Squibb, P. (1973) 'Education and Class'. *Educational Research* 15 No. 3, 194–208. 189–90.

Stacey, B. (1965) 'Achievement Motivation and Intergenerational Mobility'. *Life Sciences* 4B, 1327–32. 234.

Stacey, B. (1969) 'Achievement Motivation, Occupational Choice and Intergenerational Occupational Mobility'. *Human Relations* 22 No. 3, 275–81. 234.

Statistics of Education 1961, Supplement (1962) London: H.M.S.O. 174.

Statistics of Education 1963 Part 3 (1964) London: H.M.S.O. 218.

Statistics of Education 1964, Vol. 3. (1966) London: H.M.S.O. 219.

Statistics of Education 1970, Vol. 4, Teachers (1972) London: H.M.S.O. 20.

Statistics of Education 1974, Vol. 2, School Leavers, C.S.E. and G.C.E. (1976) London: H.M.S.O. 218–19. *Vol. 5, Finance and Awards* (1976) London: H.M.S.O.

Statistics of Education 1975, Vol. 1, Schools (1976) London: H.M.S.O. 32. *Vol. 2, School Leavers, C.S.E. and G.C.E.* (1977) London: H.M.S.O. 219. *Vol. 4, Teachers* (1977) London: H.M.S.O. 20.

Statistics of Education 1976, Vol. 1, Schools (1977) London: H.M.S.O. 65, 199.

STUBBS, M. (1976) 'Keeping in Touch: Some Functions of Teacher-Talk', in Stubbs and Delamont 1976. 95.

STUBBS, M., and DELAMONT, S. (1976) *Explorations in Classroom Observation.* London: John Wiley.

SUGARMAN, B. (1966) 'Social Class and Values as Related to Achievement and Conduct in Schools'. *Sociological Review* 14 No. 3, 287–301. 194.

SUGARMAN, B. M. (1967) 'Involvement in Youth Culture, Academic Achievement and Conformity in School'. *British Journal of Sociology* 18 No. 2, 151–64. 57, 59.

SUGARMAN, B. M. (1968) 'Social Norms in Teenage Boys' Peer Groups, their Implications for Achievement and Conduct in Four London Schools'. *Human Relations* 21 No. 1, 41–58. 58.

SUGARMAN, B. M. (1970) 'Classroom Friends and Leaders'. *New Society* 15 No. 382, 141–2. 58.

SWIFT, D. F. (1967) 'Social Class, Mobility Ideology and 11+ Success'. *British Journal of Sociology* 17 No. 2, 165–86. 195–6.

SYNDER, E. (1966) 'Socio Economic Variations, Values and Social Participation Among High School Students'. *Journal of Marriage and the Family* 28 No. 2, 174–6. 57.

TAYLOR, G. (1971) 'North and South: The Education Split'. *New Society* 17 No. 440, 346–7. 200.

TAYLOR, G., and AYRES, N. (1969) *Born and Bred Unequal.* London: Longman. 200–2.

TAYLOR, M. T. (1976) 'Teachers' Perceptions of their Pupils'. *Research in Education* 16 No. 1, 25–35. 38, 80.

The Times House of Commons (1970 and 1974) London: Times Newspapers. 118.

THOMPSON, K., and TUNSTALL, J. (1971) *Sociological Perspectives.* Milton Keynes: Open University Press. 6.

THOMPSON, P. G. (1971) 'Some Factors in Upward Social Mobility in England'. *Sociology and Social Research* 55 No. 2, 181–90. 240.

TORODE, B. (1976) 'Teachers' Talk and Classroom Discipline', in Stubbs and Delamont 1976. 100.

VAN DEN BERGHE, P. L. (1963) 'Dialectic and Functionalism: Toward a Theoretical Synthesis'. *American Sociological Review* 28 No. 5, 695–705. Reproduced in Wallace 1969. 11, 44.

VAN DER EYKEN, W. (1973) *Education, the Child and Society.* Harmondsworth: Penguin. 124.

VAUGHAN, M., and ARCHER, M. S. (1971) *Social Conflict and Educational Change in England and France 1789–1848.* Cambridge: Cambridge University Press. 153–9.

VERMA, G. K., and BAGLEY, C. (1975) *Race and Education Across Cultures.* London: Heinemann.

WALKER, R., and ADELMAN, C. C. (1976) 'Strawberries', in Stubbs and Delamont 1976. 96.

WALLACE, W. L. (1969) *Sociological Theory.* London: Heinemann. 5, 6, 7.

WALLER, W. (1932 and 1965) *The Sociology of Teaching.* New York: Wiley. 39, 40, 45, 54.

WEEKS, D. R. (1972) *A Glossary of Sociological Concepts.* Bletchley: Open University Press. 28, 35.

WERTHMAN, C. (1963) 'Delinquents in Schools. A Test for the Legitimacy of Authority'. *Berkeley Journal of Sociology* 8 No. 1, 39–60. Reproduced in Cosin, Dale, Esland and Swift 1971. 75–76.

WHITLEY, R. (1973) 'Commonalities and Connections among Directors of Large Financial Institutions'. *Sociological Review* 21 No. 4, 613–32. 118.

WILLIAMS, F., WHITHEAD, J. L., and MILLER, L. M. (1972) 'Relations Between Language Attitudes and Teacher Expectancy'. *American Educational Research Journal* 9, 263–77. 141.

WILLOWER, D. J. (1969) 'Schools as Organisations: Some Illustrated Strategies for Educational Research and Practice'. *Journal of Educational Administration* 7 No. 2, 110–26. 43.

WOODS, P. (1975) ' "Showing them Up" in Secondary School', in Chanan and Delamont 1975. 99, 102.

WOODS, P. (1976) 'Having a Laugh: An Antidote to Schooling', in Hammersley and Woods 1976. 102.

WRIGHT MILLS, C. (1959) *The Sociological Imagination*. London: Oxford University Press. 25.

YOUNG, M. (1958) *The Rise of the Meritocracy*. London: Thames and Hudson. 243.

YOUNG, M. F. D. (1968) Book review in *New Society* 12 No. 303, 98. 22.

YOUNG, M. F. D. (1971) *Knowledge and Control*. London: Collier-Macmillan. 8, 231.

YOUNG, T. R., and BEARDSLEY, P. (1968) 'The Sociology of Class-room Teaching – Microfunctional Analysis'. *Journal of Educational Thought* 33 No. 2, 175–86. 48.

ZENTER, H., and PARR, A. H. (1968) 'Social Status in the High School – An Analysis of some Related Variables'. *Alberta Journal of Educational Research* 14 No. 4, 253–64. 56.

Subject index

Figures which follow a semi-colon refer to Tables

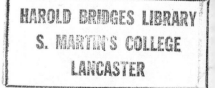